The Complete
Direct Marketing
Sourcebook

The Complete *Direct Marketing* Sourcebook

A Step-by-Step Guide to Organizing and Managing
a Successful Direct Marketing Program

John Kremer

JOHN WILEY & SONS, INC.
New York ▪ Chichester ▪ Brisbane ▪ Toronto ▪ Singapore

Copyright © 1983, 1990, 1992 by John Kremer.

Published by John Wiley & Sons, Inc.
All rights reserved. Published simultaneously in Canada.

Library of Congress Cataloging in Publication Data:

Kremer, John, 1949–
    The complete direct marketing sourcebook: a step-by-step
guide to organizing and managing a successful direct marketing
program / by John Kremer.
        p.   c.—(Wiley series on business strategy)
    Rev. ed. of: Mail order selling made easier. c1990.
    Includes bibliographical references and index.
    ISBN 0-471-55386-7 (cloth)—ISBN 0-471-55387-5 (paper)
    1. Mail-order business—Handbooks, manuals, etc.   2. Direct
marketing—Handbooks, manuals, etc.   3. Mail-order business—
Forms.   4. Direct marketing—Forms.   I. Kremer, John, 1949–
Mail order selling made easier.   II. Title.   III. Series.
HF5466.F665   1992
651'.29—dc20   91-34102

Printed in the United States of America

10 9 8 7 6 5 4

Preface

Direct Marketing in the 1990s and Beyond

Direct marketing has always been an effective way to market goods and services, but three recent trends have challenged the practicality and profitability of going direct:

1. *Rising postage costs.* The costs of mailing promotions have continued to rise, and there's no end in sight. The costs of shipping packages and fulfilling orders have also continued to rise.
2. *Government regulation.* More and more states are going after mail order companies to get them to collect state sales taxes even if they have no physical presence in the state. The nationwide impact of direct marketing will continue to draw regulatory interest, not just in the area of tax collections but in the areas of privacy of credit transactions, abuses of 900 numbers, and indiscriminate telemarketing.
3. *Ecological concerns.* The growing interest in recycling and waste reduction will cause more people to react negatively to so-called junk mail. People (and businesses) are tired of receiving direct mail solicitations that do not interest them.

To succeed under these changing conditions, direct marketers will have to be even more vigilant in using the tried and tested methods outlined in this book, as well as the latest technological innovations.

To counteract rising postage costs, for instance, direct marketers can use database modeling techniques to prospect for new customers who match the demographics of the company's current customers. By screening outside lists before mailing to them, direct marketers can cut postage costs while increasing their chances of getting a high response rate.

Even without sophisticated computer modeling techniques, direct marketers can cut mailing costs by being more selective when reviewing outside lists. Use the checklist in Chapter 5 to help you select the best lists for direct mail offers, and see Appendix I to help control postage costs.

By targeting direct mail promotions and by offering great customer service, companies can also limit their exposure to the growing governmental regulation of direct marketing firms. For more information on how to offer great service to customers, see Chapter 10. For details on how to target direct mail promotions, Chapter 5 on selecting lists and Chapter 8 on tracking responses to promotions are helpful.

Finally, your company can show that it is ecologically responsible in one of several ways. You can, for example, target promotions more carefully so you don't mail to people who have no likely desire for your product or service. Keep track of responses to your current promotions and note which lists and media work best, so you can target future promotions more carefully. Make a genuine effort to reach true prospects rather than mere suspects. A second way is to use recycled paper in promotions (letters, brochures, catalogs, etc.). For details on how to get the best printing values and lowest paper prices, see Chapter 3. A third way is to cut down on marginal mailings. Use the break-even worksheet in Chapter 3 to help you determine which mailings will be most profitable, and test mailings before you roll out to a large list. For more information on how to test mailings and how to project responses, see Chapter 5.

Despite all the recent technological innovations (home shopping networks, long-form television infomercials, computer shopping services, fax machines) and all the social changes, direct marketing still works. And it will continue to work for any company that is committed to operating according to the basic rules and principles of direct marketing that are described in this book—rules that were learned and relearned in the school of hard knocks by hundreds of individuals and companies.

You don't have to be one of those individuals or companies. You don't have to reinvent the wheel. All of the basic principles of direct marketing are described in this book. And to make it easier for you to put them into practice, I have designed simple worksheets that will take you step by step through all the points you need to consider in designing and developing a successful direct marketing program.

The 1990s need be no riskier than the 1980s—if you know how to do your numbers. This book shows you how.

JOHN KREMER

Fairfield, Iowa
March 1992

Contents

Appendix III: Sources and Resources   233

Introduction

How to Get the Most Out of This Book

Of the thousands of ways to market a product or service, I prefer direct marketing. Why? Because if you do your testing and numbers properly, direct marketing is so predictable. And yet to be truly effective, direct marketing also requires considerable creativity and inventiveness. The most successful direct marketers are those who combine both qualities: creativity and organization. I like that challenge.

In consulting with many smaller mail order companies and start-ups, I have discovered that most have plenty of creativity. What they often lack, however, is a sense of organization. Too many fail because they don't plan properly, and, perhaps more important, they don't follow through.

The Complete Direct Marketing Sourcebook is designed to make it easier for anyone to handle all the details involved in planning and carrying out a successful direct marketing program. The best way to handle these details is to develop worksheets that lay out all the necessary steps (or points to be covered) in a simple, easy-to-use format. This book does that.

This book is not a general introduction to the subject of mail order marketing. Plenty of good books already cover the basics for beginners as well as for seasoned veterans. The three I recommend most often are William Cohen's *Building a Mail Order Business*, Julian Simon's *How to Start and Operate a Mail Order Business*, and Bob Stone's *Successful Direct Marketing Methods*. (For details about these books and many others, see the Bibliography at the end of this book.)

I have designed *The Complete Direct Marketing Sourcebook* as a hands-on working supplement to those basic guides. It includes all the worksheets, sample letters, charts, checklists, and procedures you might need to apply the basic principles of mail order marketing in your own business.

GARBAGE IN, GARBAGE OUT

Most of the worksheets and procedures outlined in this book are designed to be used in any direct marketing program regardless of its size, product, or method of promotion. These worksheets are generic, so don't take them as the last word on mail order operations. Use them instead as guides to developing worksheets and procedures to suit your own needs.

For instance, if your operation is computerized (as most mail order companies are), you wouldn't fill out many of these worksheets by hand. More likely, you would generate these worksheets as reports direct from your order entry database. To be able to do this, however, you have to design your database so it contains all the information required to create the reports you need to fulfill your orders, track your promotions, and maintain your in-house mailing list. Remember the cardinal rule of computer databases: Garbage In, Garbage Out. For that reason, as I describe each worksheet that might have an impact on your order entry database, I will alert you to the information that needs to be keyed into your database.

FOUR CATEGORIES OF WORKSHEETS

The worksheets in this book fall into four basic categories, all of them easy to use. Just follow the directions in each case, as outlined below:

1. **Master copies.**   You may use these worksheets as they are. If you would like to have 8½" x 11" master copies, enlarge them using a photocopier. Examples of such master copies include the advertising record worksheets, the inventory control form, and the project priority log. In this book, you will often find two copies of these worksheets: one in the main body of the book, illustrating how the worksheet should be filled out, and the other in Appendix II, which contains samples of all the master copies.
2. **Sample letters.**   Use the many sample letters as guides in writing your own standard letters. Examples include testimonial request letters and sample refund letters. Read the instructions that accompany the sample letters to get an idea of how to adapt the letters to your own needs.
3. **Letterhead required.**   Some of the worksheets and sample letters should not be copied until you have added your letterhead to them. These include the request for quotation and the ad insertion order. To use these, first make a standard-size master copy; then paste your letterhead (address and company logo) at the top; finally, photocopy onto appropriate paper. Or white out the "Your Letterhead Here" statement on the standard-size master copy and then photocopy direct to your printed letterhead stationery. Another option is to make up your own master copy using ours as an example.
4. **Charts and procedures.**   A number of the worksheets are designed to be used directly in your operations. You can use them right out of the

book, or make copies so you can keep them where they will be handy. For example, the postage rates comparison chart might be kept near your postage scale, or the test sample probability table might be kept near your computer terminal when you are projecting probable responses to your mailings.

A TRAINING MANUAL

Besides being of use to owners or managers of a mail order business, this book also makes a superb training manual. *The Complete Direct Marketing Sourcebook* gives new employees an insider's look into the business of direct marketing and provides them with a detailed understanding of the mechanics of running a mail order operation. With such an overview, they will learn their duties more quickly and will also be able to work more efficiently and effectively with others in the organization.

YOU CAN FIND THE ANSWER HERE

As one reader of a previous edition of this book said, "If you have any questions about the nitty-gritty of mail order, you can find the answer here." Besides providing worksheets and instructions for handling the details of running a mail order operation, this book also contains four bonus sections.

Appendix I: How to Reduce Rising Postage Costs, describes 15 techniques other direct mailers are using to cut their postage costs by as much as 33%.

Appendix II: Master Copies of the Worksheets, provides blank copies of all the worksheets described in the following chapters. Use these blank worksheets to plan, develop, and carry out your direct mail programs.

Appendix III: Sources and Resources, includes many resources that a direct marketer might need when creating, producing, and carrying out various promotions. Among other things, this resource list will tell you where to find inexpensive full-color printers for test mailings, how to set up charge card privileges, where to go to set up an in-house toll-free telephone line, where to locate professional direct mail copywriters, and which trade magazines serve the market. It's a one-of-a-kind resource listing.

The Bibliography reviews 100 books about marketing, advertising, mail order, publicity, graphics, printing, and publishing. These are the books I recommend most often. Even after many years in this business, I still find inspiration, guidance, and good sense in many of these books.

HOW TO USE THIS BOOK

If you want to get the most out of this book, you have to put the ideas and principles into practice. Don't just read this book, and don't just let it sit on your shelf. Use it. First and foremost, try out some of the worksheets to see if they will fit in with the way you do business. If so, then adapt them to your needs, and begin to use them right away.

Feel free to mark up this book—unless, of course, you've borrowed this copy from an associate or from the library. As you read, make notes. Use a marker to highlight the sections or ideas that make the most sense to you and that have the greatest potential for your own marketing program. Use this book as you would a dictionary or workbook. Keep it handy, mark it up, and scribble notes to yourself.

Above all, don't just glance through this book once and then toss it aside. If you do, you'll miss many opportunities to make your company grow and grow and grow.

MARKETING IS THE MEANS, NOT THE GOAL

It is easy to get caught up in the details of running a business and forget why you are in it in the first place. I know because it has happened to me. One way to free yourself from the crush of these details is to organize them using the worksheets in this book. But they are not enough. You still have to remember why you are doing what you are doing. Direct marketing is just a means to a goal; it is not the goal itself.

Set your goals high, and then live up to them. That is the only way to ensure that you won't be inundated or overshadowed by the little details of day-to-day operations.

I wish you the best of luck—and skill.

1

Planning for Success

To make the optimum use of your time and resources (and to ensure your success in mail order), plan your projects carefully. What is the best product to sell? At what price? By which means? These are just a few of the questions you must answer before you begin a direct marketing operation or start up a mail order business. And to answer these questions, you need to know your costs, capital requirements, profit potential, and time schedules.

The worksheets and formulas in the first two chapters of this book will help you to decide which projects offer the best profit potential and the best odds of success. They cannot guarantee you success, but they can help you to

1. avoid time-consuming projects that offer little reward,
2. keep closer tabs on your projects as you carry them out,
3. select the most appropriate products for your promotions,
4. set the price for your products,
5. choose the most cost-effective promotions, and
6. minimize the downside risk while maximizing your profits.

This chapter contains two generic worksheets to help you set priorities and keep track of your projects. The worksheets will come in handy whenever you need to prioritize your activities or make sure that no important steps are overlooked in any project you carry out.

The second chapter will help you choose which products to promote, calculate the cost of producing the products, select the manufacturers of the products (or the parts, if you are putting the product together yourself), and set the retail price.

HOW TO CHOOSE THE OPTIMUM PROJECT

The project priority worksheet (Exhibit 1-1) can be used whenever you need to set priorities—whether selecting which products to produce, which promotions to carry out, or which media to use. In the sample, the worksheet is used to select the promotions that will give the company the best return on its time and resources. In this case, as with many other mail order companies, the house lists and newsletter are most likely to give the best return.

The project priority worksheet is easy to use. Just list each of your potential products, which promotions you will use (whether direct mail, magazine ads, other ads, a catalog, or something else), and which audiences you want to target. Be as specific as possible in making your lists.

Then assign a number from 1 to 10 to each project under each of the following categories (the numbers refer to the columns on the worksheet):

Promotion timing (1), the time required to get the promotion off the ground. Allow time to design and write the advertisement or sales literature, to prepare the copy, to print, and to mail (plus advertising lead times). For this category, assign the number 10 to the least amount of time and 0 to the maximum amount of time. I suggest the following values:

10 =	2 weeks	4 =	14 weeks
9 =	4 weeks	3 =	16 weeks
8 =	6 weeks	2 =	18 weeks
7 =	8 weeks	1 =	20 weeks
6 =	10 weeks	0 =	+20 weeks
5 =	12 weeks		

Adjust these values to fit your own projects.

Product timing (2), the time required to have a finished product. Allow time for designing, tooling, producing, and shipping. Be conservative. Also consider how long it will take to obtain reorders.

If you are obtaining your product from another company, the time values you used for promotion timing might also be suitable for this category. If, however, you are designing and producing the product yourself, allow for more time. Designing and manufacturing a product can take anywhere from two or three months up to five or six years. Set your time values to allow for the range of times involved in acquiring a finished product.

Capital requirements (3), how much up-front cash the project will require. How much will you need for designing, tooling, ad copy prep work, initial product inventory, and promotion? The higher the capital requirements are, the less desirable the project will be, especially if your financial resources are limited.

PROJECT PRIORITY WORKSHEET

Product	Promotion	Audience	1	2	3	4	5	6	7	Total
1001 Ways	Direct Mail	Open Horizon list	10	9	10	10	10	9	10	68
"	"	Bowker list	8	9	3	7	8	7	8	50
"	"	COSMEP list	8	9	6	8	8	8	8	55
"	"	MAP members	10	9	8	9	9	9	8	62
"	"	PMA members	8	9	6	8	9	8	8	56
"	"	PW list	8	9	3	7	8	7	8	50
"	Co-op	PMA Libraries	6	9	7	5	5	8	5	45
"	Insert	WD Book Club	6	9	5	4	4	6	5	39
"	Display Ad	BMU	9	9	10	10	10	10	10	68
"	"	MSPA News	7	9	7	7	7	7	6	50
"	"	Small Press	5	9	5	6	7	7	6	45
"	"	Personal Pub.	7	9	4	3	4	4	2	33
"	"	PW 1/6 page	8	9	5	4	8	6	4	44
"	"	The Writer	7	9	5	3	3	4	3	34
"	"	Writer's Digest	7	9	5	3	4	5	3	36
Mail Order Selling	Direct Mail	Open Horizon list	10	8	10	10	8	9	9	64

1 — Promotion Timing
2 — Product Timing
3 — Capital Requirements
4 — Profit Potential
5 — Back End Potential
6 — Ease of Operation
7 — Odds of Success

For each of the seven numbered columns, assign a value of 0 to 10. For the number assignments shown at the left, follow the guidelines in the text. If you want to assign other meanings to the numbers, you may do so. When you have completed filling in the numbers, add up the total for each project. Generally, the project with the highest total will allow you to make optimum use of your time and resources.

Exhibit 1-1   Project priority worksheet.

To make this category more objective, you can assign concrete values to each number—for example, 10 = $1,000 or less, 9 = $1,001 to $5,000, 8 = $5,000 to $10,000, 7 = $10,000 to $25,000—or some other such ranking that reflects the range of potential capital requirements. Note that for this category, 0 is high (that is, assign 0 for projects requiring a large up-front investment) and 10 is low (requires low up-front investment).

Profit potential (4), how much profit you can expect to earn from each project. Assign a dollar value to each number from 1 to 10 (0 is the lowest and 10 the highest). Be realistic in evaluating the potential profits. Use the cost analysis and profit formulas described in Chapter 2 to determine potential profits for each project.

Back end potential (5), the potential for repeat sales. Will your customers come back for more? Does the product itself get used up or wear out so the customer will need to buy more (e.g., vitamins or clothing)? Can you develop an appropriate line of products that can be offered to your customers (e.g., a catalog of kitchen gadgets or a series of books)? Repeat customers are the foundations of all enduring mail order businesses. The greater the back end potential, the higher the assigned value should be.

Ease of operation (6), whether the product is something you can handle. Does it draw upon your talents and interests? Will it be easy to set up and continue? If it is impossible, assign a 0, if you could do it in your sleep, assign a 10. The more suitable the operation is, the higher the number will be.

Odds of success (7), the most subjective of the rankings. How appealing is the product? How large is the customer base? Will it play in Peoria? The rating should reflect your enthusiasm for the product, plus—more important—the results of any market testing you have done. Zero indicates no chance of success; 10 indicates that the sky is the limit.

The project priority worksheet is designed to be flexible. You can assign whatever meaning you like to the seven numbers on it. The seven meanings I have assigned are the ones I have found to be most valuable in predicting the success of a project.

You might also want to weight some factors as more important than others and assign higher numbers to them. For example, if you have little money to start with, capital requirements could be the determining factor in your decision and, hence, should carry greater weight (have a higher number assigned to it). Or if your time is limited because you are employed full time elsewhere, the promotion and product timing or the ease of operation might be the most significant factors and carry the greatest weight.

Once you have assigned number values to all the categories, add them up. In most cases the project with the highest total should be given first priority in your plans. Generally this project will be the one that allows you to make optimum use of your time and resources.

> Use the project priority worksheet to help you choose which projects to pursue first, but don't let it be the sole determiner. It should supplement your intuitive judgment, not replace it.

A master copy of the project priority worksheet (as well as all other sample worksheets) is reproduced in Appendix II. Copy it and fill in the blanks to suit your needs.

HOW TO MAKE THE BEST USE OF YOUR TIME

Project Log

Whenever you start a new project, lay out a schedule detailing each activity you must complete. The project log (Exhibit 1-2) ensures two things: that no essential activity will be forgotten and that each job gets done in sequence and, it is hoped, on time.

If you note the actual starting and finishing dates for each job, the project log can also help you in planning future projects. By providing you with a record of how long each activity actually took (as compared to what it should have taken), the project log should make it easier for you to set a realistic schedule for forthcoming projects.

The project log shown as Exhibit 1-2 was used to schedule the production of a display advertisement for a book. It does not necessarily cover all steps that might be necessary in producing a display ad, but it can serve as a starting point for setting your own production schedules. If you adapt the sample ad production schedule, you might want to schedule time to rewrite copy and approve it before sending it to typesetting.

Schedule-at-a-Glance

If you are visually oriented, you might want to draw up a schedule on a calendar or on a one-page worksheet that I call a schedule-at-a-glance (Exhibit 1-3). To keep it in front of you at all times, make a large one that will fit on your wall.

The sample schedule-at-a-glance in Exhibit 1-3 is designed to track the production schedule for a catalog or direct mail package that involves some full-color printing. This schedule begins after the products have been selected, all photographs have been taken, and the copy has been

PROJECT LOG

Project Name: Display Ad Production
Schedule for *1001 Ways*

Starting Date: 3/9/92

Target Completion Date: 5/18/92

| Scheduled | | Actual | | Actions to Be Accomplished | Done |
Start	Finish	Start	Finish		
3/9/92	3/16/92			Set publication date. —> Committee	
3/9/92	3/16/92			Set advertising budget. —> Committee	
3/9/92	3/16/92			Select media for placement. —> John / Jane	
3/9/92	3/16/92			Specify ad sizes needed. —> John / Jane / Mary	
3/9/92	3/16/92			Approve media choices and budget. —> Committee	
3/19/92	3/29/92			Prepare layout for space ads. —> Mary	
3/19/92	3/29/92			Take photos of book cover. Farm out to Kelly & Company.	
3/19/92	4/16/92			Write copy for space ads. —> David	
3/29/92	4/16/92			Prepare other illustrations. —> Mary	
4/16/92	4/20/92			Approve copy and illustrations. —> Committee	
4/23/92	4/27/92			Typeset copy. —> Mary / Elaine	
4/23/92	4/30/92			Prepare finished art. —> Mary	
4/30/92	5/4/92			Proofread ad. Check pasteup. —> Mary / David / Jane	
5/4/92	5/11/92			Approve final ad. —> Committee	
5/11/92	5/15/92			Make camera-ready copies with keys. —> Max	
5/15/92	5/18/92			Send copies to appropriate media. —> John / Jane	
8/15/92	9/30/92			Ads appear in magazines.	
8/15/92	12/15/92			Monitor sales from ads. —> Jane / John	

Exhibit 1-2   Project log.

Production Schedule for Catalog or Direct Mail Package

Jobs or Actions to Be Accomplished	Week 1	Week 2	Week 3	Week 4	Week 5	Week 6	Week 7	Week 8	Week 9
Approve copy and illustrations									
Design a comprehensive layout									
Approve layout									
Send specifications and RFQ to printer									
Select and specify type									
Typeset copy									
Proofread galleys									
Correct typeset galleys									
Paste up mechanicals									
Proofread mechanicals									
Correct mechanicals									
Select a printer									
Get color separations									
Approve separations									
Make negatives and strip in separations									
Make blueline proofs									
Make four-color proofs									
Proofread and approve bluelines									
Examine and approve four-color proofs									
Make corrections or adjustments to negatives									
Make plates									
Print catalog or direct mail package									
Approve print job before goes to bindery									
Print job goes to bindery									
Accept delivery of printed material									

Exhibit 1-3   Schedule-at-a-glance.

written. It makes it easy for you to visualize the flow of the various production jobs and how they interact. It clearly shows that every person must meet deadlines or the entire process gets out of kilter. Lay out a schedule-at-a-glance for every project you begin; it will help everyone keep on track.

Note that the production of an actual full-color catalog or direct mail package could well take much longer than the 9 weeks allotted in this sample schedule. Rarely, however, will it take much less than 9 weeks. This sample schedule, for instance, assumes that the printer and typesetter are local. If that is not the case, allow more time for sending proofs and approvals back and forth between you and your suppliers. This schedule also allows little room for possible delays.

A generic schedule-at-a-glance can be found in Appendix II. Many office supply stores stock such forms in large sizes for displaying on office walls.

You can adapt the schedule-at-a-glance to meet your needs. To clarify the dates involved in the project, for example, you might change the top headers to indicate the actual days involved—for example, May 1-5 rather than Week 2. Or you could color code the shadings to represent the people responsible for seeing that the actions are accomplished—for example, a blue shading for Bill in graphic design, a red to represent Mary in production, and a green to represent Albert in purchasing.

GET ORGANIZED; THEN TAKE ACTION

The information in this chapter was presented first for a good reason. If you're not organized, you are not likely to be successful in the mail order business. Direct marketing requires great attention to detail. Sure, you can get by for awhile without attending to the details, but then you are simply playing a game of chance. The great power of direct marketing versus other forms of advertising is that you can directly measure your success and adjust your program accordingly. To take full advantage of this power, you need to plan and organize your activities so you can adapt to the demands of your customers.

2

How to Find a Product, Produce It, and Set a Price

HOW TO SELECT A PRODUCT

The first step in establishing a mail order operation or, for that matter, any other business, is to find something to sell—some service or product that people need or desire. Generally the best products are somehow unique. They are one of a kind, they offer some new twist on a tried-and-true idea, or they are better than all the rest. In other words, they stand out.

In my business of publishing, I have no competition because nobody can begin to match the amount of hands-on detail that I put into every book or newsletter I write. There are, of course, other books on the subjects I write about, but I never write a book that simply duplicates someone else's work. Why waste my time or the reader's? So when I write, I either make my book the best on the subject or I add a new twist. This book, for example, is clearly not the most comprehensive one on the subject, but it is the only one that puts so much attention on the nitty-gritty of mail order and provides a way to understand and make use of those details to operate a successful direct marketing program. As a bonus, it also lists hundreds of resources—something few other books come close to matching.

To find a product that truly stands out, you need to do some research. Begin by becoming a close observer of your day-to-day life and of the lives of those around you. What do they need? What do they want? Can you make something better? Can you solve a problem for them? Can you entertain them? What do *you* need? What do you want? Can you solve a problem for yourself—something that would also interest others?

To supplement this casual research, read magazines, especially those covering your special areas of interest. Ask questions of anyone involved in that area—the retailers, the customers, the hobbyists. Join relevant associations and clubs. Attend conventions and seminars serving that area of interest. Keep your eyes and ears—and mind—open.

If you do this, sooner or later you will come across one or two ideas that truly deserve to be marketed. It may be something you have to create, something someone else has created but not yet marketed effectively, or something that has been on the market for some time but never marketed in the way you intend to do.

Once you find one or more products that you think will sell well via direct marketing, evaluate them to make sure that they truly suit your resources and capabilities. To ensure that you consider all the major points that determine whether a product can be sold successfully via mail order, use a checklist, worksheet, or spreadsheet similar to the new product evaluation worksheet shown as Exhibit 2-1. This worksheet can be customized to your needs in three ways:

1. Add selection criteria that you feel are appropriate to your product, market, or approach to that market.
2. Set your own scale for weighing the relative importance of the various selection criteria. In the sample, I used a scale of 1 through 5. I also kept the average weight (the sum of the assigned weights divided by the number of criteria) equal to the midpoint on the scale (3). If you don't keep the average weight close to the midpoint, your results will be biased.
3. Establish a different scale for rating the importance of the criteria for your marketing program (I used a scale of 1 through 10). You might want to assign meanings to each point on the scale, similar to what I did for the project priority worksheet (Exhibit 1-1).

In the sample worksheet, I came up with a product rating of 474 out of a possible 600 (see the explanation in the boxed material). That's a good rating. Using the scales in the example, any product with a total rating over 400 would be a good prospect—provided you did not let your enthusiasm bias your ratings. Any product that rates a total below 200 or even 300 should probably not be pursued. It doesn't have the juice.

> The Total (the last column) is obtained by multiplying the relative importance (RI) times the rating (RA) in column 3. The highest possible rating (600) is calculated by multiplying the average weight (in this example, 3) times the highest possible rating (10) times the number of criteria (20).

The new product evaluation worksheet cannot, and should not, eliminate subjectivity in product selection. What it can do is help you to weigh all the relevant factors that influence the success or failure of a

New Product Evaluation Worksheet

Product: Widget

Date: June 6, 1992

Description: A practical whatchamacallit that does everything you ever wanted it to do

Selection Criteria	Relative Importance	Rating (1 thru 10)	Total (RI x RA)
Is the market for this product large enough?	5	8	40
Is the audience or market easy to target?	5	9	45
Is there any competition (potential or established)?	2	5	10
Can it be competitively priced?	3	7	21
Is the cost low enough to justify a high markup?	3	7	21
Does it offer real value for the price asked?	4	9	36
Is the product original? Unique?	2	8	16
Does it fill a need?	4	7	28
Is the product easy to use? To understand?	3	6	18
How safe is the product?	1	10	10
Is the product readily available or easy to manufacture?	3	8	24
Does the product require any special packaging?	2	9	18
Is the product suitable for shipping? Easy to ship?	2	10	20
Does the product require any service or follow up?	2	8	16
Does the product have a long life expectancy?	2	7	14
Is the product exclusive? Patentable?	2	7	14
Does the product encourage repeat business?	4	8	32
Is it compatible with the current product lines?	4	8	32
Is the expected return on investment high enough?	4	8	32
Will it contribute to the long-range growth of company?	3	9	27
Average Weight:	3	Total:	474

Exhibit 2-1   New product evaluation worksheet.

mail order product. Use it to substantiate your gut feelings about a new product. And, perhaps more important, use it to sell the idea to others: your banker, your sales force, your investors.

HOW TO QUERY SUPPLIERS AND MANUFACTURERS

Once you have decided on a product, you need to figure out what it will cost you to produce or obtain it. If you are buying the product as is direct from another company and reselling it to your own customers, you can use the merchandise data sheet in Chapter 9 (Exhibit 9-3) to figure your costs and query your suppliers. If you will be manufacturing the product, assembling parts, or modifying the product in some way, use the worksheets in this chapter to solicit bids and calculate the costs of the product.

To locate the names and addresses of prospective suppliers, look in the *Thomas Register of American Manufacturers,* a multivolume set available in most public libraries. I have found this directory, supplemented by the Yellow Pages of most large city telephone books, to be indispensable in locating suppliers for almost anything one would want to manufacture. Ask your librarian for help in locating other suitable directories if these are not available.

You can also locate appropriate suppliers by attending trade conventions in your area of interest and reading the trade publications. For example, if you are interested in toys, read *Playthings* and *Toy and Hobby World.*

Once you have located the names and addresses of some potential suppliers, send them a request for quotation (RFQ, Exhibit 2-2). Query at least three to four suppliers for each finished item or raw material you require. I have found that suppliers vary considerably in the prices they charge, the quality they produce, and the services they provide. Besides, if you want to avoid the problems that arise from calamities and vicissitudes of people and nature, you should have at least one alternative supplier for every product you sell.

Filling Out the RFQ

One advantage of using a standard RFQ form is that it guarantees that all potential suppliers have the same specifications to bid upon. Nonetheless, be alert to check that the suppliers don't change any of the specifications in preparing their quotes, especially if they provide their quotes on a different form (rather than returning your RFQ). For that reason, keep a copy of your RFQ for your own reference.

Before sending out a standard RFQ, you have to fill out some of the information yourself:

Request for Quotation

Issued by:	ABC Company
	Jack Smith, Production Supervisor
	459 Broadway
	Fairfield, NJ 07889
	(201) 444-4444

This is a request for quotation, not an order. Please provide us with your best prices and delivery times for the following described products or services. Please sign and date this RFQ and return to us by the date noted below. Thank you.

Vendor:	XYZ Company
	Attn: Estimator
	9238 W. Henderson Street
	Newark, NJ 07045

RFQ Number: 376

Date of RFQ: 7/9/91

Reply Not Later Than: 8/1/91

Delivery Required By: 11/15/91

Terms: Net 60	F.O.B. Fairfield	Ship via truck: CFS	Ship Wgt.

Quantity	Item	Description	Unit Cost	Total
5,000	Purple Widgets	Some of the best things incorporated into a bunch of gooey stuff and colored purple.		
10,000	Purple Widgets	Some of the best things incorporated into a bunch of gooey stuff and colored purple.		
50,000	Purple Widgets	Some of the best things incorporated into a bunch of gooey stuff and colored purple.		
5,000	Yellow Widgets	Some of the best things incorporated into a bunch of gooey stuff and colored yellow.		
5,000	Red Widgets	Some of the best things incorporated into a bunch of gooey stuff and colored red.		

Special charges (dies, plates, set-up charges, etc.):

Shipment can be made within _____ days after the order is placed.

Prices quoted include all costs, except where noted. Prices firm until:

_____	_____
Date of Quotation	Authorized Signature
_____	_____
Telephone Number	Name and Title

Exhibit 2-2   Request for quotation.

Issued by. Type in the name of your company, your name and title, the company address, and your telephone number. Include your fax number if you have one.

Vendor. Type in the name and address of the potential supplier or manufacturer.

RFQ Number. This is your reference number; it should be the same for each supplier queried for a particular item. When suppliers call you about the quote, they will refer to this number.

Date of RFQ. The date the RFQ is sent out.

Reply Not Later Than. The latest date you will accept any quotations. To allow for late quotes, set a date that is at least a few days before your deadline for deciding which supplier you will use.

Delivery Required By. If you need the item by a certain date, say so.

Terms. If you want specific terms (e.g., net 30), list them here; otherwise, leave the space blank so the suppliers can list their usual terms.

F.O.B. If you want the price to include delivery to your firm, list your location (e.g., F.O.B. Fairfield); otherwise prices usually do not include delivery charges to your firm.

Ship via. If you want delivery by a specific carrier, indicate that here, or if you want delivery via first class mail rather than fourth class, indicate that. If you have no preference, write "best way."

Quantity. List the specific quantity or range of quantities for which you want quotes.

Item. List each item or variation separately by name or number.

Description. Describe the item you want to buy. Specify the size, shape, colors, composition, and any other pertinent characteristics. Be as specific as possible.

All other items in the RFQ will be completed by the supplier: shipping weight, unit cost, total, special charges, lead time (how soon shipment can be made), how firm the prices are, the date the quotation is made, plus name, title, and telephone number of the person who prepared the quote.

How to Keep Track of Your Suppliers

As you receive quotations from potential suppliers, transfer the information to a vendor record such as the one shown as Exhibit 2-3. The vendor record allows you to track the pricing and performance of the suppliers you choose to use. Make a vendor record for each potential supplier so you will have ready access to alternate sources just in case your prime suppliers raise their prices or are not able to deliver on time.

The vendor record shown as Exhibit 2-3 has been designed to complement the request for quotation so you can easily transfer the information from one form to the other. The sample vendor record illustrates how the record should be filled out:

Item. The raw material or finished good supplied by the vendor.

Product. The name of the product of which the item is either a part or, in some cases, the whole (the product is the item and nothing else).

Vendor. The name of the company supplying the item.

Address. The vendor's address.

Phone. The telephone number of your contact.

Fax No. If the supplier has a fax machine, note the number here.

Contact. The name and title (if known) of the person who is your contact in the company. It might be the sales manager, a telephone sales rep, or the estimator.

Terms. How soon do you have to pay for the item once you receive it? Generally, this will be net 30 or net 60.

F.O.B. If F.O.B. your location, the supplier pays shipping. If F.O.B. their plant, you pay the shipping. Generally you pay the shipping.

Ship via. If you have a preferred way for shipping items from their location to your warehouse, indicate it here.

Ship Wgt. How much does the item weigh? Generally this will be indicated in terms of carton weight (with so many items per carton) or weight per thousand items.

Item. The name of the item.

Description. Describe in detail the item to be supplied by this particular vendor (dimensions, color, composition, etc.). Be as specific as possible.

Quantity. List the various quantities for which you want quotes.

Unit Cost. List the price quoted by the supplier—whether it is expressed as cost/M (cost per thousand pieces), cost per item, cost per carton quantity, or something else.

Total. Indicate the total cost for each quantity. For example, 5,000 widgets @ $2.45 each would cost $12,250 for the entire lot.

Special Charges. Any one-time charges for dies, molds, and other tooling costs, as well as any setup, color change, imprinting, or other special charges that occur every time the supplier sets up to produce your widget. If the special charge is a one-time tooling cost, amortize these charges over the projected lifetime of the product. If these special charges recur each time you order more widgets produced, these charges should

Vendor Record

Item: Widgets	Product: The Widget Collectors Series

Vendor XYZ Company	Phone 201-123-4567
Address 9238 W. Henderson Street	Fax No. 201-123-7890
Newark, NJ 07045	Contact David Smith-Jones

Terms: Net 60	F.O.B. Fairfield	Ship via Jim's Trucking	Ship Wgt. 8 oz. each

Item	Description	Quantity	Unit Cost	Total
Purple Widgets	Some of the best things incorporated into a bunch of gooey stuff and colored purple.	5,000	$2.45	$12,250.00
Purple Widgets	Some of the best things incorporated into a bunch of gooey stuff and colored purple.	10,000	$2.29	$22,900.00
Purple Widgets	Some of the best things incorporated into a bunch of gooey stuff and colored purple.	50,000	$2.03	$101,500.00
Yellow Widgets	Some of the best things incorporated into a bunch of gooey stuff and colored yellow.	5,000	$2.45	$12,250.00
Red Widgets	Some of the best things incorporated into a bunch of gooey stuff and colored red.	5,000	$2.45	$12,250.00

Special charges (dies, plates, set-up charges, etc.): One-time die charge for widget: $12,000.00
Set-up charges for widget production: $300.00
Color change charge: $35.00 per color

Lead Time: 25 days from time of order	Estimated Shipping Charges: $325 / 5000

Special Ordering Instructions: Be sure to tell them to ship via Jim's Trucking Service.

COMMENTS

Quality: According to Jim at RFQ Company, XYZ offers superb quality and service.

Cooperation: They are very cooperative, flexible, willing to work with us.

Dependability: According to Jim at RFQ, they've never missed a deadline.

Exhibit 2-3   Vendor record.

be added to the total costs. See the product costs worksheet (Exhibit 2-4) for details.

Lead time. How many days or weeks does it take to produce and ship your order? If a mold has to be created, how many additional days are needed?

Shipping charges. If no estimate is provided by the vendor, estimate the charges by calculating the weight of a full shipment and then calling the local agent for a national trucking company to get a quote for trucking the shipment. Trucking costs depend on two major factors: (1) the length of the journey from the pickup point to your warehouse (2) and the type of product being shipped. (Perishables and breakables cost more to ship; if the product is odd-shaped, it might also cost more to ship.)

Special ordering instructions. If the vendor requires partial prepayment or has other ordering restrictions such as minimum quantities, note them here. Also note any special instructions you need to give them when ordering.

Comments. Once you have narrowed the choice to two or three vendors, have each provide you with the names and telephone numbers of at least two other companies they supply. Call these companies and ask for references regarding the quality, cooperation, and dependability of the vendor. Note their comments here. If you have previously dealt with this vendor, make notes of your own experience as well.

The information in this vendor record can be used to place orders with your primary and alternate suppliers, to track how well they follow through, and to estimate your initial product costs.

HOW TO CALCULATE THE COST OF YOUR PRODUCT

Before you can determine the selling price for your product and its potential profitability, you need to calculate how much the product will cost you to produce (or buy). To assist you in doing a careful cost analysis of your product, use the product costs worksheet shown as Exhibit 2-4. Even if someone else is manufacturing your product, you still have to consider any additional packaging, inbound freight, and handling costs.

Your product may be a simple one-component item (for example, a coffee mug), or it might involve many parts or raw materials, or both. This worksheet allows room for four component parts and their costs, plus assembly, finishing, packaging, overhead, royalty, and miscellaneous. Note some of the potential costs for a component:

Raw material. This may consist of actual raw materials, a molded part, a partially finished piece, or a finished item. Under the unit cost, indicate the quoted price for the item at different quantities. For example, if the vendor quotes the cost of a maple wood handle as $250/M ($250 per

Product Costs Worksheet

Product: Widgets			Qty: 5,000	Qty: 10,000
Item	**Description of Part or Labor**		**Unit Cost**	**Unit Cost**
Part #1	Raw Material	maple wood handle	0.25	0.20
	Set-up Charges	$100.00	0.02	0.01
	Tooling Costs	$200.00 for model (amortize over 10M)	0.02	0.02
	Inbound Freight	from Maine — $100 / M	0.10	0.10
	Labor	50¢ per piece	0.50	0.50
Part #2	Raw Material	plastic doodad injected by XYZ	0.13	0.11
	Set-up Charges	$100.00	0.02	0.01
	Tooling Costs	$8,000 for die (amortize over 10M)	0.80	0.80
	Inbound Freight	trucked to us at no charge		
	Labor	none		
Part #3	Raw Material	metal clip supplied by SSS Corp.	0.15	0.12
	Set-up Charges	none		
	Tooling Costs	none		
	Inbound Freight	local		
	Labor	none		
Part #4	Raw Material	electronic chip from Intel	0.10	0.08
	Set-up Charges	$100.00	0.02	0.01
	Tooling Costs	$3,000 programming (amortize 10M)	0.30	0.30
	Inbound Freight	from Texas — $200 / 5M	0.04	0.04
	Labor	none		
Labor	Assembly of product	Labor at our plant — 54¢ per unit	0.54	0.54
Labor	Finishing Labor	Wax and polish — 32¢ per unit	0.32	0.32
Packaging	Package	Box from Georgia Pacific	0.31	0.28
	Set-up Charges	none		
	Tooling Costs	standard box		
	Inbound Freight	FOB Fairfield		
	Labor	insert product and seal — 36¢	0.36	0.36
Royalty	Inventor:	$1.50 per unit to Jay Frederick	1.50	1.50
Overhead	Plant Overhead	$1.45 per unit	1.45	1.45
Misc.				
		Total Unit Cost	6.93	$6.75
	Quantity times total unit cost = **Total Product Cost**		$34,650	$67,500

Exhibit 2-4   Product costs worksheet.

thousand) in quantities of 5,000 and $200/M in quantities of 10,000, your unit costs would be 25¢ and 20¢, respectively.

Setup charges. Many manufacturing processes require some setup time, which is usually charged separate from the per piece price. Some production companies incorporate these charges into the per piece price they give you, and others tack it on. Special setup charges might also apply to other processes, such as a color change in the middle of a production run, that require extra labor. These setup charges should be broken down to a per unit cost. For example, a $100 setup charge breaks down to 2¢ per unit in a run of 5,000 and 1¢ per unit in a run of 10,000.

Tooling costs. For printed products, tooling costs include copy layout, typesetting, pasteup, halftones, and printing plates (if reuseable). For other products, you might have to buy a mold or die. Tooling costs can be amortized over the lifetime of the product (the expected volume of sales). For example, if you expect to sell 10,000 items, divide the tooling costs by 10,000 to obtain your unit tooling cost (even if you are producing only 5,000 units in the first production run).

Inbound freight. If you pay for the shipping, include those charges in the product cost. To figure unit cost, divide the shipping costs by the number of items in the shipment. If you import your product or some of its components, you will have to pay for ocean freight, brokerage fees, duties, terminal fees, and trucking. You can include all of these costs as part of inbound freight.

Labor. If you are buying a finished product, the labor will already be figured into the costs, but if you are producing the item yourself, you need to include your labor costs. Note that these labor costs encompass more than just the hourly wage; they also include social security, unemployment taxes, insurance, vacation time, and other benefits.

To assign a labor cost to an item, you need to know how many items an average worker can produce in an hour (or in a standard day). Divide the hourly wage cost by the number of items produced to come up with a unit labor cost. For example, if the hourly wage including all taxes and benefits is $12 and an average worker can produce 200 items in an hour, the unit labor costs are 6¢. However you calculate your unit labor costs, be sure to allow plenty of leeway for break times, downtimes, setup times, and any other factors that might affect production.

Besides the costs of each part, consider a number of other costs that contribute to the per unit cost—for example:

Assembly labor. If you must assemble the component parts to make a finished product, include the cost of labor.

Finishing labor. If your product requires any finishing touches (polishing, painting), add these labor costs as well.

Packaging. Most products require packaging. Be sure to include these costs in your product costs. Such costs might include the actual cost of the package (box, bag, tube) plus any setup and tooling charges (color changes, color separations, imprinting, dies), freight, and labor for packaging the product. If your packaging consists of two elements such as a plastic bag and a header card, calculate each cost separately.

Royalties. If you are licensing the product from the original inventor, writer, or rights owner, include the cost of royalties (usually a percentage of unit selling price).

Overhead. As part of the product cost, assign a certain percentage of the overhead for the manufacturing operation. Overhead costs include factory rent, heat, and power; the plant manager's salary; insurance; and similar other items.

If you have only one product, you amortize the manufacturing overhead over the lifetime of the product. If you have many products, you will probably assign a specific amount to each product. Ask your accountant for advice.

Miscellaneous. Other costs to consider include an allowance for spoilage, overruns, quality control, inventory costs (if not part of plant overhead), and instruction sheets. Be sure to include anything that has an impact on the unit cost of your product.

Once you have calculated all the component costs on this worksheet, add them up to find out your **total unit cost** for each production quantity. Use this total unit cost to figure a selling price for your product and to calculate the break-even points for your direct mail and advertising programs.

To calculate **total product cost,** multiply the total unit cost times the production quantity. Since, in many cases, much of the total product cost must be paid for before you have any income from sales of the product, you need to know this total so you can arrange to have enough money to cover these costs plus your administrative overhead and original marketing expenditures.

You might want to enter the numbers from the product costs worksheet into a spreadsheet program so you can more readily see the impact that various changes in costs might have on the total unit cost of your product.

HOW TO SET A PRICE FOR YOUR PRODUCT

Two Basic Factors in Pricing

Pricing your product depends on two factors: (1) your manufacturing costs and desired profit and (2) what the market (your customers) will pay for the product. The first factor—your costs and desired profit—

determines the **price floor,** which is the lowest price you can sell the product for and still make the profit you want. The second factor—what the market will bear—determines the **price ceiling,** which is the highest price customers will pay; in other words, if your price went any higher, you would lose a significant number of customers.

You can determine the price floor by doing the appropriate research and calculations. The only ways, however, that you will be able to determine the price ceiling are to run market tests or to guesstimate based on your knowledge of what similar products are selling for. Once you have established a price floor and a price ceiling, test to see what price between the two will bring you the greatest return.

Establishing a Price Floor

You can establish the price floor by any of at least three different methods: (1) taking costs into consideration, (2) targeting your desired profit margin, or (3) targeting your desired percentage return on investment.

Cost-Based Pricing

There are two cost-based methods of pricing you can use: full-cost pricing and incremental cost pricing.

Full-cost pricing is calculated by marking up your total variable costs per unit by a certain percentage (total variable costs are discussed in the next chapter). Most mail order firms consider a 200% to 300% (two to three times) markup safe for most products. The markup could be less for higher-priced items (over $40) and more for an item priced under $10 (to allow for advertising costs). For example, if your total variable costs were $7, you would want to sell your product for somewhere between $14 and $21.

Incremental cost pricing is calculated by marking up the total unit cost of your product by a certain percentage. Average markups range from 400% (four times) to 1,000% (10 times). The higher the expected selling price is, the lower the markup will have to be in order to produce a fair profit. Conversely, the lower the expected selling price is, the higher the markup will have to be. For example, if your product cost was $4, you would want to sell your product for between $16 and $40.

These cost-based pricing guidelines are generally appropriate for direct response selling. If you were selling to retail stores or wholesalers, your markups would probably be different. For instance, a book publisher could not afford a 400% markup on a product sold to bookstores since book distributors, the middlemen, require as much as a 65% discount off the retail price. If the book cost $2.50 to manufacture and sold for $10.00 at retail (a 400% markup), the book publisher would receive as little as $3.50 after the distributors took their 65% discount. That would leave the publisher with only $1.00 to pay all marketing, administrative, and distribution costs and return a profit. That's not enough. Hence, most book publishers use markups of 8 to 10 times unit costs.

Target Profit Margin Pricing

You can price your product by targeting the profit margin you want to earn. To do this, determine your variable costs per unit product **(C)** and your sales costs as a percentage of total sales income. When you do a break-even worksheet (like the one in Exhibit 3-4), you determine your total variable costs. Your sales costs should generally be no more than 50% of your sales income. Allow 50% in those cases where you do not know your sales cost percentage.

The formula to find your price is as follows (where **P** = selling price, **C** = total variable costs per unit, **SC%** = your sales cost percentage, and **PM%** = your desired profit margin):

$$P = \frac{C}{100\% - (SC\% + PM\%)}$$

Target Profit Margin Pricing

In real-life terms, here is how that would work out. If you desired a profit margin of 20% and your total variable costs per unit were $7.00, then your selling price would need to be $23.33 (if you assign a sales costs percentage of 50%):

$$P = \frac{\$7.00}{100\% - (50\% + 20\%)} = \frac{\$7.00}{30\%} = \frac{\$7.00}{.30} = \$23.33$$

Target Profit Margin Pricing (sample)

Target Return on Investment Pricing

A third way to establish price is by deciding what kind of return on investment you want to earn. For instance, you might want to target a return on your investment that equals, if not surpasses, what you could earn by putting your money into a money market account.

To set prices by targeting a specific return on your investment, you must have a reasonably accurate estimate of the expected response to your promotion (that is, the number of orders per thousand mailed).

The target return on investment pricing formula works like this (where **P** = selling price, **ROI** = your desired return on investment expressed as a decimal percentage, **I** = your total investment per 1000 circulars, and **R** = your expected number of orders per 1000 circulars you mail):

$$P = \frac{(ROI \times I) + I}{R}$$

Target ROI Pricing

Here is an example of how this formula works in an actual case. If your desired return on investment is 20% (.20 when expressed as a decimal), your total investment is $520, and your expected response rate is 3%, or 30 orders/M, then your selling price would need to be $20.80:

$$P = \frac{(.20 \times 520) + 520}{30} = \frac{104 + 520}{30} = \frac{624}{30} = \$20.80$$

Target ROI Pricing (sample)

Deciding on a Price

As you can see, the various methods of determining price produce a wide range of potential prices, since all of the examples could easily have resulted from calculations concerning the same product:

Full-cost pricing: $14.00–$21.00.
Incremental cost pricing: $16.00–$40.00.
Target profit margin: $23.33.
Target return on investment: $20.80:

Taking all four pricing methods into consideration, I would probably price the product somewhere between $19.95 and $24.95—probably at the higher price if, and only if, I felt that the product would be perceived by the customer as being worth $24.95. Of course, I would then do a test mailing to verify that the $24.95 price produces the expected returns (around 30 per thousand).

All four of the pricing methods have their weaknesses. Both cost pricing methods are rather arbitrary; they can at best suggest a range of possible prices. The target profit margin pricing formula requires that you know your selling costs percentage or arbitrarily select 50% as the percentage (a percentage that may be too low or too high). And the target return on investment pricing formula relies too heavily on the estimated returns to be reliable without further testing.

Nevertheless, the four methods used together provide a reasonable range of potential prices, which, combined with your knowledge of the market (what competitors with similar products are charging) and further testing, should allow you to set a selling price that is reasonable for consumers and profitable for you.

One of the great strengths of direct marketing is that you can test. If you are not sure you have selected the best price, you can always do a split mailing that tests which of two prices offers the better return.

A Few Pricing Tips

Here are a few final pointers on what to do (and not do) when setting your price:

- Look at what your competitors are charging for identical or similar products. Unless your product offers a significant advantage, stick close to your competitors' pricing strategies.
- Don't use any one pricing formula as the only factor in determining your price.
- Test your prices.
- Although you should consider short-term profits, plan for the long term.
- If you change prices, monitor sales to see if you made the right move.
- Don't charge too low a price. In many cases, it is better to start a bit high and then work down if your target consumers resist the price. In one case, I raised the price of a book from $19.95 to $25.00 and, to my surprise, met absolutely no price resistance.

3

How to Make a Profit with Direct Mail Promotions

Many elements go into creating a successful direct marketing promotion: a great offer (product), creative direct mail packages, good customer service, the right lists. But none of these will ensure that you make a profit if you don't control costs and don't test promotions before rolling out to a wider audience.

This chapter is designed to help you in two ways. It will help you to gain greater control over the costs of your direct mail promotions, and it will teach you how to calculate the possibilities of your success (that is, whether you will make any money on your direct marketing promotions and get a decent return on your investment).

HOW TO GET THE BEST PRINTING VALUES

The first step in controlling promotional costs is identical to the first step in controlling product costs: you must get some price quotations. As a direct response marketer, you will need printed brochures, catalogs, letters, envelopes, and other sales literature. Since price quotations for different print jobs can vary considerably from one printer to another, query at least three or four reliable printers.

To ensure that all printers are quoting the same specifications, use a standard request for quotation (RFQ) form. Exhibit 3-1 shows a simple RFQ form for printing that you can reproduce on your letterhead. Exhibit 3-2 contains a more complex RFQ form; it ensures that you cover most of the details that allow a printer to provide a more accurate quotation.

Open Horizons Publishing, P. O. Box 1102, Fairfield, IA 52556
(515) 472-6130 / Fax: (515) 472-3186

Request for Quotation

Contact: John Kremer

Please quote by January 20, 1992

To: ABC Printers
      234 West Broadway
      Tinseltown, USA

Please quote your best price and turnaround time for the following job:

Specifications:

Title of Job:	Recommended Books brochure
Quantity:	23,000
Total Pages:	4 pages
Page Size:	8 1/2" x 11"
Text Paper:	60 lb. ivory vellum
Text Ink:	2 colors: black and reflex blue
Cover Stock:	self-cover
Cover Ink:	not applicable
Bindery:	Fold 3000 to 4-page brochure.
	Fold 20,000 to letter-fold (to fit #10 envelope).
Packing:	Pack in tightly sealed cartons (275 lb test) not to exceed 40 lb.
Material Provided:	Camera-ready copy
Special Instructions:	Quote separately the costs to add a third PMS color.

Quote:

Price: $_____

Estimated Delivery: _____ working days from receipt of camera-ready copy.

Terms: Net 30 (credit references available upon request).

Remarks:

Signed:_____

Thank you for your quote. We look forward to working with you.

Exhibit 3-1   Request for printing quotation: Simple form.

If you do not know much about printing, rely on your advertising agency or designer to handle the printing queries. If you'd like to learn more about how to talk to printers and designers, read *Getting It Printed* by Mark Beach et al. (see the Bibliography for details). This book is the best on the subject. Indeed, the RFQ shown in Exhibit 3-2 is adapted from a two-page RFQ in that book.

How to Prepare a Request for Quotation: Simple Form

Regardless of whether you are printing a catalog, a brochure, a leaflet, or some other piece, you have to provide printers with certain basic information so they can prepare a valid quotation. At the very least, they need to know the following points:

- **Title of job.** A description of the job.
- **Quantity.** The number of copies you wanted printed. You may request quotations for several different quantities.
- **Total pages.** The number of pages or the number of sides to be printed.
- **Page size.** The size of the page or sheet to be printed.
- **Text paper.** The kind of paper you want to use for the text (60 lb. white offset, 24 lb. ivory laid, or something else).
- **Text ink.** The color of ink, especially if other than black. If you plan to use more than one color, that needs to be noted.
- **Cover stock.** The cover stock you want to use if there is a cover.
- **Bindery.** The finishing operations you want the printer to do (saddle stitch into a booklet, use a letter fold or a Z-fold, or something else).
- **Packing.** How you want the finished job packed (e.g., rubber bands or paper to wrap the printed pieces, shrink wrap, pack in cartons, or load onto a skid).
- **Material provided.** Whether you will supply camera-ready copy or whether you want them to typeset and pasteup the job. If you are using photos, will you provide the halftones and color separations, or will they? Are there any bleeds? Screens? Reverses? (These require extra prep time for the printer and will cost more.)

The more complicated your print job is and the more pieces are involved, the more accurate you need to be in describing the complete job. Otherwise you will not get an accurate quotation.

When querying a printer, also ask for the following information:

- **Prices.** The printer should provide you with a price quotation for the quantities you request.
- **Estimated delivery.** How many working days (weekdays not including holdays) will it take the printer to complete your job once you have provided the camera-ready copy or other material?
- **Terms.** What are the printer's terms for payment? You may indicate what terms you would like.

Request for Quotation

Company: Open Horizons Publishing Company

Contact: John Kremer

Address: P. O. Box 1102, Fairfield IA 52556

Phone: (515) 472-6130

To: ABC Printing Company
234 First Street
Anywhere ST 12345

Please quote your best price and delivery on the following job. Please quote:

[X] as firm price   [ ] verbally

[ ] as rough estimate   [X] in writing

Job Name:	Marketing Brochure
Date of RFQ:	1/15/912
Date quote needed:	2/3/92
Date job to printer:	2/10/92
Date job needed:	2/24/92

This job is a: [ ] new job   [ ] exact reprint   [ ] reprint with changes_____

Quality desired: [ ] basic   [ ] good   [ ] premium   [ ] showcase

Quantity: 1) _____   2) _____   3) _____   [ ] additional _____

Format

Product Description: _____

Trim Size: Flat: _____ x _____   Bound or folded: _____ x _____

No. of pages: _____   [ ] self cover   [ ] plus cover

Copy

Design features: [ ] bleeds   [ ] screen tints #____   [ ] reverses #____   [ ] comp enclosed

Art provided: [ ] camera-ready   [ ] negatives   [ ] printer to typeset and paste up

Extras: [ ] halftones #____   [ ] duotones #____   [ ] color separations #____

Proofs: [ ] galley   [ ] blueline   [ ] composite color   [ ] progressive

Paper

	weight	name	color	finish	grade
Cover					
Inside					

Printing

	ink colors / varnish	ink colors / varnish
Cover	side 1 _____	side 2 _____
Inside	side 1 _____	side 2 _____
_____	side 1 _____	side 2 _____

Bindery

Operations: [ ] deliver flat   [ ] trim   [ ] collate & gather   [ ] fold _____
[ ] round corner   [ ] punch   [ ] drill   [ ] score / perforate

Bindings: [ ] saddle stitch   [ ] side stitch   [ ] perfect bind   [ ] case bind
[ ] spiral bind   [ ] plastic comb   [ ] Wire-O   [ ] pad

Packing: [ ] band in #____ s   [ ] wrap in #____ s   [ ] bulk in cartons   [ ] skid pack

Shipping: [ ] will pick up   [ ] send UPS   [ ] ship via truck   [ ] deliver to _____

Comments: _____

Exhibit 3-2   Request for printing quotation: Complex form.

Get a firm commitment on delivery time for your printing needs. Also request work samples so you can check the quality of the work each printer produces. Finally, always ask the printers to provide quotations by a specific date so you can make a purchasing decision before preparing your final copy.

How to Prepare a Request for Quotation: Complete Form

Exhibit 3-2 is a more complete form for requesting printing quotations. In some ways it is also easier to fill out but only if you know how to speak printerese. Don't use this form if you don't know what you are talking about (unless you work on it with your graphic designer or local printer). Here are some of the points covered in this RFQ:

- **Addresses.** In the top left box, type in your company name, your name (or whoever should receive the price quotations), your address, and telephone number. Include your fax number if you would be open to receiving the quotation via fax. In the "To" box directly below, type in the name of the printing company you are querying.
- **Quote check boxes.** Check whether you would like the price quotation to be a firm price or a rough estimate. Check also whether you would like a verbal or written quotation (or both).
- **Job Name.** Give either a title to the job or an RFQ number. When talking to the printer about the job, you will use this information to identify which job you are talking about.
- **Date of RFQ.** The date you send out the RFQ.
- **Date Quote Needed.** The latest date you will accept price quotations. To allow for delays, set this date a few days before you need to make a decision on which printer you will be using.
- **Date Job to Printer.** The date you will send the camera-ready copy and other materials to the printer.
- **Date Job Needed.** The date the finished print job should arrive at your warehouse or at your mailing house.
- **This job is a . . .** Indicate if this is a new job, an exact reprint of a previous job, or a reprint with some changes (indicate changes).
- **Quality Desired.** These classifications provide the printer with an indication of the quality you desire. "Basic," the quality of everyday work produced by quick printers, is good enough for local advertising fliers, business forms, and newsletters. "Good" quality, which most commercial printers can readily provide, is often seen in books, magazines, direct mail letters, and average catalogs. "Premium" quality requires great attention to detail and the use of high-grade materials; 4-color upscale catalogs and magazines such as *National Geographic* exhibit premium quality printing. "Showcase" quality, which requires careful planning and execution, is used only for the most expensive publications, such as museum-grade art books, expensive brochures, and some annual reports.

- **Quantity.**   Indicate what quantities you would like prices for. You may indicate three different quantities. And if you want to know the cost for additional thousands, check the last box and write "1000s" in the blank that follows.
- **Product Description.**   Describe the print job. Is it a full-color catalog with insert? A letter? Brochure? Something else?
- **Trim Size.**   Indicate the trim size for either flat sheets or for the bound or folded job. For example, a catalog might have a trim size of 8" × 10" when bound, or a brochure might be 4" × 7" when folded.
- **No. of Pages.**   How many pages will there be in the catalog, letter, or brochure? Will the catalog or brochure have a self cover (the cover is of the same stock and color as the rest of the text) or a separate cover? If the catalog has a self cover, the number of pages includes the cover; if the catalog has a separate cover, it is considered separate from the number of pages you indicate.
- **Design Features.**   Check whether the job will require any bleeds (printing to the edge of the page), screen tints (shading), reverses (white on black, etc.), or other frills that require extra prep work for the printer. Indicate how many screens or reverses will be required.
- **Art Provided.**   Check how you will be providing the material to the printer—camera-ready copy, negatives, or ready for typesetting by the printer.
- **Extras.**   Will the print job involve any halftones, duotones, or color separations? Indicate how many and whether you will be providing them or you want the printer to provide them from your materials.
- **Proofs.**   If you want to see what the job looks like once the printer has completed the prep work, you can ask for a proof in galley form, bluelines, composite color, or progressives. A simple black and white job with no extras or design features might not require proofing, but any color work should be proofed.
- **Paper.**   Indicate the weight, trade name, color, finish, and grade of paper you want to use. If you will be supplying the paper, let the printer know. If you want them to supply it, make sure they have it in stock or can order it in time. If you don't know how to specify the paper, enclose a sample of what you want with the RFQ.
- **Printing.**   Indicate the ink colors you want for the print job. If possible, specify as PMS numbers or include samples.
- **Bindery Operations.**   Indicate what you want them to do with the printing once it comes off the press. Do you want them to deliver it flat (if you were going to have another company do the bindery work), trim it, do any folding (Z-folds, letter folds, accordion folds, gatefolds, etc.), collate and gather it, drill any holes, or something else?
- **Bindings.**   If the printed piece is to be bound, indicate what kind of binding you want. The variations are described in *Getting It Printed* and in the *Directory of Book Printers*.
- **Packing.**   Indicate how you want the printed pieces to be packed.
- **Shipping.**   Check if you will be picking the job up or if you want the printer to send the finished pieces via UPS or truck. If the pieces should be delivered somewhere other than your company address, type in the address where the finished job should be delivered.

- **Comments.** Write any additional instructions that might be required to identify clearly what you want done.

If your direct mail package involves many pieces (a letter, a brochure, several envelopes, a lift letter, etc.), consider sending out separate RFQs for each item. Indeed, you might want to use different printers for various parts of the job.

If you don't know much about printing, it is best to work with an advertising agency, graphic designer, or printer to write out the specifications for these queries. If you feel you can do it yourself but need to know the meaning of certain terms, most of the words used in these two sample RFQs are defined in the glossaries of *Getting It Printed* and the *Directory of Book Printers*.

How to Calculate the Costs of Your Promotions

Once you have received the printing quotations, begin to add up the total costs of your direct mail promotions. You need to know these costs before you do any testing, because these costs are part of the calculations you must make to determine whether a mailing has paid off.

Use the direct mail promotion costs worksheet (Exhibit 3-3) to add up the costs of your promotions. This worksheet ensures that you will not leave out any major costs when adding them up.

For direct mail programs, calculate either total costs or costs/M (costs per thousand pieces). To figure costs/M, though, you need to know how many thousands you intend to mail since creative and prep work costs should be amortized over the entire mailing (or series of mailings). Other production costs also vary depending on quantity (for example, the cost/M for 1,000 letters might be $36, whereas for 20M it might be $29).

Here are the major costs to consider when calculating total promotional costs:

- **Creative.** All creative costs, including salaries or fees of the writers and artists, costs of materials, photographs, modeling fees, and retouching.
- **Prep.** The costs of typesetting, proofing, corrections, pasteup, color separations, negatives, stripping, and platemaking.
- **Printing.** Costs for all the pieces in the direct mail package: letters, envelopes, response vehicles, brochures, catalogs, and so forth. Use the price quotations you've received from your RFQs.
- **Lists.** The cost of renting the list, any special selections, and any merge/purge you require. If you are using your own list of customers, include the cost of maintaining and updating your list. (For details on the various options and costs of using mailing lists, see Chapter 5.)
- **Lettershop.** If you have a lettershop handle the mailing, inserting, addressing, sorting, and mailing, these charges may be grouped as one cost. If you do the mailing yourself, consider the costs of inserting all pieces into the outer envelope, the costs of labeling the envelope, and

Direct Mail Promotion Costs Worksheet

Product: Widgets		Promotion: Mailing to Widget Lovers of America	

Dept.	Description of Job	Cost/M	Total Costs
Creative	Writing copy (revisions and updates)	$22.50	$2,250
	Design and layout	3.50	350
	Artwork (mechanicals and finished art)	5.60	560
	Photography (photos, models/talent, retouching)	18.80	1,880
Prep	Typesetting (typography, proofing, corrections)	2.80	280
	Paste up camera-ready copy	1.20	120
	Halftones, color separations	4.30	430
	Platemaking (camera work, proofs, negatives, stripping, plates)	1.70	170
Printing	Letter	32.50	3,250
	Outer envelope	29.50	2,950
	Reply envelope	19.50	1,950
	Order form, response vehicle, reply card	12.50	1,250
	Brochure, catalog	71.65	7,165
	Other inserts (lift letter, buck slip, etc.)	7.75	775
Lists	List rental	60.00	6,000
	List selects (zip code, hotline names, etc.)	5.00	500
	Merge/purge		
Lettershop	Inserting	15.00	1,500
	Addressing or labeling	15.00	1,500
	Sorting, metering, and mailing	15.00	1,500
Overhead	Percentage of overhead for advertising and mailing departments		
Misc.			
	Production Costs Subtotal	343.80	34,380
Postage	First class, bulk rate, alternative delivery methods	167.00	16,700
Notes: 100,000 rollout mailing with revisions in copy, includes: 4-color brochure, 2 envelopes, 4-page letter, BRC, lift letter mailed with bulk mail stamps affixed, no merge/purge	Totals	$510.80	$51,080

Exhibit 3-3   Direct mail promotion costs worksheet.

the costs of bagging, sorting, and mailing. Be sure to include all labor costs.

- **Overhead.** A percentage of your overhead for the advertising department and mailing operations. Some mail order people include it; many don't, though, because they consider overhead a fixed cost.
- **Misc.** Any other products or services that might affect the costs of your promotions.
- **Production Costs.** Total production costs for the direct mail promotion may be totaled from all the items above. To get the total costs of your promotion, however, also add in the cost of the outgoing postage.
- **Postage.** Postage costs vary depending on whether you use first class, third-class bulk rate, or some other means of delivery, such as by hand, by mailgram, by UPS, by birds, or by lizards. You can be creative. To find out more about the options available for cutting down on postage costs, see Appendix I.

This promotion costs worksheet comes in handy not only in calculating break-even points, but it also gives you a fairly accurate picture of your total upfront investment for the promotion. You need to know this so you can be sure to have the money available when you are ready to roll out the promotion after doing test mailings.

How to Determine Your Break-Even Point

Now that you have calculated product and promotion costs, you can determine your break-even point for profitable mailings and ads. The break-even worksheet shown as Exhibit 3-4 makes it easy for you to consider the major costs of running any direct mail promotion, add them up, and then determine your break-even point. It also allows you to calculate your contribution margin, a figure that plays an important role in enabling you to project the profit potential of any program.

At the top of the worksheet, fill in the name of the product being promoted and indicate which promotion is being considered (an ad, a specific mailing, or a series of mailings). Then fill out each blank in the "Subtotals" and "Totals" columns.

Before you can calculate all the costs of handling a promotion, determine the adjusted selling price of the product so that you can calculate sales taxes, bad debts, and credit card charges.

1. Adjusted selling price. To determine the adjusted selling price, enter any postage and handling or credit card charges you require into 1-B. Then add these charges to the retail selling price of the product (1-A) to determine the adjusted selling price. This adjusted price should be the actual amount you receive from your customers.

2. Total costs of filling the order. To find out how much it costs to fill an order, add the following:

A. **Product unit cost.** The unit cost you calculated using the product costs worksheet (Exhibit 2-4).

Break-Even Worksheet

Product: Widget   **Promotion:** Mailing to Widget Lovers of America

Item #	Description of Item	Formulas	Subtotals	Totals
1 - A	Price of product or service being sold		$24.95	
B	Other charges (postage & handling, etc.)		3.00	
C	Adjusted price of product	(1A + 1B)		$27.95
2 - A	Cost of product or service		$3.67	
B	Handling expense and order processing		1.10	
C	Package expenses (mailing carton, tape, etc.)		.70	
D	Shipping (postage or UPS charges)		2.30	
E	Premium costs including handling (if premium offered)		0	
F	Sales or use tax, if any	(1C x 5%)	1.40	
G	Total costs of filling the order			9.17
3 - A	Estimated percentage of returns (expressed as a decimal)		.05	
B	Postage and handling of returns	(2B + 2D)	$3.40	
C	Refurbishing returned merchandise	(10% of 2A)	.37	
D	Total costs of handling returns	(3B + 3C)	3.77	
E	Chargeable costs of handling returns	(3A x 3D)		.19
4 - A	Estimated percentage of bad debts (expressed as a decimal)		.05	
B	Chargeable costs of bad debts	(1C x 4A)		1.40
5 - A	Estimated percentage of sales via credit cards (as a decimal)		.50	
B	Credit card processing charge	(4.0% of 1C)	$1.12	
C	Chargeable cost of credit	(5A x 5B)		.56
6 - A	Administrative overhead	(10% of 1A)		2.50
7 - A	Miscellaneous costs			0
8 - A	Total variable costs	(2G + 3E + 4B + 5C + 6A + 7A)		$13.82
9 - A	Unit profit after variable costs	(1C - 8A)		14.13
10 - A	Percentage of final sales (expressed as a decimal)	(1.0 - 3A)	.95	
11 - A	Net unit profit	(9A x 10A)		13.42
12 - A	Credit for returned merchandise	(3A x 2A)		.18
13 - A	Contribution margin (net profit per order)	(11A + 12A)		$13.60
14 - A	Mailing or advertising cost per thousand		$510.80	
B	Number of orders per M to break even	(14A / 13A)		38 orders

Notes:

Exhibit 3-4   Break-even worksheet.

B. **Order processing.** All labor expenses involved in handling the order, including opening the mail, adding the name to your customer list, packing the order, and shipping it out.

C. **Package expenses.** The costs for the mailing carton, tape, label, packing peanuts, and anything else you put into the package.

D. **Shipping.** Weigh a sample package (including the product, the packaging, and any other inserts) to figure out the cost of shipping. If you use more than one method of shipping (for example, UPS and post office), estimate what percentage of packages will be shipped via each method and then average the costs taking these percentages into account. For example, if it cost $3.43 to ship the package via UPS (80% of orders) and $2.67 to ship via the post office (the other 20%), the average would be: ($3.43 × .80) + ($2.67 × .20) = $3.28.

E. **Premium costs.** If you offer a premium as part of the promotion, add in the unit cost of the premium plus any additional handling expenses.

F. **Sales tax.** If your state has a sales tax or you are subject to sales taxes in any other states, multiply the tax percentage times the total selling price (1-C) to figure your costs. Adjust this figure to match the percentage of total orders received from in-state buyers (or buyers from other states where you are subject to the sales tax).

G. **Total fulfillment costs.** Add up 2-A through 2-F.

   3. Returns. To find out what returns will cost you to handle, enter the following information and do the following calculations:

A. **Percentage of returns.** Estimate the percentage of returns, refund requests, or order cancellations expected. This percentage can vary from 1% to 15% or more. Most mail order programs allow for a 5% to 10% return rate. The return percentage depends a lot on your product, credit policies, advertising pitch, and customer base. The best way to calculate return percentage is by past experience from similar programs you have run or, better yet, from tests of the program itself. When in doubt, estimate toward the high side rather than the low side of your expectations.

B. **Handling of returns.** To figure your costs for returns, add the return postage and handling costs, which should be equivalent to your original postage and handling expenses (2-B + 2-D). Include postage costs because some people send returns collect or without postage. Also, some packages are refused and then returned to you by the post office at your expense (if you have guaranteed return postage, which you should if your product costs more than the postage and handling expenses).

C. **Refurbishing.** Allow at least 10% of the cost of the product (2-A) for refurbishing returned materials for resale. This assumes, of course, that the product can be refurbished for resale. Otherwise enter the unit cost of the product here.

D. **Total costs.** Add 3-B and 3-C to calculate the total costs of handling a return.

E. **Chargeable costs of returns.**   The total costs of handling returns must be multiplied by your estimated return percentage to obtain the chargeable costs of returns. These chargeable costs should be included in the total costs of the program. For example, if you expect 5% returns and your cost of handling returns is $3.77, then add 19¢ (.05 × $3.77) to your program costs.

4. Bad debts.   Just as you must allow for returns, allow for bad checks, no pays, and other assorted duds.

A. **Percentage of bad debts.**   If you invoice customers, the bad debt rate could go as high as 25%. It is best to estimate the percentage based on your past experience with similar products and customers. If this is not possible, then allow at least 5% to 10%. My company's bad debt percentage among book publishers is less than 1%, but it is more than 3% among direct marketers. What does that say about our business? Of course, generally that 3% consists of opportunity seekers and dabblers rather than serious entrepreneurs or full-time professionals.
B. **Chargeable costs of bad debts.**   Multiply your estimated percentage of bad debts times the total selling price (1-C) to calculate how much to allow for bad debts in the total program costs.

5. Credit costs.   If you take payment by credit card, allow for the percentage the bank charges for processing these orders.

A. **Percentage of credit card sales.**   Estimate how many customers will use credit cards. In my business, it's about 30%. But if your customers are consumers rather than professionals, the percentage could be much higher. Also, if you heavily promote the use of credit cards and a toll-free number, the percentage will be higher.
B. **Credit card processing charge.**   Add in the fees that the bank charges when processing credit cards. Generally this is a percentage of the total charge. Hence, multiply the percentage the bank charges times the adjusted price of the product (1-C) to obtain the total processing charge.
C. **Chargeable cost of credit.**   To calculate the chargeable cost of credit, multiply the estimated percentage of credit card sales (5-A) times the bank processing charge (5-B). This calculation tells how much it costs to provide charge card privileges.

If your bank charges you 5¢ to 10¢ for every check you cash, you might also include this check charge as part of the credit costs. The **chargeable costs of cashing checks** equals the check charge multiplied by the estimated percentage of customers paying by check. Alternatively, you may consider the check charge as part of your regular administrative overhead expenses.

6. Administrative overhead. Some mail order people do not include administrative overhead in these calculations because they consider overhead a fixed rather than a variable cost. Many others do assign a percentage of the retail price (1-A) to administrative overhead costs since these costs (office salaries, rent, utilities, telephone, office supplies) can vary with the sales volume. If you do include overhead, allow from 5% to 20% (10% is average). Assigning administrative overhead to variable costs is reasonable if you expect to sell a large quantity of units or if your administrative overhead expenses per promotion are low.

7. Miscellaneous costs. If you receive a large percentage of orders via a toll-free number or fax, you should probably include these costs in your calculations (since you pay for the toll-free calls and the fax paper). Estimate what percentage of customers will use the toll-free number or fax machine to send orders, and then multiply by the average costs of using these alternatives.

8. Total variable costs. To calculate the total variable costs of your promotion, add up the costs of filling the order (2-G), processing returns (3-E), bad debt allowance (4-B), credit costs (5-C), overhead (6-A), and any miscellaneous costs (7-A).

9. Unit profit after variable costs. Subtract the total variable costs from the total selling price (1-C) to obtain the unit profit.

10. Percentage of final sales. To calculate the percentage of sales that are final (with no refunds), subtract the estimated percentage of returns for refunds after the initial sale (3-A) by the total percentage of sales (100% or, expressed as a decimal, 1.0).

11. Net unit profit. Multiply the percentage of final sales (10-A) times the unit profit after variable costs (9-A).

12. Credit for returned merchandise. If you can resell merchandise that has been returned to you, add the value of that merchandise into your calculations. Calculate how much this refurbished merchandise is worth to you by multiplying the percentage of returns (3-A) times the cost of the products (2-A).

13. Contribution margin. The contribution margin, or net profit per order, equals the selling price minus the total variable costs. It is the amount of money still available to pay for advertising (and allow for a profit) after all the variable costs are taken care of. The contribution margin is calculated by adding the net unit profit (11-A) to the credit for returned merchandise (12-A). As you can see, returns play an important role in the overall costs of any mail order program.

This break-even worksheet is probably the most important worksheet in this book. If you learn nothing else from this book but use this form when calculating your break-even points, you will earn back the cost of this book manyfold.

HOW TO CALCULATE YOUR BREAK-EVEN POINT

Break-Even Points for Direct Mail Programs

The **break-even point** is the point at which you make no profit but lose no money; in short, you break even. Any orders exceeding the break-even point make money for you.

To calculate your break-even point (BE), divide the mailing costs per thousand (the total cost/M calculated in the direct mail promotion costs worksheet) by the contribution margin (CM), which is on line 13-A of the break-even worksheet.

For example, if your mailing costs per thousand circulars were $510.80 and your CM were $13.60, your BE would be 38 orders (actually 37.56) per thousand. This means you need a response of almost 4% to make a profit on this promotion.

> The 4% response rate in the example is figured by dividing the BE point of 38 orders per thousand by 1,000. This gives a result of 3.8%, which was then rounded to 4% since you need to get *more than* 3.8% to make a profit.

Break-Even Points for Magazine Ads

You can also use the break-even worksheet to figure your break-even point for a magazine ad. Substitute the cost of the ad in line 14-A, or divide the ad cost by the contribution margin. For example, if your ad costs were $2,850 and your CM was $13.60, the BE would be 210 orders (actually, 209.56).

To figure out how many orders you need per thousand subscribers, divide the circulation of the magazine by 1,000 and then divide the BE by the resulting number. For example, if the circulation of the magazine were 434,000, you would need .48 order per thousand to break even (210/434). This means you would need a response rate of almost .5% (or about 1/2 percent) in order to make a profit.

> If you did not include administrative overhead costs in line 6-A of the break-even worksheet but do expect the mailing or ad to cover these expenses, then you must still take them into consideration before calculating your break-even point. To take them into consideration, add the overhead to the cost of the advertisement or to the cost of mailing 1,000 circulars (by amortizing the overhead over the entire mailing) and enter the new total on line 14-A of the worksheet. Then calculate the BE as before.

HOW TO PROJECT YOUR PROFITS

Once you know the break-even point, you can project potential profits for different rates of response. It is a simple calculation. To make it even simpler, use the projected profit worksheet (Exhibit 3-5). Enter the numbers or do the appropriate calculations for each of the following steps:

1. Make up to four estimates of the number of orders you expect to receive per thousand circulars mailed. In the example, I used 30, 35, 40, and 45 orders. Enter enough numbers to reflect what you believe is the range of possible response rates.
2. Write down the number of orders you need per thousand circulars in order to break even. Use the results of your break-even calculations (line 14-B on the break-even worksheet). Enter this number under all four response rates.
3. Subtract the break-even number from estimated responses (the number in line 1 from the number in line 2). The result is the number of orders expected to produce a profit. In the example, the response rates of 3% and 3.5% do not produce a profit, but the 4% and 4.5% response rates do.
4. Write your contribution margin on line 4 under all four response rates. The contribution margin is the number on line 13-A of the break-even worksheet.
5. To discover your profit for each thousand circulars mailed, multiply profit-producing orders (line 3) times contribution margin (line 4).
6. To find out total net profit for the entire mailing, write down the total number of circulars you plan to mail and divide by 1,000. In the example, the company mailed 100,000 circulars.
7. Multiply the results of line 5 times line 6. If the company in the example were to go ahead with the mailing and it got only a 3% response, the company would lose $10,880. If the response rate were 4.5%, the company would make a profit of $9,520.

For magazine advertisements, if your break-even is already expressed in total number of orders from the entire readership, then you need only go through the first five steps in the worksheet. Make four estimates of the total number of orders you expect from the ad; subtract the number of orders needed to break even; and then multiply the result by your contribution margin. You will then have a projection of the potential profits for various response rates to the magazine ad.

HOW TO DETERMINE YOUR RETURN ON INVESTMENT

Even when you make a profit on a mailing or ad, you still need to know whether the potential profit is worth the investment of your time and money. Hence, before going ahead with a project, calculate the percentage

Projected Profit and Return on Investment Worksheet

Product: Widgets

Promotion: Mailing to Widget Lovers of America

No.	Profit Projects Calculations	Formulas	Projected Rates of Response (Pull)			
			Rate 1	Rate 2	Rate 3	Rate 4
1	Estimated number of orders / M		30	35	40	45
2	Break-even number of orders / M	(line 14-B, B-E)	38	38	38	38
3	Profit-producing orders	(#1 - #2)	- 8	- 3	2	7
4	Contribution margin	(line 13-A, B-E Worksheet)	$13.60	$13.60	$13.60	$13.60
5	Profit / M circulars	(#3 x #4)	($108.80)	($40.80)	$27.20	$95.20
6	Total number of circulars mailed divided by 1000		100	100	100	100
7	**Total net profit**	(#5 x #6)	($10,880)	($4,080)	$2,720	$9,520

No.	Profit Projects Calculations	Formulas	Rate 1	Rate 2	Rate 3	Rate 4
8	Total variable costs	(line 8-A, B-E Worksheet)	$13.82	$13.82	$13.82	$13.82
9	Promotion Costs / M	(line 14-A, B-E Worksheet)	$510.80	$510.80	$510.80	$510.80
10	Investment / M circulars	[(#8 x #1) + #9]	$925.40	$994.50	$1,063.60	$1,132.70
11	Selling price (adjusted)	(line 1-C, B-E Worksheet)	$27.95	$27.95	$27.95	$27.95
12	Total Income / M circulars	(#1 x #11)	$838.50	$978.25	$1,118.00	$1,257.75
13	Net Income / M circulars	(#12 - #10)	($86.90)	($16.25)	$54.40	$125.05
14	Return on Investment	(#13 / #10)	(.094)	(.016)	.051	.110
15	**Return on Investment as a %**	(100 x #14)	(9.4%)	(1.6%)	5.1%	11.0%

Notes: The actual break-even point is 37.56. If we used that number, our profit figures would improve. For example, at a 4% response rate, our total net profit would be $3,318.40.

If we can cut our promotion costs by $40.00, we would make a slight profit at a 3.5% response rate, since the break-even point would then be 34.6 orders per thousand ($470.80 / $13.60).

Again, if we can cut our promotion costs by $40.00, our return on investment would also be much greater. For instance, with a 3.5% response our ROI would be 2.5% rather than a negative. At 4.5% response, our ROI would be 15.1%.

Exhibit 3-5   Projected profit and ROI worksheet.

return on your investment (ROI). If you cannot get an ROI that is at least equal to the interest your bank would pay for your money, why bother? Keep it in the bank. It's safer.

To calculate your ROI, you need to know the following:

- Selling price of your product.
- Total variable costs per unit product
- Response, or the number of orders per thousand circulars you mail.
- Promotion costs, that is, the cost per thousand circulars you mail.

Your total investment for each 1,000 circulars you mail is equal to your variable costs times the response per 1,000 plus your promotion costs. Your percentage ROI then equals your selling price times the response per 1,000 plus your investment per 1,000 divided by that same investment.

That all sounds very complicated, and in some ways it is. But it is easy if you use the bottom half of the projected profit and return on investment worksheet (Exhibit 3-5). Fill in the numbers (all taken from the break-even worksheet) and do the simple calculations.

1. *Line 8.* Enter the total variable costs per unit (from line 8-A of the break-even worksheet).
2. *Line 9.* Enter the promotion costs per thousand circulars that you mail (from line 15-A of the break-even worksheet or from the total Cost/M at the bottom of the promotion costs worksheet).
3. *Line 10.* Calculate your investment per thousand circulars mailed. Calculate that investment by multiplying total variable costs per unit times the estimated rate of response (line 8 times line 1), and then add the result to promotion costs (line 9).
4. *Line 11.* Enter the adjusted selling price of your product (from line 1-C of the break-even worksheet).
5. *Line 12.* Determine total income for each thousand circulars mailed by multiplying adjusted selling price (line 11) times the estimated response rate (line 1).
6. *Line 13.* Calculate net income per thousand circulars mailed by subtracting total income (line 12) from your investment (line 10).
7. Calculate the ROI by dividing the net income (line 13) by the investment per thousand circulars (line 10).
8. To express the return on investment as a percentage, multiply the results you entered in line 14 by 100.

In the example, only a response rate of 4.5% gives a return on investment (11%) that competes with what you could receive by putting your money into a money market account. At the lower response rates, you would do better with a bank (at least, for this example).

Don't give up if your initial calculations lead to a poor ROI. Look to see if you can change something. Here are just a few of the things you could do (and their effect on your ROI):

- **Test different prices.** Often a higher price will sell as well as or better than a lower price. If the selling price for the widgets were $29.95, the ROI would be 5.4% at a 3% response rate and 19% at a 4% response.

- **Try to lower your costs**—either your promotion costs or your variable costs or both. There are ways to cut costs without hurting the product quality or response. For instance, if promotion costs were cut by $40.00, the ROI would be 2.5% at 3% response and 15.1% at 4.5%.
- **Try to increase response rates.**   Test different offers, selling packages, or payment terms—all of these are known to affect response rates. In the example, the higher response rates produced a better ROI.

> The calculations in this book for break-even points, projected profits, and return on investment are given only as examples. They will work in most cases as a quick check on your profitability. But before acting on these calculations (and the underlying assumptions), always check with an accountant or comptroller to make sure that you figure all expenses and income in a way that is compatible with your accounting system.

4

How to Design an Effective Direct Mail Package

THE ADVANTAGES OF DIRECT MAIL

Of all direct marketing methods, I prefer direct mail. Following are just a few of the advantages of direct mail:

- **It is quicker to produce.** You can prepare and mail a small promotion within days or weeks rather than months. Hence, it is perfect for testing prices, products, offers, and potential audiences. More elaborate and carefully targeted promotions do take longer to prepare, but even then they usually require a shorter lead time than most other media.
- **Response is quicker.** You can project the final results of a mailing more quickly and accurately than you can with most other advertising.
- **It can be cheaper, especially for smaller tests.** Using a computer to generate the sales letters, I have done personalized first-class mailings to lists as large as 500 for only the cost of paper, envelopes, and postage (about 30¢ per piece).
- **It does not require as much design time.** A standardized direct mail format (letter, response card, folder or brochure, and return envelope) is much easier to design and produce than a direct response magazine advertisement or a television commercial.
- **It can be highly targeted.** If you choose lists carefully, you can target your mailings much more selectively than you can with most other media. You can reach almost any market segment, buyer profile, or area of the country you feel is most appropriate for your offer.
- **It allows you to target hard-to-reach consumers.**
- **It is more flexible.** After testing a promotion, you can change almost

anything right away without waiting. You have complete control over the media, the audience, and your offer.

- **It can offer more details.**   You can pack a lot of information into one envelope—far more than you can on a full-page magazine or newspaper ad, or in two minutes or even a half-hour on radio or television.
- **There is less competition.**   Your advertising message does not have to compete with other advertising messages or editorial matter. At least, it doesn't have to compete once the envelope is opened.
- **It can be more personal.**   Not only can letters be personalized via mail-merging techniques, but you can use more informal language in writing your letter and can direct your letter to the specific interests of the reader.
- **It is easier to respond to.**   The inclusion of an order card and return envelope makes it easier for the consumer to respond to direct mail as compared to magazine ads (unless you include a bind-in card opposite the advertisement or include a toll-free order number).
- **It is easier to keep.**   A direct mail piece is more likely to be retained for future reference than a magazine ad since many readers find it inconvenient to tear an advertisement out of a magazine or will be reluctant to do so. Other forms of advertising (radio, television, newspapers, billboards, and telemarketing) offer nothing to retain.
- **It can build a list of loyal customers.**   It allows you to build and maintain an in-house list of prime prospects for future products or current related products. Furthermore, you can make money renting the list to other direct marketers.
- **It can be used to test.**   You can build an advertising campaign with more confidence by testing small lists, then building to larger lists, and then rolling out to a full list or lists. I saved the best reason for last.

THE MANY WAYS YOU CAN USE DIRECT MAIL

Direct mail can be used for many other reasons besides making a direct sale: to increase the sales of your products via other distribution channels, to enhance your company's reputation, to service customers, or any number of other reasons:

- **Obtain inquiries.**   You can use an inexpensive direct mail package to obtain inquiries about your product, which you then follow up with a more expensive and elaborate informational package to obtain a sale.
- **Obtain leads.**   Use direct mail to obtain leads for direct sales representatives or telemarketing staff.
- **Offer free trials.**   One of the most effective ways to sell expensive products is to offer a 15- (or 30-) day free trial period. When a customer sends in a request, send the product with an invoice. Upon receipt, the customer has 15 days to return the product if not satisfied or pay the accompanying invoice.
- **Supplement retail sales.**   Harlequin, a romance book publisher, uses direct mail to make sales they would not reach through retail stores.

According to its president, Harlequin's direct sales do not cut into retail sales. This additive effect of direct mail sales has also been noticed in many other industries (such as the toy and gift industries).

- **Boost retail sales.**   The publishers of Reader's Digest Books have found that many of the people they mail to actually buy the book at a retail bookstore rather than order direct by mail. Inevitably when they make a mailing on a backlist title, bookstore sales also increase.
- **Make special sales.**   To reach potential volume buyers (for premium or catalog sales), direct mail followed up by telephone calls is the most cost-effective way to advertise.
- **Sell licensing rights.**   One of the most cost-effective ways to sell licensing or other subsidiary rights to your products is to reach potential buyers via direct mail and then follow up with telephone calls.
- **Publicize your product.**   Most publicity is generated by direct mail, followed up by telephone calls.
- **Maintain contact with key customers.**   Direct mail can be used to send newsletters, updates, and other customer communications to help you maintain contact with your key customers. Such continuing contact can lead to better customer relations and, hence, to more sales.
- **Build your customer list.**   One of the great advantages of direct marketing is that you can build up a list of buyers who are interested in the areas related to your specialty. Many direct marketers even lose money on their first mailings just so they can build up their list—not only for their own future use but also to rent to others.
- **Conduct research.**   Use direct mail to do market research and surveys. Many opinion polls and other market research are already conducted by this method. By doing market research you can discover what's right and what's not so right about your product.
- **Sell advertising.**   If you publish magazines, directories, or other reference books where advertising is accepted, you can sell advertising space by mail.

THE THREE FUNDAMENTALS OF DIRECT MAIL

The following three elements are vital to the success of any direct mail promotion. If any of these is missing or inadequate, the chances of success are slim.

1. **The offer.**   Your product must be worth the cost. Make an irresistible offer, and your chances of success are much greater than if the product is inadequate or the price is too high (or too low).
2. **The advertising copy.**   The format of direct mail is not nearly as important as its message. The copy must speak to the interests of the reader. The letter, brochure, order form, lift letter, and other enclosures must stimulate the reader to act.
3. **The list.**   You can have the best offer and the most irresistible copy in the world, but if you mail to the wrong list, none of that will have any

effect. Hence, of the three fundamentals, many direct marketing professionals would insist that the list is the most important.

HOW TO IMPROVE YOUR OFFER

The most important element of your offer is the product itself. If the product answers a definite need, your offer may need little else to be effective. Nonetheless, here are a few suggestions on how to improve your offer to make it more enticing to the mail order buyer.

To help you cover all the possibilities when designing your direct mail offers, I have provided a checklist of these points in Appendix II (Exhibit 4-1—Direct Mail Checklists). Make extra copies to use each time you sit down to design an offer.

- **Offer a premium for buying your product.** When Open Horizons first offered the *Directory of Book Printers* for direct sale, we offered a choice of four reports for ordering early: (1) *20 Ways to Save on the Printing of Your Books*, (2) *16 Points to Consider When Selecting a Book Printer*, (3) *70 Full-Color Catalog and Brochure Printers*, or (4) *68 Books about Publishing—a Bibliographic Review*. We found the response to these free premiums to be so great (indeed, many people bought the other three reports) that we included the first two reports in the third edition of the *Directory*. Whatever premium you do offer, be sure it has a high perceived value regardless of its actual cost.

- **Set a time limit.** If you limit the availability of the product or a special offer, you can increase the response. At the very least, most people respond more quickly (which can be important if you require a faster inflow of cash).

- **Offer a discount for ordering within a certain time limit or for a volume order.** For years, my company has offered a 10% discount to anyone ordering three or more books at the same time. And because of this offer, I seldom get orders for two books. When customers order more than one book, they invariably order three or more. Indeed, I have gotten many comments from customers saying that they simply could not resist the discount. A study of "What Works Best" by the American Advertising Distributors of South Jersey found that discounted offers generally worked best for pulling in new customers for retail stores that used direct mail.

- **Offer payment options.** Allow payment by credit card, check, billing, or some other option. The billing option is almost a necessity if you are selling to companies. Indeed, a credit or bill-me offer has been known to improve results by 50% or more. Installment payments, for items costing more than $25, can also improve results. (You will have to allow for credit or collection costs in your break-even analysis if you extend liberal payment options.)

- **Make it easy to order.** Allow ordering by telephone, by collect call, or by a toll-free number. Provide a BRE (business reply envelope) to make it easier for customers to send in the order. Since Open Horizons installed a toll-free order number, about 35% of our orders and about 60% of our dollar volume now comes over the telephone.

• **Offer a free trial period.** The free trial period works particularly well for advertising in card decks where your advertising message is so limited by the available space that you almost have to offer people a chance to try the product before they buy it. "What Works Best" found that a free week's trial membership was the most effective offer for bringing in new members for health clubs.

• **Offer a demo.** Computer software companies have discovered that one of the best ways to attract the interest of potential buyers is to offer a demonstration diskette of their program. Perfume manufacturers have discovered that scent strips are a superb way to give consumers an experience of their product.

• **Buy one, get one free.** This ploy has been used for years by some marketers of vitamins. It is, according to "What Works Best," also the best way to pull in new customers for local restaurants that do direct mail: "Buy one entrée; get a second entrée free."

• **Make your unique selling proposition stand out.** Be sure that your product is seen as unique. Establish a point of difference in your offer. For instance, to promote its frequent flier program from those that restricted travel to U.S. destinations, Pan-Am made it clear that fliers could go anywhere in the world using its frequent flier program.

• **Enhance your product.** Look for ways to make it better, or ways for it to serve another audience, or ways for it to serve other needs of prime customers. To encourage people who use MCI telephone service at their offices to use it also in their homes or when they travel, MCI developed the MCI calling card.

• **Offer several versions of the product.** One version could be standard and the other a higher-priced and more exclusive version. Generally you can never sell two items through one mailing package (unless your mailing package is a catalog), but you can sell two different versions of the same item—and make it work for you. In a mailing for the third edition of the *Directory of Book Printers*, we offered both the standard book (for $13 postpaid) and a Deluxe MailMerge Edition (for $30 postpaid). About 15% of the resulting orders were for the higher-priced edition.

• **Make a special offer.** For example, send discount coupons to all customers in celebration of your company's anniversary saying, "It's our birthday, but you get the present!" The coupon could, for instance, offer $3 off for any order regardless of size.

The more believable your special offer is to your target audience, the more likely it is that it will succeed.

- **Offer special benefits to repeat buyers or previous customers.**   Some credit card companies offer special discounts or premium points the more you use their cards.

- **Guarantee satisfaction.**   Offer a 30-day money-back guarantee, a lifetime replacement warranty, or some other form of guarantee that assures customers that you will stand by your product. Then stand by it.

- **Run a sweepstakes.**   Sweepstakes can increase orders by 50%. Other contest offers can also increase reader participation and response.

- **Offer rush service.**   People appreciate fast service. If you offer special shipping, people respond. Quick service is especially important for seasonal products such as holiday gifts.

HOW TO WRITE EFFECTIVE DIRECT MAIL LETTERS

Although the format of your direct mail package is not nearly as important as the advertising copy itself, variations in format can have measurable effects on the response. When you write advertising copy:

- **Sell the benefits.**   Above all, write copy that sells the benefits that can be derived from using your product. Don't leave any doubt about what the benefits are, and don't expect the readers to guess what the benefits are from a listing of the product's features. Tell them. Spell it out in clear language that anyone could understand.

- **Offer a benefit right away.**   The first paragraph—indeed the first line—should pique the interest of the reader; it should inspire the reader to read on. You must capture the reader's interest right away, or the entire letter will fail because the reader stops too soon.

- **Use "you" copy.**   Write in a personal, comfortable style. Don't use overly long sentences or paragraphs. Underline words to make a point. Vary the length of paragraphs. And even begin sentences with *and* or *or* or *but*. In short, write in a conversational tone as if you were writing to a friend rather than being graded by the queen's grammarian.

- **Remember the classic formula for writing direct mail copy that sells: AIDA (attention, interest, desire, action).**   First, get the reader's attention. Second, once you have their attention, keep them interested by asking questions, answering questions, giving examples, and stating benefits. Third, stir their desire by demonstrating to them all the advantages of owning the product you are offering. And, finally, inspire them to act. Ask for the order. Make it easy to order. And don't let them delay.

- **Above all, ask for the order.**   Make your offer clear. Repeat the offer on your response card or order form.

- **Don't be afraid to be redundant.**   Repeat if necessary. Say the same thing several times to be sure that the reader has gotten the point. You don't have to repeat everything in the same paragraph, but you should repeat your main offer and the major benefits of your product several times in the mailing package—at least three times. Repetition helps to make your point clear and avoids any possible misunderstandings. (You can even repeat the exact same sentence again later on in your letter. If it's a good sentence, it can bear repeating.)

• **Use key words that people respond to.** Here are a few of those key words: *you, your, free, new, bonus, satisfaction guaranteed, order now, success.* According to research done at Yale University, the following 12 words are the most persuasive: *discovery, easy, guarantee, health, love, money, new, proven, results, safety, save, you.* There are, of course, many more key words, but these are among the most effective. To help you remember these key words and think of other effective words when writing your direct mail copy, make a copy of the words that work checklist in Appendix II.

• **Use testimonials in your letter.** When we mailed out a letter offering the *Directory of Book Printers*, we included the following testimonial as teaser copy on the front of the envelope and as the lead to our letter: "Without Kremer's *Directory* I paid $12,500 for the first printing of one book—and got plenty of production hassles. With the *Directory* I paid $4,500 for the identical job—and no problems!" That testimonial not only allowed us to sum up the two main benefits of the *Directory*, but it did it in an objective yet dramatic way.

• **Direct your offer to the people reading the letter.** If you switch lists and customer profile is different, rewrite the letter if necessary to appeal to the new audience.

• **Write as much copy as you need to tell your story—no more, no less.** But note: A two-page letter tends to pull better than a one-page letter, and a four-page letter tends to pull better than a two-page letter.

• **Use details.** Use specifics to boost the credibility of your letters. Whenever you make a general point, back it up with detail. Use numbers, testimonials, success stories, case studies, and statistics.

• **Offer free information.** Give the reader some free information in your letter: predictions that affect his or her well-being or business, news, trends, unusual facts, advice, or how-to instructions. Make sure it offers the reader a reason to continue reading your letter.

• **Personalize your letter.** Don't use computers just to merge the recipient's name into the greeting and body of the letter. Have a reason for using the person's name. Better yet, use some other details that demonstrate you know the reader's background. For instance, Merrill Lynch sent a personalized letter to some of its key Investment Retirement Account clients detailing what their present holdings were and how their retirement value would change if they switched to a new program Merrill Lynch was offering. To personalize the letter even more, each letter was signed by the client's financial consultant. Sales for the program doubled as a result of this single mailing.

• **Develop more personal salutations.**   Rather than writing "Dear Customer" or "Dear Reader," start your letter with "Dear Plant Lover" or "Dear Fellow Publisher." Address the audience directly.

• **Change style to suit your audience.**   Use a casual style when writing to sportswear buyers. Use a more technical style when writing to a medical audience about a new drug or treatment. For most letters, an enthusiastic personal style is probably best—almost as if you were writing to your best friends to tell them about a great new product you've just discovered.

• **Be honest.**   Keep your words and style believable. Don't exaggerate, and don't use hype. I have always found it to be more effective to be completely open and honest in my letters.

SOME DESIGN TECHNIQUES TO ENLIVEN YOUR LETTERS

Here are some techniques you can use to involve readers more and enliven the look and feel of your letters.

• **Add a P.S. at the end of your letter.**   Time and again, a postscript has proved effective in increasing orders. Use it to restate the key benefit of your product, to offer an added inducement to order, or to offer a guarantee. The P.S. is one of the most read parts of any direct mail letter. Most people read the postscript before they read the letter.

• **Letters should look like letters.**   Use typewriter type in your direct mail letters. It still works better than fancy typefaces—perhaps because it seems more personal and less high tech.

• **Use involvement devices, such as stickers, tabs, stamps, rub-offs, or tokens to get the reader involved.**   Involvement devices almost always improve results. But you don't always have to be elaborate. You can also get readers involved by asking them to check boxes, answer a question, fill in a blank, jot down some numbers, or circle some words. *Games* magazine used an unusual involvement device (that was also a personalization) at the top of one of their letters: a connect-the-dots puzzle that spelled out the last name of the recipient.

• **Enclose money.**   Paste or tape it onto your letter. People always respond to money, even if only a nickel. *Graphics Arts Monthly* enclosed a quarter with a request for reader feedback. They wrote, "There's no way we can pay for your time ... perhaps the coin will help brighten the day of a child you know."

• **Use handwriting.**   Besides underlining sentences, circle certain words or write something in the margin (using legible handwriting). Don't overdo this, but use whatever seems appropriate to emphasize a point or make the letter more personal. In several test mailings designed by Herschell Gordon Lewis, author of *Direct Mail Copy That Sells*, a handwritten overline outpulled a typed overline. When using handwriting in a letter, he recommends that you make sure the handwriting is legible, that the handwritten note is short, and that the note adds some spice to the letter.

- **Highlight with a second color.** Blue is the most common color used to highlight points in direct mail letters because it allows the writer to sign the letter in blue ink, the standard color for signing letters. But red stands out more, and you might want to use it to highlight important benefits or key points in your letters. You might experiment with pastels or fluorescents if they are appropriate to the audience.

- **End each page of your letter with an incomplete sentence so the reader will turn the page.** Or end the page by offering a special benefit or by asking a question. How would you then begin the next page? By answering the question from the previous page. The question is an irresistible lure. The reader is forced to turn the page to find out what the answer is.

- **Use a Johnson box.** That's the box at the top of many direct mail letters that is made up of asterisks. It contains one or two sentences that serve the purpose of a headline or lead.

- **Use short paragraphs.** No paragraph should be more than seven lines long. Indent the beginning of paragraphs. Indent the entire paragraph. Every so often, use a one-sentence or one-line paragraph.

- **Use a rebus letter.** A rebus is a picture used in place of a word—for example, an illustration of an eye for the word "I" or a picture of a bee as part of the word "beware." Such a letter might be unusual enough to work for certain audiences.

These are just some of the techniques you can use to make your direct mail letters more appealing and, thus, more effective. But remember that these are just the frills. Your offer and your copy are far more important.

To help you when you need an idea for something different in your own mailings, start up a swipe file. Save every direct mail package, catalog, flyer, advertisement, or letter that you find effective (whether because of its copy, its layout, its color, its graphics, or some other feature). File these away under appropriate categories: words that sell, great openings, fantastic layouts, effective order forms, unusual formats, and so on. Refer to them when you need fresh ideas or even tried and true ideas.

Start a collection of reference books on the subject. Here are a few that I recommend most often (besides the basic introductory guides I recommended in the Introduction to this book). For details about these and many other books, see the Bibliography in the back of this book.

Cash Copy, by Jeffrey Lant
Words That Sell, by Richard Bayan
Direct Mail Copy That Sells, by Herschell Gordon Lewis
More Than You Ever Wanted to Know about Mail Order, by H. G. Lewis

Tested Advertising Methods, by John Caples
Create the Perfect Sales Piece, by Robert Bly
The Direct Marketer's Idea Book, by Martin Gross
Direct Marketing Success: What Works and Why, by Freeman F. Gosden, Jr.
The Solid Golid Mailbox, by Walter H. Weintz

TIPS FOR CREATING MORE EFFECTIVE ENVELOPES

One of the first barriers any direct mail letter faces is at the mailbox. Many letters are thrown away without being opened because the outside envelopes did not inspire the recipient to open the letters. Here are a few techniques other direct mailers have used to get their envelopes opened:

• **Use teaser copy.**   One way to get an envelope opened is to print some teaser copy on it that suggests a benefit to interest the recipient. The best teasers are the ones that target your intended audience and offer an enticing reward for opening the envelope. For example, the *Games* magazine mailing that featured the connect-the-dots puzzle used the following teaser on its envelope: "Connect the dots and discover a surprise from *Games* magazine! Gift pencil enclosed." Anyone interested in *Games* magazine would open such an envelope.

   Here's the teaser I used on one of my most successful mailings: **"Inside: 112 book marketing contacts—and a $5,000 guarantee."** The mailing, which sold subscriptions to the *Book Promotion Hotline* newsletter, was read. I know, because I counted the returns.

• **Use windows to pull in interest.**   The *Games* magazine mailing envelope had a window that featured a set of numbered dots that, when connected, spelled out the recipient's last name.

• **Make the envelope look important.**   You can make it look like a telegram, a bill, a check enclosure, a priority letter, or an important business letter. Such letters have to be opened in case they are the real thing. Of course, you risk alienating the recipients if you deceive them into opening your letter. Yet this technique apparently works for some companies because they use it again and again.

• **Make it look like a personal letter.**   The most important letters of all to most of us are personal letters. You make a mass mailing look personal by printing the address rather than affixing a label; by using a return address made up of your first initial and last name, plus your address; by not using a company logo, stationery, or teaser copy; and by using a first class stamp.

• **Use actual stamps.**   Use precanceled bulk mail stamps or first class rather than a printed bulk mail indicia. If you're making a large mailing, use metered bulk mail rather than a printed indicia (bulk metered mail is not easily distinguished from first-class metered mail; hence, it actually looks very businesslike). Finally, have a bulk mail indicia printed in red ink

THE HUNGARIAN COUNT? THE RUSSIAN PRINCESS?
COLONEL ARBUTHNOT? THE SECRETARY? VALET?

WHODUNNIT

FREE

Invitation to a murder.

Figure 4-1   An unusual envelope.

so it looks exactly like metered mail. (Check with the post office to make sure you do this so it meets their specifications).

• **Use some special effects on the outside of the envelope.**   Possibilities are stickers, seals, commemorative stamps, tokens, cartoons, rub-offs, and embossing.

• **Use an unusual envelope.**   For instance, use an extra-large envelope, an envelope with multiple windows, a flaming red envelope, a full-color envelope, a brown paper bag, a popcorn bag, or a mailing tube. Figure 4-1 shows a great envelope. Wouldn't you open it? It was used by Bantam Books to advertise a line of mysteries.

TIPS FOR CREATING MORE EFFECTIVE RESPONSE VEHICLES

How do you get people to use your order forms, reply cards, or other response vehicles? Here are a few tips (again derived from what's working for other direct mailers):

• **Make it look like an order form.**   Don't have readers trying to guess which piece to send in.
• **Keep it as clear and simple as possible.**   Make it easy for them to fill it out and return it. Allow plenty of room to write in their name, address, credit card number, signature, or whatever else you require.
• **Print the reader's name and address on the order form.**   This makes it easier for them to check off a box or two and pop it into the mail.
• **Limit the number of choices.**   For mailings other than catalogs, you are better off giving only one or two choices—no more. People seem to put off making a choice when too many are offered. The result is that they choose, by default, not to order.
• **Make sure your offer is clear.**   Your offer should be readily understood by anyone. The complete offer should be outlined on the form.
• **Make sure it has all the information needed to order.**   Repeat your

offer. Include the prices. Give the payment options. Note any deadlines or special premium offers.

- **State your guarantee.**   Make it clear, bold, and unconditional.
- **Use involvement devices.**   Order forms that require the recipient to remove a sticker from one part of the form and put it on another part almost always pull better than order forms without such an involvement device. Or use punch-out tokens or stamps.
- **Code your forms so you know where the order came from.**   Generally this code can be on the label or on the return address side.
- **Include a reply envelope in your mailing, with or without return postage guaranteed.**   A preaddressed reply envelope makes it easier for the person to respond. It's also more secure than a reply card by itself. Any time you ask for a check or credit card payment, include a reply envelope.
- **Two response devices are often better than one.**   Use both an envelope and a reply card, or include a second order form in your mailing package and perhaps one printed in the brochure. Not only does a second form reduce the chances of a person's losing the ordering information (price, address, etc.), but it also encourages pass-along orders.
- **Print your name and address in many places (at least once on each enclosure in the mailing package).**   This prevents the loss of an order when the customer misplaces the order form and adds a greater measure of credibility to your offer. If you were not proud of your product, you would try to hide your name.
- **Offer a toll-free order option.**   If you have a toll-free order number, make sure that number is printed in large, bold letters on the order form. The more ways you give them to respond, the more likely it is that they will respond.

These various options for using envelopes and order forms are included in the direct mail checklists in Appendix II. You may copy these and post it above your desk to make sure you cover all the options when working on your next direct mail package.

YOUR DIRECT MAIL PACKAGE OPTIONS

When using direct mail, you have a number of different formats to use—formats that have proved successful for other companies. If any seems appropriate for your company, test that format against your current direct mail package. If it proves successful for your products, you might switch all or a large portion of your mailings to that format.

Classic Letter Package

Perhaps the most common direct mail promotion is the classic letter package consisting of a letter (anywhere from 2 to 12 pages in length), an outer envelope, a BRE (business reply envelope), an order form, and a lift letter, brochure, or both. It is so common because it works, time and time again. If you use a **brochure,** remember that a two-color brochure almost always outpulls a one-color brochure. Put your selling message, the prime benefit, on the front cover. (Most people never read past the front cover if it does not pull them in.) And make sure your brochure describes the complete offer; even if the brochure gets separated from the rest of the mailing package, the customer can still place the order.

Lift letters are short letters usually printed on half-sheets of paper to supplement the sales story laid out in the longer full-size letter. When original, they can be effective in increasing results.

Catalogs

Why do people buy from catalogs? According to a Gallup survey, 36% of the respondents buy from catalogs primarily because they are more convenient than shopping in retail stores, 19% like the variety available in a catalog, 17% like the lower prices, and 6% like the higher quality. Remember these percentages when planning and designing your catalog.

Tabloid Catalogs

New Society Publishers prints its seasonal catalogs on tabloid-size newspaper stock, which allows plenty of room for describing and illustrating new and backlist titles while being inexpensive to print. It's also more in keeping with their alternative political stance. A glossy catalog wouldn't fit their image.

Catalog in Magazine Format

One advantage is that such a mailing format is more likely to be saved during the first sorting of mail, and it also has a better chance of being read. A mailing that can produce those effects has a much better chance of making the sale than a mailing that gets tossed out without being opened at all.

Self-Mailers

Self-mailers are mailing formats that do not require an envelope. They come in many different sizes and formats—from simple folded leaflets to large folded brochures printed on card stock. Self-mailers offer several advantages. Because they tend to be shorter and less involved, they are generally easier and quicker to produce. Since they require no outside envelope, they are cheaper to produce. And because they are in one piece with no outside envelope, they require no collating and stuffing; hence, labor costs for preparing them for mailing are much lower.

Postcards

Some book publishers have used simple postcards to announce single titles. Postcards have a sense of urgency and informality that might be appropriate for some products.

Double Postcards

These have proved to be effective for magazine subscriptions/renewals and for some other offers where the mailer is well known among the target audience. Double postcards are easy for the recipient to use: just tear off the return postcard, check the right boxes, and put it in the mail. And since a postcard mails first class for less than a letter goes bulk rate, you are assured of greater delivery rates at lower costs. Financial Sourcebooks, a publisher of bank marketing newsletters, books, and reports, got responses ranging from 2.2% to 8% for the double postcard pictured in Figure 4-2. Because they put labels on both parts of the postcard and offered to invoice, they made it even easier for their audience to respond.

Card Decks

Rather than just mail one or two cards in another company's card deck, offer your entire line of products in card deck format, with one or two products offered per card. St. Anthony Messenger Press replaced its Christmas gift catalog with a card deck format to offer its line of religious books to half a million customers. Results were "beyond anything else we've ever done."

Statement Stuffers

You can print small 8 1/2" × 3 1/2" flyers announcing new products to send out with invoices and statements. These statement stuffers can be cheap to produce and effective in selling related products or impulse items. To promote their Boston guidebook, *In and Out of Boston (with or without) Children*, Globe Pequot Press inserted stuffers with the billing statements for the *Boston Globe*. As a result of this promotion and many others, they sold over 300,000 copies of the guide.

The Memo

For years, the *Kiplinger Letter* used a letter written by a secretary. Several years ago, however, someone bettered it with something that looks more like a miniature memo than a letter.

NO POSTAGE
NECESSARY
IF MAILED
IN THE
UNITED STATES

BUSINESS REPLY MAIL
FIRST CLASS   PERMIT NO. 1133   NAPERVILLE, IL

POSTAGE WILL BE PAID BY ADDRESSEE

Financial Sourcebooks
P.O. Box 313
Naperville   IL   60566-0313

Attn: *SourceBank* MCIF Special Issue Order

Ι.ΙΙ..ΙΙ....Ι.Ι..ΙΙ....ΙΙ..Ι.Ι..Ι.Ι....ΙΙ..ΙΙ......ΙΙ.Ι

Understanding Our Customers--The Cornerstone of Market Planning
In this **56-page** special issue of our new newsletter, we've compiled a series of
articles and reports which examine marketing databases (MCIFs) and the role they
can play in better understanding financial services customers. Articles such as:
◆ *The MCIF as a Marketing Management Tool*
◆ *Trigger Mailing Systems Puts MCIFs to Work*
◆ *How Valuable are Your CD or Loan Customers*
◆ *Customer/Household Profitability Analyses Using an MCIF*
◆ *Structuring Your Relationship With Your Marketing Database Supplier*

We've also included important information such as. . .
A **glossary of MCIF terms & directory of MCIF vendors** with product descriptions

This issue is our way of introducing you to our new bimonthly newsletter *Source-Bank*. A newsletter that is deeply focused around the issues of the day (through
in-depth reports such as this one), and also provides easy access to the evolving in-
formation sources in the industry. Thus in this issue, you'll also find updates of
recent research, including government information, a column of recently released
books in our area, and articles on **Competitive Intelligence** (A topic to which we'll
be devoting a full issue in December) and Surviving the Current Job Turmoil.

Relationship marketing and the understanding of customers on which it must be
based are the key to solid market planning. We've put together a report that can
help. Because we believe this to be a topic of particular importance to you, we've
made it **easy to order**--just tear off the postcard above and drop it in the mail.
We'll send you this special report immediately and bill you for it.

Figure 4-2   Double postcard mailing.

SourceBank

resource guide in financial services

312-961-2161 ■ Naperville, IL 60566 ■ P.O. Box 313 ■ Financial Sourcebooks

MCIF Special Issue Request Card

Yes! Please send me a copy of the *SourceBank* Special Issue
entitled *Understanding Your Customers:MCIFs In Action*
❏ I'll take advantage of a 1-year subscription to *SourceBank* for
the introductory price of $150 (20% off the regular price of $189)
❏ I'd like just the 56-page report for the discounted price of $42
Please make any necessary corrections or additions to label below

```
PLAT 688 CODE A
MARIE KIEFER
AD LIB PUBLICATIONS
P.O. BOX 1102
FAIRFIELD,      IA 52556
```

Over the next year, we will be introducing some new books,
please check off those about which you would like to be notified:
❏ *Competitive Intelligence*   ❏ *Online Sources: A Step-by-Step*
  in Financial Services: Finding   *Guide to Accessing and Using*
  and Using it Effectively   *Business & Financial Databases*
❏ *The MCIF Applications Workbook* ❏ *The Annotated Financial*
❏ *The Banking Job Market*   *Marketing Plan*

FIRST CLASS MAIL

```
00352 R
PLAT 688 CODE A
MARIE KIEFER
AD LIB PUBLICATIONS
P.O. BOX 1102
FAIRFIELD,      IA 52556
```

**A New
Special
Report
from
*SourceBank***

Figure 4-2   (Continued)

The Dover Format

Besides mailing special interest catalogs, Dover Publications also mails up to eight 11″ × 17″ flyers folded to fit inside a normal number 10 business envelope. Each flyer features a separate line of about 40 books (for example, paper dolls, crafts, graphic arts, or science). Although most books sell for under $7, Dover does well with these mailings because the average order is much higher, with most customers ordering three or more books.

Stamps

Little, Brown & Company uses a sheet of full-color stamps, each bearing a cover illustration for one of their medical books. Recipients need only select the stamps for the books they want to receive, stick them on the order form, and send it in. Such offers work well if your products photograph well and if you offer billing privileges.

Newspaper Clippings

Sales & Marketing Digest enclosed only one item in its direct mail letters: an ad that appears to have been torn out of the financial section of a newspaper. They used this format for several years, so it apparently worked.

Broadsides or Posters

These formats can be effective for products with appealing graphics. Any use of broadsides or posters requires careful planning and graphic design.

Newsletters

Because newsletters combine useful information with an advertising message, they can be one of the most effective ways to market books and other information products. Above all, newsletters tend to be read—and that is always the first step toward selling anything by mail!

The *Book Marketing Update* newsletter was begun as an advertising vehicle for Open Horizon's books. The first two issues were sent to 20,000 book publishers for a total cost of about $10,000. From those two issues we grossed about $35,000 in sales (with about a 4% response rate). From our experience, I suggest these pointers:

Keep the newsletter short.
Publish monthly or bimonthly, because repetition is important for creating the greatest impact with newsletters.
Start small. Keep testing until you find the right format and audience.

Floppy Disks

Many major companies are now using computer floppy disks as a dramatic and often effective way to grab and hold people's attention. This new medium is still novel enough to attract attention. Computer disks are one of the greatest involvement devices. If designed well, they encourage interaction by involving recipients in answering questions, filling in the blanks, or making choices on what parts of the program to see. They can pack an incredible amount of information, with many options to choose from. Computer owners have attractive demographics: high income, college educated, home owners. And you can create animated displays with great graphics.

Here are just a few of the companies using floppy disks to market their products: General Motors received 300,000 requests for an interactive disk that demonstrated one of its new Buicks. Ford Motor distributed 25,000 disks for its upscale sports sedan, the Merkur XR4Ti, with the following selling message: "Take a test drive on your disk drive." Chase Manhattan Bank sent out a disk to demonstrate its electronic funds transfer service.

Videocassettes

If you sell a high-priced product, try sending videocassette versions of your catalog to top prospects. Not only will the videocassette attract attention, but it is also far less likely to be thrown out before it is viewed. Royal Silk, a catalog of high-priced clothing for women, offered a version of its catalog on videocassette. They charged $5 or $10 for it. They found that people who ordered from the videocassette catalog spent an average of $20 more per order than those who did not.

DIRECT MAIL PROMOTIONS THAT WORK: A SAMPLE

All of the tips, suggestions, and options presented in this chapter are not meant to be the final word about direct mail promotions. Use this chapter as a starting point for writing and designing your own direct mail promotions. You can break any rule in the book (this book or any other) if it makes sense to do so—and if you test your mailing promotion thoroughly before rolling out to a larger audience.

The four-page self-mailer reproduced as Figure 4-3 was the most successful short-term marketing promotion in the 10-year history of Calibre Press, a small Midwest publisher of law enforcement and self-defense books and videos. The mailing pulled an astonishing 12% response, and yet it violated many of the established rules of successful direct mail. Here are just a few of the "rules" it broke:

- It was a self-mailer, which usually pulls many fewer responses than a standard mailing package.
- It included no postage-paid or self-addressed envelope for returning the order.
- It featured no illustrations, although the book was highly illustrated (and much of the value of the book is in its illustrations).
- Although police are among the most skeptical of audiences, the letter included no testimonials.
- No guarantee was offered although the book was fairly high priced.
- It was sent to 50,000 names derived from a house list that was two or three years old plus some compiled names (compiled from directories that were also two or three years old).

With all these strikes against it, why did the mailing piece work?

- It was targeted to the right audience—law enforcement professionals—even if the lists were somewhat outdated.
- Calibre Press had developed a reputation for delivering high-quality products (books, videotapes, and seminars) for the same audience. Their new book built on the recognition of the previous book, and the letter suggested that the new book was even better.
- The self-mailer used many of the elements of a good direct mail letter: a Johnson box that built upon the reputation of the previous book, subheads that made great offers, lots of white space and indentations, yellow highlighting (not noticeable on the sample in this book) and two postscripts that were undoubtedly effective.
- While some of the copy was simply a self-pat on the back, much of the copy did offer specific benefits for police in the field—information that could mean their life.
- It was easy to read—an important point since police, in general, are not noted for being heavy readers.
- It made a good offer: a $5 prepublication discount.
- It created an urgency to order now by setting a deadline for getting the $5 discount and by offering an autographed copy to the first 500 buyers.
- The first edition guarantee and personal autograph appealed to this particular audience.
- The letter created an additional aura of exclusivity by stressing that the book was not available to civilians.
- By offering a toll-free 800 number and by accepting credit cards and department purchase orders, it made it easy for the reader to order

666 Dundee Road. Suite 1607 • Northbrook. Illinois 60062 • (312) 498-5680

```
***********************************************
*                                             *
* Your prompt response today will reserve     *
* your special first-edition copy of the      *
* MOST EXCITING BOOK since Street Survival.    *
*                                             *
***********************************************
```

Dear Law Enforcement Professional:

     The book you've been asking about and waiting for--the
companion volume to <u>Street Survival: Tactics for Armed
Encounters</u>--is now at the typesetter.

     It's called **THE TACTICAL EDGE: SURVIVING HIGH-RISK
PATROL**...and in short order <u>it promises to be the new bible
of law enforcement</u>.

     Written by Charles Remsberg, co-author of <u>Street
Survival</u>, and illustrated by Dennis Anderson, **THE TACTICAL
EDGE** has been more than two years in research and development. It features <u>more than 550 hardbound pages, over 600
memorable photographs and illustrations...and the best
survival tactics of hundreds of experienced officers</u> from
all types of agencies.

              Seasoned officers who've reviewed
              this unique volume in manuscript
              form say that we've achieved our
              goal: to assemble the most extensive
              treasury ever of <u>realistic tactical
              options</u> you can use to control the
              threats of high-risk calls.

     THE TACTICAL EDGE teaches you how to think tactically...
how to condition yourself mentally...how to maneuver would-be
assailants on vehicle stops, domestic disturbances, armed
robbery calls, building searches and barricade situations...
how to defeat an offender who takes you or a fellow officer
hostage...how to apply the latest in physical defense skills

Figure 4-3   A self-mailer that worked.

- 2 -

...how to determine the appropriate use of force...and much, much more.

TWO BOOKS IN ONE

THIS BOOK PROVIDES THE ANSWERS THAT YOU AND OTHER OFFICERS HAVE TOLD US YOU MOST NEED IN ORDER TO SURVIVE. It's equal to two normal-length books...and it's available only to law enforcement personnel.

Because of your loyal support in the past, we're sending you this special announcement before publication. We've included the Table of Contents so you can see for yourself the comprehensive nature of **THE TACTICAL EDGE.** You'll see that this is the ultimate source of hard-to-come-by tactical information for staying alive.

Before we place our premier advertising for the law enforcement community as a whole, you can reserve your personal copy of **THE TACTICAL EDGE.**

FIRST-EDITION GUARANTEE

Ordering now will benefit both you and us. You will be guaranteed a first-edition copy from the first shipment of bound books we receive from the printer, which is expected to be late December. By having your commitment now, we can better gauge our initial press run.

> If we receive your pre-paid order by November 15, the price of your first-edition copy will be discounted to $29.95, plus shipping. THAT'S A SAVINGS of $5.00 from the scheduled retail price.

After November 15, pre-publication orders will still be taken, but the cost will be the full retail price of $34.95.

PERSONAL AUTOGRAPH

One more advantage of responding immediately: If you are among the first 500 officers to order **THE TACTICAL EDGE,** your copy will be personally autographed by the author.

So mark "yes" on the enclosed order card today and return it in the prepaid envelope. Or call (312) 498-5680

Figure 4-3 (Continued)

- 3 -

for easy credit card reservations. The paperwork will be processed promptly so that your book(s) can be shipped as soon as we receive our first printed copies.

THE TACTICAL EDGE is a work you will want to refer to throughout your career. Considering the threats you face today, it will be one of the most valuable pieces of professional equipment you'll ever own.

Sincerely,

THE PUBLISHERS

P.S.   THE TACTICAL EDGE is not a revision of the Street Survival book. It is a wholly new text of advanced material that builds on Street Survival's foundation of basics. Whether you're a street officer, a trainer or a concerned administrator, you'll find it filled with tactics you can use immediately to enhance the safety of patrol.

P.P.S. Christmas is coming. THE TACTICAL EDGE is one gift that is sure to be a hit!

I want the most comprehensive book on officer survival ever published, **THE TACTICAL EDGE**. I accept your special pre-publication offer of $29.95 per copy, plus shipping (a $5 savings off the scheduled retail price of $34.95) **if reserved before November 15, 1985.** Please ship my first-edition order as soon as books are available from the printer.

YES!

FOR EASY CREDIT CARD ORDERING, (312) 498-5680 or TOLL FREE 1-800-323-0037. Or return this order form with check, money order, department purchase order or credit card number.

☐ Visa ☐ MasterCard # _____ Exp. Date_____

Name _____

Address _____

City _____ State_____ Zip_____

Rank/Dept. _____

☐ If my order is among the first 500 you receive, please have my book(s) autographed by the author before shipping.

NOT AVAILABLE TO CIVILIANS. OFFER EXPIRES NOVEMBER 15, 1985.

Note: Please correct mailing label errors on other side.

_____books at $29.95 each...$_____
Shipping/handling for
U.S. and Canada ($2 per copy)..._____
Shipping/handling for
overseas ($5 per copy) . . . . _____
Illinois residents add
7% sales tax . . . . _____

TOTAL $_____

PAYMENT IN U.S. FUNDS ONLY, PLEASE

Calibre Press, Inc.
666 Dundee Rd., Suite 1607
Northbrook, IL 60062
Phone (312) 498-5680

Figure 4-3   (Continued)

Here are the contents that make this the most comprehensive book on practical street tactics ever published...

I. THE MENTAL EDGE

1. **MENTAL CONDITIONING**
   The Mind/Body Partnership...Stress Response...Relaxation Response...Positive "Self-Talk"...Crisis Rehearsal...Your Survival Resource...Awareness Spectrum

2. **TACTICAL THINKING**
   Threat Assessment...Thought Processes...Analyzing a Tactic

II. THE TACTICAL EDGE

3. **BUILDING SEARCHES**
   Enter...or Wait?...Principles of Movement...Stairways ...Hallways...Doorways..."Softening" Rooms...Real World Adaptations...Canine Considerations

4. **BARRICADED SUBJECTS**
   Identifying "the Problem"...Manipulation...Escalation of Response...Team Movement...Chemical Agents... Sniper Control...Entry

5. **ARMED ROBBERY RESPONSE**
   Approach and Deployment...Verification...Confrontation...Inside Tactics...Money Escorts

6. **VEHICLE STOPS**
   Assessing Risk...Threat Zones...Searches...Extractions ...Problem Vehicles...High-Risk Stops...Biker Runs... Off-Duty Considerations

7. **DOMESTIC DISTURBANCES**
   Cycle of Violence...Unexpected Approach...Tactical Calming...Arrest Strategy..."Getting through the Night"...Safe Departure...Officer Disputants...Bar Fights

8. **HOSTAGE OFFICERS**
   Dynamics of Confrontation...Dialogue...Escape... Handcuff Defeat..."Hideout" Weapons...Persuasion

III. THE FORCE EDGE

9. **PHYSICAL CONTROL**
   The Force Continuum...Yes/No/Maybe People...Three Ds...Tactical Positioning...Escort Control...Pressure Points...Countermeasures...Neck Restraint...Tactical Handcuffing...Mopping Up

IV. KEEPING THE EDGE

10. **KEEPING THE EDGE**
    Revealing interviews with seven officers who've survived violent encounters about how they maintain their tactical superiority on the street.

Calibre Press, Inc.
666 Dundee Rd., Suite 1607
Northbrook, IL 60062

THE TACTICAL EDGE

THE BOOK YOU'VE BEEN WAITING FOR!

Figure 4-3   (Continued)

right away. It appealed to the instant gratification of action-oriented people.
• The coupon restated the benefits and the offer.

As a result of that successful mailing, Calibre Press increased the initial print run of the book from 5,000 to 10,000 copies. Within three months, they had to go back for a second printing of 7,500. Three years later, the book was still very much alive; they'd just taken delivery on the fifth printing of the book.

> Much of the analysis of the Calibre Press mailing was taken from a talk given by Charles Remsburg, the author and publisher of the book, at a conference sponsored by the Mid-America Publishers Association. The comments reflect his after-the-fact opinion of why the mailing worked. He was as surprised as anyone else at the high response.

HOW TO SPECIFY YOUR PROMOTIONAL PACKAGE

Whether you use outside contractors or prepare your promotional packages in-house, you will need to write up a set of specifications for each project. That is the only way to guarantee that the people writing and designing the promotion know exactly what you want covered. A complete set of written specifications will speed up the process of writing and designing the promotion, and it will limit the number of misunderstandings and delays that could occur without one.

To help you design a promotional package specification sheet that works for your products and promotions, a sample spec sheet is reproduced as Figure 4-4. This sample lists 23 points that need to be covered in enough detail to give the writers and designers the information they need to create an effective promotional package. Besides listing the 23 essential points, the sample asks some leading questions to aid you in writing the specifications.

You can photocopy and enlarge the sample spec sheet if you want to keep these points in front of you at all times. Since the length of an adequate specification sheet will vary with the nature of the product and promotion, there is no master copy of this spec sheet in Appendix II. Anyway, it's easy enough to reproduce the basic points without using a standard form.

HOW TO REVIEW AND APPROVE YOUR PROMOTIONAL PACKAGE

When the writers and designers have created a prospective promotion, review it before any typesetting, photography, and finished artwork gets produced. Why pay for   ething you might not like or want to use?

Promotional Package Specification Sheet

To: Name and address of company, department, or individual who will be providing the copywriting or design of the promotion.

From: Name of your company
Name of contact person
Address
Phone and fax numbers

Product: Name of your product or service

Promotion: Direct mailing, ad, or whatever

1. Description of product: What product or service are you offering? Describe it in 50 words or less. **Be sure to enclose a sample of the product.**

2. Purpose of product: What does the product do? How is it used? How does it work?

3. Product features: Give all the details about the product — color, size, weight, material, number of parts, power ratings, number of working parts, and/or whatever other facts and specifications are appropriate.

4. Main benefits of the product: What is the key sales appeal of this product? What are the other major benefits? What will it do for the user? Does it save time or money? Will it make life easier or better? Does it solve a problem? If so, what is that problem and how does it solve it?

5. Comparison to other products: How does it compare to other products already on the market (or about to come on the market)? What will it give users that they can't get anywhere else? How is it different? Newer? Better? Is it unique? An exclusive? Less expensive? A better buy? Do you provide better service?

Do you have any related products? If so, how does this product tie in with those? Will you later sell those products to buyers of this product?

6. Price: What is the price? Any extra costs such as shipping and handling? Any discounts? Any deluxe versions? Any alternatives? Any deadlines for receiving special offers?

7. Payment methods: What options will you be offering for payments? Cash with order? Billing? Purchase order required? Credit cards?

8. The offer: What is the offer? What do you want the recipient to respond to? Is this a special offer? A premium? An introductory offer? A prepublication discount? A limited-time offer? Free information?

9. The package or promotion: Direct mail package consisting of what elements? Letter? Lift letter? Brochure? Catalog? Self-mailer? Or is it a display ad? A newsletter? A postcard? An insert? An entire campaign?

Enclose samples of previous promotions for this product or other products your company has sold. Which were winners? Losers?

10. The objective of the promotion: To gain direct sales? Leads? Inquiries? Or is it to provide product information to customers? Gain an extra sale? Respond to inquiries? Announce new products? Build the company's or product's image? If so, what image should be conveyed?

Figure 4-4 Promotional package specification sheet.

11. The audience: Who is the prime prospect? What are the characteristics of the target audience or audiences? If a business audience, what is the title and/or responsibility of the prospect?

If a consumer, what are the interests, problems, concerns, demographics, and characteristics of the typical prospect?

Are there any secondary audiences? If so, is it worth preparing separate versions of the promotion for them?

12. The lists/media to be used: What lists or media will you be using? Be specific. Which have you used in the past? Which worked? Which did not?

13. Tests: Will you be conducting any tests? If so, what points will be tested? Will tests affect the design of the package? The offer? The copy?

14. Budget: What is the budget for this promotion? How much will be available for each part of the promotion? For lists? For the package? For other costs? Are there any restrictions? For example, no 4-color brochures or no flashy involvement devices.

15. Schedule: When do you need the complete package? What are the approval dates? When will you be sending out the first test mailing or placing the first advertisement?

16. Testimonials: Do you have any testimonials for the product? Celebrity endorsements? Reviews? Other media coverage? **Enclose samples.**

17. Complaints: Have you ever had any complaints about this product or any similar products? Do you have any letters from unhappy customers? Any bad reviews or media coverage? **Enclose samples.**

18. Must include the following: What points absolutely must be included in the copy? What benefits or features must be stressed? What design elements absolutely must be part of the package?

19. Any taboos?   Any points that absolutely must be avoided? Any words or phrases? Any designs? Anything that cannot be offered or promised?

20. The guarantee: What is your guarantee? How strong is it? What are its limits? 30-day free trial period? 100% money-back guarantee? Return privileges? Inspection privileges? A warranty?

21. How will orders come?   Will you provide a BRE? Accept phone orders? Accept collect calls? Will you have a toll-free phone number? Will you use a 900 phone number? What percentage of your orders are now by phone? Will orders come any other way besides mail and phone?

22. The company: What is the history of the company? Any special points? What about the personality of the owner? Any special expertise? Any points about the company or owners/managers that might have impact on sales?

23. Anything else?   Note any other information or points which could be useful to the copywriters and designers. Include any background material that you think might be helpful. Recommend additional reading material, if it is appropriate. Suggest other people they might talk to.

Figure 4-4   (Continued)

To aid you in reviewing the promotion, use an approval/review form, such as the one reproduced in Appendix II. Besides reviewing the promotion yourself, give it to some of the other people involved in the promotion (the product developer, salespeople, media buyers, and others) and ask them to fill out an approval/review form as well. Then review these reviews. Write down the major criticisms, questions, and strong points noted by the reviewers. Use this feedback to work with your writers and designers to refine the promotional package and make it even more effective.

Once they have made the revisions, review the package one more time. Then before testing the promotion, send it to several reviewers outside your company. If possible, have at least one person who is a member of the target audience review the promotion. Also, have someone who knows absolutely nothing about the subject review it.

Ask these outside reviewers to fill out an approval/review form so you are guaranteed of getting appropriate feedback from them. You might also interview them after they have filled out the form. Ask them if they understand the product. Do they understand the offer? Have them describe these to you.

These outside reviewers are invaluable. If you used only people inside the company, especially people who know the product well, you could easily overlook some major point or take something for granted that needs to be spelled out in the promotion. Outside reviewers invariably pick up on these deficiencies.

When you send out promotional packages for review, be sure to set a deadline for the return of the approval/review form and promotional samples, and make sure the reviewers know to whom they should return these materials. These points are covered when you fill out the top of the approval/review form; just be sure you complete the top information before sending the material out for review.

Once your promotional material has been written, designed, and produced, it is time to test the package. The next chapter describes how to search for targeted lists, select and rent the most appropriate ones, test them, and then evaluate those tests.

5

How to Select, Rent, and
Test Mailing Lists

Of the three fundamentals of direct mail, the most important is the list. Indeed, lists are often given up to 60% of the credit for the success or failure of any mailings. Put simply, if you mail to the wrong list, neither your offer nor your message will have any impact whatsoever.

Because the list is so valuable to any mailing effort, this chapter describes how to generate, maintain, and select mailing lists that will produce the greatest results for your direct mail program.

HOW TO BUILD YOUR HOUSE LIST

The most valuable asset of any direct marketing company is its house list of previous buyers and inquirers. Your own list will almost always offer the best return on any mailing, even when some of the buyers may have originally bought products unrelated to the product you are currently offering. Of course, previous buyers of related products are your best prospects of all.

Since your house list is so valuable, here are a few ways to maintain the list and build it up.

• **Clean your list regularly.** Since 20% to 30% of all addresses change every year, make sure to clean your own house list at least every six months. Not only do individual consumers move with such regularity, but so do businesses and personnel. Job titles change, people get promoted, people switch jobs, people switch companies, businesses expand, businesses move, businesses go out of business: these are all responsible for the deterioration of business mailing lists.

To clean your list, periodically print "Address Correction Requested" on the envelopes of bulk mailings to your list. The post office will then return to you any address that is no longer correct (at least, in theory). Of course, they charge you for this service. The post office is also supposed to return any of your first-class mailings which are not forwardable, but my experience suggests that this service is very much a hit-or-miss proposition.

If you really want your list cleaned, check with your local post office about the post office's National Change of Address program. They will give you the details on this program designed to cut down on the number of undeliverables.

   • **Use an RFM formula to prioritize your list.**   When setting up your database of customers, you should have some way of pulling out the following information:

Recency of order—When was the last time your customer ordered? Three months ago, six months ago, one year, two years?
Frequency of ordering—How often has your customer ordered? On the average of once a month? Once every quarter? Once a year?
Monetary value of orders—What is the average dollar size of an order from that customer?

Each of the three factors—recency, frequency, and monetary—should be factored into a formula (an RFM formula) and then weighted in a way that will most effectively prioritize your customers. Here is one way to prioritize customers by assigning points and then adding the points up for each customer:

Recency: 3 months	25 points
6 months	20 points
12 months	15 points
18 months	10 points
24 months	5 points
more than 24 months	0 points
Frequency: every month	50 points
every 2 months	45 points
every 3 months	40 points
every 6 months	30 points
every 12 months	15 points
every 18 months	5 points
Monetary: $100	25 points
$75	22 points
$50	18 points
$40	15 points
$30	10 points
$20	5 points

To obtain RFM totals for each customer, add the points "earned" for each of the three factors. For instance, John Smith, who last ordered from you six months ago and usually buys about once a year with an average order of $40 would earn an RFM total of 50 (20 + 15 + 15). Jane Doe, on the other hand, who last ordered three months ago and usually buys about every six months with an average order of $20 would earn an RFM total of 60 (25 + 30 + 5). In this instance, Jane is a more valuable customer for you even though the annual average dollar volume for both customers happens to be $40. She is more valuable because she orders more often (and more recently); hence, she is likely to be a better long-term customer and more likely to order from your current mailing.

To work an effective RFM analysis, you have to have an idea of how to weight each of the three factors. In the example, frequency was the most heavily weighted factor (the frequency of a customer's orders was considered the most likely determiner of who would respond to the offer). For some companies, however, the monetary value might be weighted more heavily or the recency. In my own company, we have found that the recency and monetary factors tend to be more reliable in predicting who will respond to our current offer. Hence, we weight these factors more heavily than frequency.

- **Offer low-priced promotions to qualify prospects.** Such promotions are a great way to pull in new customers who are likely to order other products from you. For example, to add names to our list, Open Horizons has offered several inexpensive reports, including a $3 report, *70 Full-Color Catalog, Brochure, Direct Mail, and Card Printers.* We offered these reports through press releases, small classified ads, and even as giveaways. Although in most cases we did not make money on these offers, we did not lose money, and we added a good number of regular customers to our in-house list. These low-priced reports function the same as loss leaders: they bring in the customers, and once these customers discover all the other books we have to offer, they order more—enough to make the entire proposition pay off.

- **Offer freebies.** Offer freebies to attract potential customers. Just be sure to offer a freebie that is related to your main line of products—one, in short, that will attract the right kind of prospects. Such free offers have been known to bring in as many as 20,000 inquiries when featured in a magazine with national circulation (such as *Family Circle*). Our free flier, *50 Creative Marketing Ideas,* has been mentioned in many publishing newsletters and has drawn hundreds of qualifying inquiries.

- **Do a friend a favor.** Add a section to your catalog order form that gives your current customers an opportunity to "do a friend a favor." Ask them to give you the names of any friends whom they think would like to receive your catalog. This has worked well for a number of mail order catalog companies.

- **Run an ad.** Put a display or classified ad (whatever you can afford and whatever works) in targeted magazines. Either go for a direct sale or aim for lots of inquiries and then try to convert them into buyers.

How do you decide whether to go for the order or an inquiry? There are many factors that go into such a decision. How large an ad can you afford? How high priced is your product? How targeted is the magazine? How good is your ad? If you can answer the four questions positively, then you could probably go for the direct order. Otherwise, you'd probably be better off taking the two-step approach: get the inquiry, and then make the sale through your direct mail package responding to the inquiry.

• **Rent other lists.**   Probably the quickest way to build your in-house list of customers is to rent other targeted lists. Most list rental contracts won't allow you to add these names to your in-house list directly, but you will be able to add the names of those people who respond to the mailing you send out to rented lists. In short, when they order from you, they become your customers.

HOW TO FIND APPROPRIATE LISTS: CODING INQUIRIES

If you are serious about using outside mailing lists, one of the first things you should do is to get yourself on lots of mailing lists, especially ones that you might use in the future. How do you do that? Simple: Order something by mail. Subscribe to a magazine. Join an association. Send off lots of inquiries.

When you do buy something (or subscribe, join, or inquire), be sure to code your order. You want to see what other companies rent the list that you've just put yourself on. Most mail order companies, as well as many magazines and associations, rent their mailing lists to other noncompeting companies. By coding your name or address, you can discover how often the list is rented and what sorts of mailers rent the list.

When coding your address, keep it simple. The easiest way I know is to use initials along with your last name. For example, you could use J. F. Kremer when you request a woodworking catalog, J. H. Kremer when responding to a classified ad, J. M. Kremer when subscribing to a specialty magazine, G. T. Kremer when ordering from a second woodworking catalog, and H. J. Kremer when joining a woodworking association. Whatever code you use, keep track of it.

To keep track of what codes you use, enter your codes into a coded lists track record (Exhibit 5-1). Not only will this record let you keep track of which codes you used, but it will also help you keep track of which other companies are renting the lists you might later want to use yourself.

To use the coded lists track record, enter the following information in the appropriate boxes:

• **Code.**   Enter the code you used for your name and/or address.
• **Type of Request.**   Did you place an order, request a catalog, make an inquiry, join an association? This detail is important to track since a buyer's name (if you ordered) is more likely to be rented than an inquirer's name (if you simply requested a catalog or made an inquiry).

Coded Lists Track Record

Code: J. F. Kremer	Type of Request: Requested catalog

Company:	XYZ Company 1234 First Street Anytown, USA 123-456-7890 800-123-4567	Date: 4/5/92
		Product: Widgets galore
		Source: Display ad in Popular Mechanics
		also saw in Workbench

Date	Response: Offers	Response: Products
4/27/90	catalog	widgets and more widgets
5/21/90	brochure offering $5.00 off	wrench set
7/7/90	discount catalog	widgets and more
10/15/90	brochure with special offer to customers only	shop organizer
10/29/90	fall catalog	full line of widgets, etc.

Date	Other Companies	Offer and Product
8/21/90	Brand X Catalog	catalog featuring wood-working tools
9/10/90	EZ Publishers	letter/brochure/card/BRE for EZ Magazine
9/24/90	ABC Company	self-mailer for snow blowers
11/19/90	MT Publishing Company	letter/brochure/card/BRE for fix-it book
1/4/91	Specialty Clothiers	catalog featuring work clothes and shoes
1/7/91	Brand X Catalog	spring catalog featuring gardening tools

Exhibit 5-1   Coded lists track record.

- **Company.**   Enter the name, address, and telephone numbers of the company whose product you just bought or inquired about. This information will come in handy later if you decide to rent the list.
- **Date.**   Write in the date you sent in the order or made the request. This will allow you to track how long it took them to respond to your order.
- **Product.**   Note the name of the product you bought, the association you joined, the catalog you requested.
- **Source.**   Where did you find out about this company or the specific product you ordered? Did you see it in a magazine? Did you respond to a direct mail promotion? A catalog? (If you saw the ad in more than one magazine, make a note of both of them, especially if they had different codes in the ad.)
- **Date.**   Enter the dates you receive any responses.
- **Response: Offers.**   Describe what offer you received for the original company. Note the kind of promotion (catalog, brochure, self-mailer, etc.) and anything special about the offer ($5 off, sale catalog, special offer for customers only, etc.).
- **Response: Products.**   What products did they offer to you? Especially note what products they offer after their initial response to you.
- **Date.**   For any promotions you receive from other companies enter the dates you receive the promotions.
- **Other Companies.**   Note the names of the companies (if known) that are renting the list.
- **Offer and Product.**   Note what products and special offers these companies are promoting to this list. (Note also any companies that use the list more than once.)

By keeping track of which other companies rent each list you are on, you will be able to go back and analyze why they chose to use that list for their offer. With practice you will begin to see which lists apparently work best for what kinds of offers. You'll also be able to note which of your competitors have used the list and how often they have used it. The longer you keep track of these list rentals, the more accurately you will be able to judge the value of that list for your own offers.

Keeping track of such lists can steer you away from inappropriate lists. For example, I've been on some lists that are rented out four or five times a week—way too often to be effective for many promotions, especially ones for higher-priced items. I've also been on lists that, it turns out, were rented primarily to chain letter opportunists—again, not a list you'd ever want to use.

HOW TO FIND APPROPRIATE LISTS: SOME POSSIBILITIES

What kind of lists should you rent? Possibilities include lists of buyers of similar or related products, exchange lists, compiled lists, membership lists, and subscriber lists.

Buyers of Similar Products

Try to rent lists of buyers of similar products from another company. If your product is not directly competitive with the other company's products, you should be able to rent the list.

Exchange Lists

In many cases, you might be able to arrange an exchange of lists with a competitor. If you do exchange lists, make sure that the lists are as nearly equivalent as possible (in terms of average unit of sale, recency of list, number of buyers in relation to inquirers, number of names on the list, etc.). For example, Open Horizons has exchanged lists with Para Publishing, publishers of *The Self-Publishing Manual* and *Business Letters for Publishers*, and with McHugh Publishing Reports.

Buyers of Related Products

When you have exhausted all lists of buyers of similar products, test lists of buyers of items that are indirectly related to the product you are now offering. For example, if you have an organic gardening book, rent a list of buyers of organic pesticides. Here are a few of the different lists available for publishers of gardening books:

[ ] 60,000 subscribers to *Fine Gardening* magazine
[ ] 189,000 buyers of products from the *Smith & Hawken* catalog
[ ] 227,000 subscribers to *Horticulture* magazine
[ ] 50,000 subscribers to *Northern California Home & Garden*
[ ] 150,000 buyers of home and garden products from Shar-Lane Industries
[ ] 99,000 buyers of items from the *White Flower Farm* catalog
[ ] 825,000 subscribers to *Home* magazine
[ ] 215,000 continuity buyers of My Green Gardens gardening cards
[ ] 55,000 subscribers to the *Weekend Gardener* magazine
[ ] 2,195 garden clubs or 72,715 garden club members (compiled)
[ ] 1,091 seed, nursery, and gardening supply catalogs (compiled)

Compiled Lists

In almost every case, a list of mail order buyers will outperform a list of inquirers or a compiled list. Nevertheless, if no other buyer lists are available, your next best choice is a targeted compiled list. Open Horizons, for example, regularly rents the R. R. Bowker list of U.S. book publishers, and this list has always performed well for us even though it is a compiled list.

You can, of course, compile your own business mailing lists by going through the yellow pages of city telephone books. Many libraries have collections of the directories from most major cities. Some also have access to an electronic yellow pages service.

Membership Lists

The members of related organizations are also prime prospects for your products. Open Horizons has used the membership list of COSMEP (an association of smaller publishers). Next to our own house list, this list has been our best performer. Indeed, our own list now includes close to 70% of the COSMEP membership.

Subscriber Lists

Because most newsletters and magazines are sold by direct mail, their subscriber lists can be very responsive. Look for magazines targeting the same audience as you are. You might well find that mailing to their subscriber list is more effective than placing an ad in the same magazine.

FINDING THE RIGHT LIST: INQUIRY LETTERS

Thousands of mailing lists are available. Only a small number, though—maybe 30 or 40—will be really appropriate for your offer. Which of these lists should you use? If you have a limited budget, you obviously can't test them all.

To choose which lists would be most appropriate, write to those companies and publications that you feel have the best lists (or know where to obtain the best lists) for your offer. Also write to several list brokers requesting information on any list they think might be appropriate for your offer.

When writing to these companies and brokers, use letters similar to the ones in Figures 5-1 and 5-2. Be sure to describe your product and offer as completely as need be to give a clear idea of your promotion. Also describe the mailing package you will be using. If possible, send a sample or mock-up of the promotion you intend to send out.

Describe any characteristics you feel an appropriate list should have (describe your target audience). If you have used other lists previously, describe them and whether they worked well for your promotion. If you are planning to roll out your promotion within a month or so, let them know how soon you need to have the list. Set a deadline for their response.

In closing, ask for a data card or data sheet on any lists they have available that they think would meet your needs. When writing to list

ABC Company
123 State Street
Anywhere, USA
(123) 456-7890

March 5, 1992

XYZ Company
456 Broadway
Anywhere Else, USA

Dear List Manager:

We are planning a major direct mail advertising campaign for the ABC Magic Widgets. We intend to offer these widgets for only $19.95 plus $2.50 shipping and handling. A $100,000 sweepstakes will be featured in a teaser on the outside envelope. We have enclosed our direct mail package so you can get a better idea of our product and promotion.

Do you rent your list of customers [or subscribers]? If so, would you consider renting it for our promotion? We would like to mail the list on June 4th if at all possible.

If your list is available, please send us a complete data card on your list detailing its source, quantity, price, minimums, selects, and order requirements.

We hope your list is available for rent. We look forward to working with you on our promotion. Thank you.

Sincerely

H. P. Doolittle, Vice-President

Figure 5-1   Letter to company or publication.

brokers, ask for their general list catalog as well (if they have one). You can model your letter after the samples in Figures 5-1 and 5-2.

Why send a letter to a list broker? Because good list brokers will be able to recommend lists that you might never have thought to use. For the names of some list brokers, see Appendix III. Write or telephone at least three of them. That way you will be sure to get a range of good recommendations (the duplicate recommendations are probably your best bet).

ABC Company
123 State Street
Anywhere, USA
(123) 456-7890

March 5, 1992

XYZ List Company
456 Broadway
Anywhere else, USA

Dear Broker:

We are planning a major direct mail advertising campaign for the ABC Magic Widgets. We intend to offer these widgets for only $19.95 plus $2.50 shipping and handling. A $100,000 sweepstakes will be featured in the outside teaser. We have enclosed our direct mail package for you to review.

Please advise us of any lists you might have available which would be suitable for our product and offer. We are especially interested in lists of previous buyers of lawn care products. We might also be interested in buyers of related products (gardening supplies, seeds, etc.).

Send a complete data card or sheet on each list you feel would be appropriate for our offer. Include source, quantity, price, minimums, and other order requirements.

Also send us your general list catalog and any other information regarding the services you offer. Thank you.

Sincerely

H. P. Doolittle, Vice-President

Figure 5-2   Letter to a list broker.

It won't cost you any extra money to get lists from a broker. They are paid a commission by the company, which provides the list. Many companies, in fact, would prefer that you worked through a list broker.

HOW TO EVALUATE LISTS

The companies and brokers you contact should send you a list data card or sheet (Exhibit 5-2). If you do not receive such a card but instead receive

OPEN HORIZONS BOOK BUYERS

9,820	24 Month Buyers	$80.00/M
5,780	12 Month Buyers	$85.00/M
1,300	Current Newsletter Subscribers	$90.00/M

PROFILE: These buyers include major book publishers, university presses, associations with book programs, independent book publishers, and self-publishers. Most have bought books on book marketing, graphics, printing, direct marketing, publicity, and advertising. 75% are repeat buyers.

SOURCE: 50% direct mail, 10% display ads, 40% publicity and reviews

SELECTIONS: Self-Publishers $85.00/M
Book Printers $80.00/M

SUGGESTED USES: This list has been used successfully by book printers, newsletters, other book publishers, publicity services, business catalogs, typesetting services, software companies, and other business services.

REMARKS: Sample mailing piece is required.
Order direct or through a recognized list broker.

Open Horizons, 51 N. Fifth Street, Fairfield, IA 52556-3226
(515) 472-6130 / Fax: (515) 472-3186

DATE	March 2, 1992
UNIT OF SALE	$32.50
SEX	65% male, no selects
ADDRESSING	4-up Cheshire labels
	2-up P/S labels
MAINTAINED	Zip code sequence
SELECTIONS	State, no charge
	SCF/ZIP $5.00/M
	Hotline $5.00/M
KEYING	$1.00/M
MINIMUM	1,000 one time use
	Sample required

Exhibit 5-2 List data card.

information less formally presented in a letter or catalog, transfer the details to a data card, which can be filed for quick reference when planning your direct mail promotions.

There is a blank list data card in Appendix II, which you can copy onto card stock or thick paper and use for recording and filing information on individual lists. To record the list data, enter the information you need to have.

To evaluate the list, review all information on the list data card. Here are the major items most list data cards provide:

• **Name of list.** Who is the list from? Often the name of the list also describes its contents—whether, for example, the list consists of buyers or catalog requests.

• **Quantity of names available.** The quantity of names available in the entire list is detailed. Often the list owner will also make the list available broken down into last 6-month buyers, last 12-month buyers, hotline names (recent buyers, usually within the past 30 or 90 days), and others. Generally, the more recent buyers will respond best to new offers. That's why hotline names usually cost more to rent.

• **Description of list.** This generally describes the names available for rent. In the sample in Exhibit 5-2, the main house list of 9,820 24-month buyers is also available as a smaller list of last year's buyers or current newsletter subscribers.

• **Price/M.** This details the charge per thousand for the various quantities available.

• **Profile.** While this section might not be labeled, most list data cards provide some sort of description of the people on the list. Such descriptions usually indicate what kind of promotion the people responded to or what they bought. It might also detail other demographics of the buyers. This profile is important because it allows you to select lists with the greatest affinity to your list or product.

• **Source.** This indicates how the buyers came to know of the original offer. Usually the source will be space advertisements, direct mail, another house list, or some publicity. Lists generated primarily from direct mail generally respond better to other direct mail offers.

• **Selections.** Most cards detail any list selections available. For example, on a data card from Leichtung Workshops, it was possible to select by multi-buyers, dollar amount of order, sex, age, whether the buyer used a credit card, product bought, and subject interests (automotive, crafts, electrical, gardening, home products, home repair, video tapes, books, and woodworking). Most selections cost extra (over and above the price/M for the base list). For example, Leichtung charges $25/M extra for five-time buyers, $20/M extra for four-time buyers, $15/M extra for three-time buyers, and $10/M for two-time buyers.

- **Suggested markets.** Many data cards indicate what other products or offers have found or should find a responsive audience with this particular list. Check with the broker to see if any product similar to or related to your product has ever been offered to the list and, if so, what the response was.

- **Remarks.** Most list owners want to see a sample mailing piece to verify that the offer does not compete directly with any of their own products and the mailing piece is suitable for their list.

- **Date.** Check to see if the list information is dated. If the date on the card is six months or a year old, the list might also be old or not as up to date as it could be. The list broker will be able to verify how up to date the list itself is.

- **Unit of sale.** Make sure that the average sale is at least as high as the price you will be asking for your product. Be sure that the people are accustomed to buying products of similar or higher prices through the mail.

- **Sex.** Some lists can be segregated by sex, thereby allowing you to target your audience. For example, if you are selling quality men's shoes, you do not want to rent an entire list, especially if your research has shown that your shoes are bought *by* men and not *for* men.

- **Addressing.** Most lists come available on Cheshire labels or mag tape without any extra charge, but you need a machine to process Cheshire labels and a computer to use the mag tape. Hence, initially you will probably have to pay the extra charge to have them printed on pressure-sensitive labels (unless you use a lettershop).

- **Maintained.** Most lists are arranged in zip code sequence at no extra charge.

- **Selections.** Many lists can be selected by a number of different criteria. For example, you could buy only the names from a certain state or zip code or names sorted by income level or repeat buyers. Some selections may be outlined on the front of the card; others may be detailed on the back side of the card or on a separate sheet. All of these selections involve more processing time, and, hence, there is usually a small extra charge per thousand to cover the costs.

- **Keying.** If you want the labels keyed with a special code on the top right of the label, some list owners charge extra for this service—generally $1/M. If you need to target a specific office or title, many business list owners will also insert an attention line for little or no cost.

- **Minimum.** Most list owners require a minimum order—usually 3,000 to 5,000 names—to cover their costs in processing the initial order. Even if you buy the minimum, you do not necessarily have to mail the entire order on your first test.

When you are considering another list, try to get samples of direct mail promotions that have worked with the list. Ask the list owner to provide you with samples or to give you the names of some previous renters. The best samples to review are those from repeat renters of the list (no good direct marketer would ever rent a list twice if it had not performed well the first time). When you do get samples, look for any similarities in appeals, copy, or format that apparently worked in the past. These should give you some insight into the best way to approach the list with your own offer.

HOW TO SELECT LISTS

When you have gathered sufficient information about the prime lists you are considering, work up a list selection checklist such as the one shown in Exhibit 5-3. This checklist will allow you to see at a glance which lists are the best for your offer. You can then prioritize the lists. In the sample checklist, I would mail to list 1 first, list 2 second, list 4 third, and list 3 fourth based on the answers given in the checklist.

Here are a few guidelines on how to complete the list selection checklist. The most important part of the checklist is the "Question to Ask" section.

- **Product.**   List the product to be promoted.

- **Promotion.**   List how you will be promoting the product. In most cases, if you are filling out this checklist, you will probably be promoting by direct mail.

- **List Number.**   Make notes about the lists you are considering.

- **Description of the List.**   Describe each list briefly, but be as specific as possible so when you go back to review this checklist, you will be able to remember the details about each list.

- **Qty.**   Note the quantity of names available for rent. You may note only those names you are considering. For instance, if the list owner breaks the list down into 12-month and 24-month buyers and you only want to mail to the 12-month buyers, then note the quantity of such buyers available for rent.

- **List Supplier.**   Who will be supplying the list? If you will be renting the list through a list broker, you might also want to know the name of the list owner.

- **Is this list related to the offer?**   Do the people who make up the list have any affinity with the product you are offering? For example, did they respond to a similar offer or buy a related product?

- **Does the list consist of buyers?**   What percentage of the list is made

List Selection Checklist

Product: Widgets			Promotion: Direct Mailing to Other Lists	

List Number	Description of the List	Qty.	List supplier (broker and/or company)	
List #1	Wood-working enthusiasts	250M	DMZ Brokers / XYZ Catalog	
List #2	Buyers of closet organizing unit	120M	DMZ Brokers / ABC Company	
List #3	Requested catalog of home tools	60M	ENA Brokers / DEF Catalog	
List #4	Members of wood-working clubs	32M	JFK Compilers	

Question to Ask	List #1	List #2	List #3	List #4
Is this list related to the offer?	yes	yes	yes	yes
Does the list consist of buyers?	yes	yes	no	no
What is the source of the original sale?	direct mail	newspaper ad	magazine ad	club members
How recent are the names?	last 12-month	last 12-month	last 24-month	?
Is the unit of sale similar?	yes	yes	no	no
Can we select multi-buyers?	yes	no	no	no
Can we make other selections?	yes	yes	yes	no
Does list have similar demographics?	yes	maybe	maybe	maybe
Does list have similar psychographics?	yes	maybe	no	maybe
Does the list have a high dupe rate?	yes	no	no	no
Do others rent this list repeatedly?	yes	yes	yes	yes
Do our competitors rent this list?	yes	no	yes	?
Does this list have continuation usage?	yes	yes	yes	yes
How did people on the list pay?	credit card	credit card	$1.00 cash	?
Does this list have rollout potential?	yes	yes	yes	yes, some
Is the list cost effective?	yes	yes	yes	yes
Is this list clean?	yes	yes	fairly	year old
Is the list available in correct format?	yes	yes	yes	yes
Are the delivery dates guaranteed?	yes	yes	yes	yes
Any negative characteristics?	no	yes	no	yes

Exhibit 5-3 List selection checklist.

up of buyers? How many are inquirers? How many simply requested a catalog? Can you select buyers only?

• **What is the source of the original sale?**   Did they purchase by mail order? Did they respond to a space or classified ad? Did they buy from a television offer? Were they sold by a field force? Did they respond to a sweepstakes offer or a standard offer? People who bought by mail are more likely to respond to your direct mail offer than people who originally bought in response to a television or a magazine ad. People who respond to a sweepstakes offer might not respond to a standard offer.

• **How recent are the names?**   Remember the RFM formula. Recent buyers (also known as **hotline names**) tend to respond better to other direct mail offers. That's why these lists are generally more expensive to rent. There's only one way, however, to find out whether 3-month buyers will respond better to your offer than 12-month buyers. You have to test.

• **Is the unit of sale similar?**   This is the M factor in the RFM formula. Is the average unit of sale similar to the price of the product you are offering? You probably don't want to promote a $99.00 product to buyers who have responded to a $9.95 offer.

• **Can we select multi-buyers?**   This is the F factor in the RFM formula. Does the list owner enable you to select only multi-buyers (people who buy frequently)? Lists of multi-buyers tend to be more expensive to rent, but they also tend to be more responsive.

• **Can we make other selections?**   Are there other selections offered that might be appropriate for your offer? For instance, the Leichtung Workshops catalog offers buyers who have bought a particular product within the past six months. Would it pay for you to order one of these breakdowns rather than the entire list? Probably—especially if you were offering an automotive product or a gardening product (two of the available selections).

• **Does the list have similar demographics?**   For instance, if you were offering an expensive children's playset, you would want to select lists of high-income families with children. You can even select a compiled list that has these demographics.

The more detailed your knowledge is of the demographics of your own customers (buyers of the product being promoted), the more closely you will be able to match the demographics of other lists. That's one reason many mail order companies ask customers for information besides their name, address, and telephone number. That's also why companies ask you lots of detailed questions on warranty registration cards. It enables them to get a better focus on who is buying their product and, thus, to target other prospective buyers better.

• **Does the list have similar psychographics?**   Can you define the life-styles of your customers? If so, you can match mailing lists to specific life-style choices. For instance, if your customers are regular church goers, you might be able to locate a list that consists of church-going customers. What other life-style choices define your customers? Are they avid hobbyists? Do they gamble? Are they political? The closer you can match the demographics and psychographics of your customers to those on another list, the better your response should be.

• **Does the list have a high dupe rate?** One of the best indicators of a high response list is the dupe rate between that list and your in-house list when you do a merge/purge (where two lists are combined into one, and the duplicates are deleted). If you've done a merge/purge on a list and end up with lots of duplicates, chances are that the remaining names on the list will be highly responsive.

• **Do others rent this list repeatedly?** If other mailers come back to a list more than once, chances are the list is working for them. No good direct marketer ever mails to the same list twice if it did not perform well the first time. If the list has lots of repeat mailers, it's highly responsive.

• **Do our competitors rent this list?** When you research lists, ask for the names of any mailers who repeatedly rent the list. If one of your competitors is on that list of repeat mailers, chances are good that the list will be responsive to your offer.

• **Does this list have continuation usage?** In other words, do companies that do test mailings to the list follow through with rollouts (continuation mailings to the full list)? If not, then the list is not passing the test. On the other hand, lists with many continuation users will probably also work well for your offer.

• **How did the people on the list pay?** What percentage paid cash with order? How many used a credit card? How many were billed? If you are going to mail an offer that requires prepayment, favor lists that have a high percentage of cash with order payments.

• **Does this list have rollout potential?** If a test mailing to a list is successful, you will want to roll out to the entire list. The bigger the list, the better. Hence, if two lists are equal in all other things but one is bigger, test that one first.

• **Is the list cost effective?** Rental rates vary considerably from one list to another. For instance, the base rate for a compiled list from one of the catalogs sitting on my desk is $50/M, while the base rate for the Swiss Colony list is $60/M. The base rate for the Leichtung Workshops catalog list is even higher: $70/M for 24-month buyers and $80/M for 12-month buyers. If your promotional costs do not allow you to pay $80/M, then the 12-month buyers' list from Leichtung Workshops is not appropriate for you. When considering costs, be sure to include all costs, including selections, keying, and addressing formats.

• **Is this list clean?** When was the last time the list was cleaned? Is the list free of duplicates? Ask the list owner how often the list is cleaned. A clean list will always outpull a dirty list, all other things being equal.

• **Is the list available in the correct format?**   If you or your mailing houses require a specific format such as pressure-sensitive labels, are these available? If so, is there any extra charge? Most list owners provide four-up or five-up Cheshire (address labels printed 4- or 5-across on plain computer paper to work with an automatic labeling machine) at no extra charge, but many charge an extra $5/M for pressure-sensitive labels. Many also charge extra for mag tape (addresses supplied on computer tape for use with mainframe computers).

• **Are the delivery dates guaranteed?**   If you want to roll out to a list on a specific date, is that date available, and can it be guaranteed? Since many list owners limit how many mailings can go out to their lists within a specific period of time, your drop date might already be taken by another mailer. If you are testing a list that you feel will produce a good response, reserve a future date for a rollout. Be sure to verify with the list owner that the lists can be delivered before that date.

• **Any negative characteristics?**   If your previous mailing experience suggests that catalog requesters do not respond well to your offers, you might not want to mail to lists with a high percentage of such names. Other possible negatives might include compiled lists or lists made up predominantly of sweepstakes respondents (even if they were buyers). What makes up a negative characteristic all depends on the offer you are making. If you were mailing a sweepstakes offer, a list of such respondents would be highly positive, not negative.

HOW TO ORDER MAILING LISTS

Once you've reviewed all the available lists and selected which ones you intend to use, place your order. Most list brokers will provide you with their catalog of lists and list order forms (or will take the order over the telephone), but some do not. Hence, when ordering from them, use a list rental order form like the one in Exhibit 5-4.

This form covers all the necessary ordering information so the list owner or broker should understand exactly what you want. You can also use the form to lay out your order before calling it in to a list broker. That way you will be sure to cover all items while on the telephone so you won't have to call back later to add something. Here are the major points that should be covered on any list order form.

• **Vendor.**   The list broker's name and address or, if you are ordering direct, the name and address of the list owner.

• **Purchase Order No.**   Your reference number in case the supplier has any questions regarding the order.

List Rental Order Form

Vendor:

ABC List Company

Attn: Jane Doe, Account Executive

456 Seventh Avenue

New York NY 10010

Purchase Order No.: 7092

Date of Order: July 16, 1992

Date List Wanted: August 10, 1992

Mailing Date: August 23, 1992

Ordered by:

David Smith, Vice President

XYZ Company

123 First Avenue

Anytown FL 23456

Phone: 123-456-7890 / Fax: 123-789-4567

Ship to:

EZ Mailing Company

Attn: XYZ Company #4 mailing

789 Fifth Street

Everywhere IL 60610

Phone: 312-456-7890 / Fax: 312-789-4567

Quantity	List / Selections	Price per M	Total Price
100,000	90-Day hotline names from JJJ Company --- Code J823	$70.00	$7,000.00
	Selects: Multi-Buyers	5.00	500.00
250,000	12-month buyers from HHH Catalog --- Code H823	65.00	16,250.00
	Selects: Multi-Buyers	5.00	1,250.00

FORMAT (Material)
- [X] Cheshire Labels
- [ ] Pressure Sensitive Labels
- [ ] 3 x 5 Cards
- [ ] Sheet Listing
- [ ] Magnetic Tape

GEOGRAPHIC SELECTIONS
- [ ] Complete List
- [X] Cross-Section of U.S.
- [ ] Selected States
- [ ] Selected SCFs, Zips

SPECIAL INSTRUCTIONS
- [X] Key Coding J823 / H823
- [ ] Title Address _____
- [X] Sample mailing piece enclosed.

List Subtotal	$25,000.00
Material	0
Options	350.00
Shipping	10.00
Total Order	$25,360.00

Exhibit 5-4   List rental order form.

- **Date of Order.**   The date the order is placed.

- **Date List Wanted.**   The date you want the list to arrive at your location or at your lettershop (generally a week or two before mailing).

- **Mailing Date.**   Date you intend to mail your promotion to the list.

- **Ordered by.**   Your name, your company name and address, and your telephone numbers.

- **Ship to.**   Address to which the list should be sent if different from your company address. If you are using a mailing service or lettershop, have the list shipped directly to them.

- **Quantity.**   The quantity of names you want.

- **List/Selections.**   Describe the list you want to order. Be as specific as necessary. If you also want to ask for certain selects, note them on a separate line under the description of the list. Note how the select is indicated in the sample.

- **Price Per M.**   Price per thousand for the list you want.

- **Total Price.**   Price per M times quantity (divided by 1,000).

- **List Subtotal.**   The total prices for all list charges.

- **Material.**   Most lists are provided at no charge in four-up Cheshire format. If you want a different format, you will probably have to pay for it. (See notes on "Format" below.)

- **Options.**   If you want key coding or a title address (an attention line), most list owners add a token charge. (See notes on "Special Instructions" below.)

- **Shipping.**   Leave this blank if you don't know what the shipping charges are. If you do know, enter the amount. If you want faster shipping, make a note of it here.

- **Total Order.**   The total charges for your list order. It should be the sum of the four boxes above it (list subtotal, material, options, and shipping).

- **Format.**   Check the box that indicates the format in which you want the list. If you check nothing, most list suppliers will provide Cheshire labels, the default label format supplied by most list owners. **Cheshire labels** are mailing labels printed four across on continuous computer paper (44 labels per page). Each label is 3.44" × 1" in size. These labels can be affixed to your mailing piece only by a Cheshire machine, which cuts the page into label segments, applies glue, and adheres the labels to your mailing piece.

Pressure-sensitive labels are peel-and-stick labels that can be pulled off the waxed paper they come on and then stuck by hand (or machine) onto your mailing piece. If you are doing the mailing in-house and do not have a Cheshire machine, this label format is the one you want. Most label suppliers charge extra for this label format because of the additional cost of the labels. Charges run $5 to $12 per M.

Three-by-five index cards feature one address (plus telephone number and other available information) per card. You might buy these to use in making follow-up calls after your mailing goes out.

A **sheet listing** is a printed listing of each name, address, telephone number, and other information that might be available. This sheet listing might be used for making follow-up calls. While 3" × 5" cards generally cost an extra $20 to $25 per thousand, sheet listings go for $15 to $20 per thousand names.

Magnetic tape, also known as mag tape, is useful if you or your lettershop plans to process the list on a mainframe computer. When ordering, specify which tape mode you require. Most list suppliers charge an additional $20 per tape to cover their costs.

Many list owners and compilers are now providing lists on floppy **diskettes** for use on personal computers. These diskettes generally have some restrictions applied to them. For example, the list owner might restrict use to only one year or a certain number of mailings. Such diskettes could, however, allow a small company to create personalized letters from the rental lists or allow you to import some of the data into databases you already use. Since this format is still relatively new, no standard charges have developed.

As a relatively small supplier of targeted mailing lists, Open Horizons provides lists in four-across Cheshire format, as two-across pressure-sensitive labels, as sheet listings, or on diskette.

• **Geographic Selections.** Most list suppliers can break down their lists into a cross-section of the United States, selected states, or selected SCFs or zip codes. Most charge extra for SCF (Sectional Center Facilities, or addresses based on the first three digits of the zip code) or zip code selections.

• **Special Instructions.** If you want each list to be key coded so you can track which lists are producing the orders, specify that in your order. Indicate what codes you want to use for each list. Most list suppliers can code labels and charge only a token amount to do so (generally $1 or $2 per thousand).

If you want an "Attention" line on the label rather than a name, most list suppliers will run the list that way for an additional charge ranging from $2.50 per thousand up to $5.00 per thousand. You might want to use an "Attention" line if you are renting a compiled list of business names and want to make sure your piece gets to the right department, even if the individual in the compiler's database has moved on to another department or company.

Here are a few other things you should know about renting lists:

• Most list owners (not compilers) require that you enclose a sample of the mailing piece you intend to use with their list. Why? Because they may not want any direct competitors to use their list. Also, it allows them to weed out any inappropriate mailings to their list. Since the house list is one of the most valuable assets of a mail order company, they don't want their customers deluged with inappropriate offers.

• If this is an order for a test mailing, indicate how you want the names selected (every *n*th name, for example). Note that many list suppliers provide a random selection by selecting zip codes ending in the same two digits (e.g., 56—52556, 10256, 34556, etc.). This selection can make it easy to reorder the list without duplicating any names, but it does have one major drawback. If the wrong last two digits are used, it could skew the results. One company, for instance, received a list that included 100 names in a small New Hampshire town and just five in New York City—hardly the cross-section they were looking for when they rented the list.

• When you receive your list, scan a half-dozen pages or so to see how many duplicate names appear on the list. If any do, question the list owner, especially if three or more appear on a page (since that would amount to as much as 6% of the mailing).

• Scan the list for any tears or severe wrinkles that could slow your lettershop and make it impossible to affix those labels by machine.

• Most list suppliers can provide a list within about 10 working days after approval of the mailing piece, but allow up to three weeks.

• Lists are rented for one-time use only unless you specifically buy rights to the list (such rights are usually available only for compiled lists). List owners seed their lists with **decoy names** to allow them to check up on usage of the list. Not only do such names allow them to verify that renters use their lists only once, but it also allows them to double-check that the renters used their lists for the mailing pieces they sent in as samples.

• Most lists are not subject to return or exchange.

HOW TO TEST MAILING LISTS

Before rolling out any mail order promotions, do some test mailings. There are five major elements you can test: the lists you might use, the offer, the various parts of the direct mail package, the timing, and the copy. Of these, the most important to test is the selection of lists. The next most important is the offer.

To test lists, mail your promotion to a random selection of the names from each of the lists you are considering using. Be sure to code each mailing. Then track the response to each list (you can use the ad response record in the next chapter to record and compare the responses). To find out how many names you need to test for any list, use the test sample sizes probability chart (Figure 5-3).

Test Sample Sizes — Probability Chart

Resp. %	LIMITS OF ERROR (EXPRESSED AS PERCENTAGE POINTS)										
	.10	.12	.14	.16	.18	.20	.30	.40	.50	.60	.70
.2	7,667	5,324	3,911	2,994	2,366	1,917	852	479	307	213	156
.4	15,303	10,627	7,807	5,977	4,723	3,826	1,700	956	612	425	312
.6	22,908	15,908	11,687	8,948	7,070	5,727	2,545	1,432	916	636	467
.8	30,482	21,168	15,552	11,907	9,408	7,621	3,387	1,905	1,219	847	622
1.0	38,026	26,407	19,401	14,854	11,736	9,506	4,225	2,376	1,521	1,056	776
1.2	45,539	31,624	23,234	17,788	14,055	11,385	5,060	2,846	1,821	1,265	929
1.4	53,021	36,820	27,051	20,711	16,364	13,255	5,891	3,314	2,121	1,473	1,082
1.6	60,473	41,995	30,853	23,622	18,664	15,118	6,719	3,780	2,419	1,680	1,234
1.8	67,894	47,148	34,639	26,521	20,955	16,973	7,543	4,243	2,716	1,886	1,385
2.0	75,284	52,280	38,410	29,407	23,235	18,821	8,365	4,705	3,011	2,091	1,536
2.2	82,643	57,391	42,165	32,282	25,507	20,661	9,182	5,165	3,306	2,295	1,686
2.4	89,972	62,480	45,903	35,145	27,769	22,493	9,997	5,623	3,599	2,499	1,836
2.6	97,269	67,547	49,627	37,996	30,021	24,317	10,807	6,079	3,891	2,701	1,985
2.8	104,537	72,595	53,335	40,834	32,264	26,134	11,615	6,534	4,181	2,904	2,133
3.0	111,773	77,620	57,026	43,661	34,497	27,943	12,419	6,986	4,471	3,105	2,281
3.2	118,979	82,623	60,702	46,476	36,721	29,745	13,220	7,436	4,759	3,305	2,428
3.4	126,154	87,607	64,364	49,278	38,936	31,538	14,017	7,884	5,046	3,504	2,574
3.6	133,298	92,568	68,009	52,069	41,141	33,325	14,811	8,331	5,332	3,702	2,720
3.8	140,412	97,507	71,638	54,848	43,336	35,103	15,601	8,776	5,616	3,900	2,865
4.0	147,494	102,426	75,252	57,615	45,522	36,874	16,388	9,218	5,900	4,097	3,010

Figure 5-3 Test sample sizes probability chart.

To test your offer, package, timing, or copy, you need to use two random samples from the same mailing list. One key rule in testing is that you cannot test for two things at the same time. This means that if you want to test your offer, you cannot use different lists, packages, copy, or drop dates at the same time. Similarly, if you want to test your package, you cannot vary your offer, lists, copy, or drop dates. That is the reason you need to mail to two random samples from the *same* list when you want to test your offer or package or timing or copy.

Once you have done the test mailings and tracked the responses, how do you know that any variance in response is anything more than chance? The only way to be sure is to check the results against probability theory. To make your job easier, I have prepared a test sample sizes probability chart. The chart provided here will help you decide whether to go ahead with the rollout of a list after the test mailing. It also allows you to compare two test samples and determine the minimum test sample size. This probability table is based on a 95% level of confidence: 95 times out of 100 the results of any follow-up mailing will be within the same limits of error as the original test mailing—provided the following three points are taken into account:

1. The conditions are identical or as nearly identical as you can make them (same list, same offer, identical mailing package, etc.)
2. The original test samples were made up of a random cross-section of the entire list or lists.
3. Seasonal variations are taken into account (see the chart on p. 100).

> The probability table shown as Figure 5-3 only covers possible responses up to 4%. If your mailing requires a larger response to break even, you will not be able to use this table. If your response falls between two of the response points on this chart (for example, 2.5 falling between 2.4 and 2.6), you use an average of the values for the two points.

HOW TO PROJECT PROBABLE RESPONSE TO A ROLLOUT

If you wanted to project the probable response when you roll out to an entire list, you can use the probability chart. Suppose you did a test mailing to 5,000 names and received a 3% return. In that case, look down the response percentage column in Figure 5-3 until you find 3.0, and then look across until you come to the closest figure to your 5,000 name test sample. Now look up at the column's heading: .50 (a limit of error of .5%, or half a percent). This heading (.50) indicates that the response from a follow-up mailing to the same list would produce results within .5 percentage points of the test results of 3%. In other words, you can expect any further identical mailings to that list to produce results ranging from a 2.5% to a 3.5% response rate.

To be safe, use the low point on the range of possible response rates (in this case, 2.5%) when making your profit and loss projections for the rollout of this promotion. Then determine (within a 95% certainty) if a 2.5% response is an acceptable risk given your costs, contribution margin, and profit expectation.

HOW TO FIND MINIMUM TEST SAMPLE SIZES

If you have a good idea what your expected response rate will be and are willing to accept a certain limit of error, you can determine the minimum number of names you will need to test. You could save money, then, by not mailing to a larger test list than absolutely necessary to make projections.

Suppose your anticipated response rate is 2%, and you cannot afford a variation of response less than 1.8% (a limit of error of .20). Look down the response column to 2.0% and across to the column headed by .20. The minimum sample size required under these two conditions is 18,821 names, or, for simplicity, 19,000 names.

If a test sample of 19,000 names actually produced a response rate of 2.0% as anticipated, then a follow-up mailing would produce a response rate between 1.8% and 2.2% (again, with a 95% level of probability).

HOW TO COMPARE TEST SAMPLES

You can also use the chart in Figure 5-3 to compare two random test samples from the same list. If you want to verify whether the results from two test mailings are within the acceptable level of variance, follow these steps.

Suppose you were to test two random samples of 5,000 names from a list and received responses of 1.8% and 2.2% from the two samples. To verify whether they fall within the acceptable level of variance, average the two response rates (2.0% is the average of 1.8% and 2.2%).

Use the probability chart to check to see what the limit of error is for a mailing of 5,000 names at 2.0%. Look down the response column to 2.0, and then scan across until you find the number closest to 5,000 (in this case, 4,705). Now look up the column to see what the limit of error is (in this case, .40).

In this example, the two different response rates (1.8% and 2.2%) fall within the limits of error for a test mailing of 5,000 names since the limit of error allows for a .40 range of response from the average of 2.0%. Responses on a test mailing to 5,000 names could range from 1.6% to 2.4% under these circumstances.

What this means is that you may consider the response from the two test mailings as being representative of a 2.0% response rather than being indicative of major differences between the two random lists. These results also mean that if you were using the two random samples to test variations in your offer, you could not draw any conclusions about which offer was better.

On the other hand, if the differences had fallen outside the normal allowable range of responses (for example, if the response rates for this test had been 1.5% and 2.4%), you could conclude that the one offer was better than the other. To be absolutely sure that one offer was better than the other, you would test the two offers on another list.

SEASONAL VARIATIONS IN MAIL ORDER RESPONSES

The following seasonal variations in mail order list (adapted from Stone, *Successful Direct Marketing Methods;* see the Bibliography) illustrates seasonal variations in responses to nonseasonal, general mail order offers (it does not apply to Christmas gifts, seed catalogs, swimsuits, and other seasonal offers):

Month	Rating
January	111.2
February	106.8
March	79.0
April	79.5
May	79.5
June	74.5
July	81.5
August	96.8
September	87.9
October	100.0
November	90.1
December	87.9

This list reflects an averaging of the results from many mail order companies. Use it only as a general guide. As you send out more promotions and keep your own records, you should be able to develop your own seasonal response chart that will be even more reliable.

The list uses October as a base month. Any month that produces better responses on the average will have a higher rating (greater than 100.0), and any month that produces poorer responses on the average than October will have a lower rating (less than 100.0). As you can see, most mail order companies get better responses for their general offers in January and February than any other month. That's one reason so many companies mail right before the new year or early in January.

Here are two examples to show how this list can be used to take seasonal variations into account when projecting responses to mailings.

- If you were to test a list in October and then roll out to the entire list in January, you can expect an 11.2% better response (*if* the general seasonal variations hold for your offer). In other words, for every 100 orders you received in October, you should receive 111.2 in January.
- If, on the other hand, you did your test mailing in January and rolled out to the entire list in April, you can expect a poorer response—as much as 28.5% worse (April's rating divided by January's rating = .715, or 28.5% worse). That means for every 100 orders you received in January, you can expect to receive only 71.5 orders in April (again, only *if* the general seasonal variations hold for your offer).

This list should be used only as a general guide and not taken as the one and only truth. It does demonstrate, however, that seasonal variations in response to mail order offers do occur and should be taken into account when making projections. But the only reliable way that you can come close to quantifying the effect on *your* offers is to keep good records of the responses to your previous offers for similar products.

RENTING YOUR LIST TO OTHERS

At some point in the development of any mail order company, the question comes up, "Should we rent out our in-house list to other companies?" The answer that most mail order companies come up with is a resounding "Yes!" List rentals bring in more money (some companies bring in over $1 million in list rentals every year). What's more, such list rentals have little or no negative impact on a company's sales to its customers (according to companies that have studied the effect of list rentals on their own lists). If anything, such list rentals may actually increase sales by making regular mail order buyers out of the customers on your list.

If you do decide to rent out your in-house list, you can market the list yourself (on your own or through list brokers) or arrange to have a list management firm handle the rentals. In most cases, where you have at least 20,000 names on your customer list, you will be better off having a list management firm handle the list. Not only will they generally get more rentals for you, but they will also work to get your house list in shape (get rid of duplicates, make sure all the necessary data are included in the list, etc.) and show you how to safeguard your ownership of the list. Some list management firms that will work with smaller lists (as few as 5,000 names) are noted in Appendix III.

Before putting up your list for rental, draw up a list data card like the one in Exhibit 5-2. You can enlarge the master copy of the list data card in Appendix II and then type out your list data right on the form. Send this customized list data card to any company that inquires about your list and to any list management firms or brokers interested in representing your list.

How much should you charge for rental of your list? The going rate for names of buyers is at least $60 per thousand. Many companies now charge anywhere from $70 all the way up to $100 per thousand. The more hotline buyers or unique (and very targetable) names you have on your list, the more valuable your list will be. On the other hand, the more inquirers and old names (people who have not bought from you in a year or more) you have on your list, the less valuable it will be.

Because our list of book publishers is a select list of buyers, Open Horizons charges $80 per thousand for list rental. We handle our own rentals because our list is still quite small (just 10,000 names). Without any promotion at all, we rent it out about once a month. We also rent out many smaller but very targetable lists of specialty booksellers, book clubs, bookstore chains, wholesalers, radio shows that do telephone interviews, other media editors, and book printers (all at a rate of $8 per hundred). This list rental income currently represents about one-fifth of our total income. A nice piece of change.

6

Selling Direct Using Other Media

WHICH MEDIA SHOULD YOU USE?

Although targeting your prime prospect by direct mail is generally the most effective way to reach them, many mail order companies supplement their direct mailings with classified and display ads in magazines and newspapers. Other mail order companies also use telemarketing, radio ads, long-form (more than 5 minutes) and short-form (generally 30 seconds, or 1 or 2 minutes) ads on television (network, local, and cable), card packs, and even billboards. All of these media have been found to be effective for some advertisers.

To help you decide which media might be most effective for your promotions, review the competitive media analyzer in Exhibit 6-1. While this analysis presents only my view and is clearly simplistic, it should be useful in getting an overview of your media options.

The chart lists 33 positive qualities that might make any media more attractive for direct marketers to use. Then each of 11 media options is rated using a four-star system (four stars being highly positive, no stars being neutral or negative, and one, two, or three stars being relatively more positive). The ratings in the chart reflect my evaluation of the various media for an average mail order promotion.

The ratings should be adjusted depending on the requirements of the promotion (the product, the offer, the copy, the audience, the amount of money available for promotion, the selling price of the product, etc.). Because the ratings are variable, you might want to configure a competitive media analyzer customized to your own promotions. To help you do this, a master copy of this chart is included in Appendix II.

The competitive media analyzer in Exhibit 6-1 compares 11 media that could be used for direct marketing: direct mail, magazines, newspapers,

Competitive Media Analyzer

	Direct Mail	Magazines	Newspapers	Network TV	Short-form TV Spot / Cable	Long-form TV Spot / Cable	Network Radio	Spot Radio	Outdoor Billboards	Telephone Marketing	Card Packs
Highly targetable audience	****	***	*		*	**	*	**		****	***
Geographic selectivity	****	**	****		****	***	*	****	****	****	
Demographic selectivity	****	***	*	**	*	**	*	**		****	*
Psychographic selectivity	****	***	**	**	*	**	**	***		****	*
Low cost per thousand (CPM)		**	*		***	**	***	**	**		***
Low cost per actual exposure	**	**	*		*	*	*	*		*	**
Inexpensive to produce	**	**	***		*	*	**	**	*	****	***
Flexible costs	****	**	**	*	**	**	**	***		**	**
Low clutter / no distractions	*	*	*	*	*	*	**	*		**	*
Wide penetration of market	***	*	*			*	*	*		**	**
Broad reach / mass market	*	**	***	****	***	**	**	**	**	*	
High frequency possible	****	**	****	*	**	**	***	***		*	*
Flexible timing	****	*	****		**	**	**	***	**	****	*
Short lead time / quick roll-out	***	*	****		**	*	*	****	*	****	*
Quick response time	****	**	****	****	****	****	****	****		****	**
Measurable response	****	***	***	*	**	***	*	*	*	****	****
Numerous response options	****	***	**	*	*	**				*	**
More testable / lots of options	****	**	*		*	***	*	*		****	**
Lots of room to state message	****	***	**			***				*	*
Lots of creative flexibility	****	***	**	**	**	****	**	**	*	**	**
Excellent reproduction	****	****	**	****	***	****	***	***	***	**	**
High graphic impact	****	***	**	****	****	****	*	*	****		**
Involves all senses	****	***	*	***	***	***	*	*	*	*	*
Highly participatory	****	**	**			**				**	*
Intrusive	***	**	**	****	****	**	***	***	*	****	*
Compatible editorial environment		****	**			**	*	**			*
More flexibility in making changes	****	*	***			*	*	***		****	**
A long life-span	*	****	*								*
Great pass-along rate	*	****	**								*
Repeated exposure	*	***	*						***		*
Reach audience where you want to	***	***	**	**	**	**	**	**		***	****
No wasted circulation	***	**	*	*	*	**	*	*		**	***
Media help in preparing ads		*	**		*	*		**	**		**

Exhibit 6-1   Competitive media analyzer.

network television, short-form and long-form spot/cable television, network radio, spot radio, outdoor billboards, telephone marketing, and card packs. Direct mail (clearly my bias) earns the most four-star ratings.

To help you in developing a custom chart for your promotions, here are some of my reasons for rating the various media as I did:

- **Highly targetable audience.** One of the great advantages of direct marketing is being able to target an audience. Of the 11 media, direct mail and telemarketing clearly offer the greatest chance to target an audience, while network television offers little opportunity. True, you can make some demographic and psychographic differentiations between the people who watch "Golden Girls" and those who watch "MacGyver," but network television doesn't come close to the kind of selectivity that direct mail offers. Spot and cable television offer perhaps a bit more selectivity since you can target specific cable channels with highly identifiable viewers (e.g., ESPN versus Lifetime). Radio offers little selectivity unless you are trying to reach certain psychographic groups via their taste in music (news, talk, and sports stations may offer greater selectivity). Outdoor billboards offer little selectivity and are rarely used for direct marketing. Magazines and card packs, on the other hand, can have very targetable audiences and are perhaps the best direct marketing media after direct mail and telemarketing.

- **Geographic selectivity.** While many direct marketers need not concern themselves with specific regions, some do. For these marketers, direct mail and telemarketing are still tops, but spot radio and television can also target regions selectively. Used in conjunction with direct mail or telemarketing, spot broadcasts can be very effective.

Outdoor billboards also offer specific geographic selectivity. 1-800-FLOWERS, for instance, used that selectivity to test 20 billboards in the New Jersey counties of Bergen and Morris (because these two counties have favorable demographics and are close to the company's New York offices). The message was short and sweet (as it needs to be on a billboard): 1-800-FLOWERS—ANYTIME, ANYWHERE, TO ANYONE.

- **Demographic selectivity.** Direct mail and telemarketing win hands down, but magazines and some radio/television shows can also offer demographic selections.

- **Psychographic selectivity.** Because some television shows and most radio formats appeal to or reflect certain life-styles, they can be useful in targeting specific psychographic groupings. Most magazines also target a specific style (note, for instance, the difference between *Gourmet* and *Good Food*). Newspapers, via their various sections (sports, news, business, arts, etc.), can target specific life-styles as well. A growing number of specialized newspapers (for ethnic groups, fashion, computers, business, etc.) also offer psychographic selectivity.

- **Low cost per thousand (CPM).** The cost of reaching people is always a factor in direct marketing yet not nearly as important as selectivity. For instance, direct mail and telemarketing have among the highest costs per thousand yet are used extensively because they can target the right people.

- **Low cost per actual exposure.**   Some media might offer a low cost per thousand, but if no one notices your ad, what difference does it make? Direct mail, although high in cost per thousand, offers a low cost per actual exposure. Of the thousands who receive a direct mail offer, more will read it than would listen to or notice a radio commercial that offers a very low cost per thousand.

- **Inexpensive to produce.**   Network television is an obvious loser here since for anything to work, it must have the quality and pizzazz of network shows. That's hard to match without spending lots of money. Radio commercials are less expensive to produce because you have to deal with only one sense. Card packs are inexpensive to produce because the cost covers production (except for the development of the copy and camera-ready art) as well as distribution. Since many newspapers help with ad production, such ads can be inexpensive.

- **Flexible costs.**   Of all the media, direct mail offers the most flexibility on how much to spend. You can go from a simple postcard mailing to an elaborate four-color mailing with many involvement devices. Most other media, except billboards, also offer some flexibility in how much you spend.

- **Low clutter/no distractions.**   Clutter and distractions are hard to get away from. Telemarketing rates two stars because once you have the person on the line, you can hold his or her attention more readily than less participatory media. Of course, you still have to fight for the person's attention against the television blaring, kids fighting, or some other distraction, but at least you have a sporting chance.

- **Wide penetration of market.**   This category refers to a wide reach within a specific market, not to a broad mass reach. With the right lists, direct mail can achieve the greatest penetration of a market. Some highly targeted card packs also offer a wide reach within a specific market.

  Some specialized magazines offer a wide reach. One that doesn't is *Publishers Weekly*, the major trade magazine in the book publishing industry. Less than one-fifth of all book publishers in the ISBN database subscribe to the magazine. To reach the other 80%, you have to mail to them direct.

- **Broad reach/mass market.**   Network television undoubtedly offers the broadest reach. Direct mail can offer a broad reach, but that is not its strong point. Few direct marketers require a broad reach. Such broad reaches are probably most important to certain mail order catalogs and for companies doing market research or sampling.

- **High frequency possible.**   If something works, direct marketers like to know that they can readily come back to that medium as often as they like. Frequency is then important. While network television could offer high frequency, I assigned it only one star because of its high cost, which, for most companies, would practically rule out any high frequency.

- **Flexible timing.** The more flexible the timing is, the more you can test offers and the more quickly you can roll out when you want to. Among the most flexible media are direct mail, telemarketing, newspapers, and radio (primarily because of their short lead times). Radio is a bit less flexible than newspapers because the station might not have any unsold time when you want to air your ad and it can't simply add more pages (more commercials per hour) just because you want to run your ad right away.

- **Short lead time/quick roll-out.** Since flexible timing is so closely related to short lead time, most media rate the same for both of these. Direct mail is rated lower in this category because of the turnaround time to produce the mailing package (especially if it's a four-color catalog). Radio rates higher because radio ads can be produced and aired in a matter of hours (at least locally and if the changes are minor).

- **Quick response time.** If you want to test an offer immediately and verify the response within hours, use telemarketing. If you can wait a few days, try newspapers and radio. Television also offers a quick response time, often within minutes of the commercial, but only after you have spent lots of time on production.

- **Measurable response.** The more readily you can measure the response to an offer, the quicker you can expand that offer to other markets or media. Telemarketing rates tops here since you don't hang up without some sort of measurable response. Direct mail is a close second, though it is quite possible to get a response to direct mail that you cannot assign to any specific list. For example, the person responding to the offer might have received your letter from a friend, jotted down your address, and sent in an order. If your address wasn't coded or the customer left the code out, you won't be able to track the order.

- **Numerous response options.** The more response options people have, the more likely they are to order. If they can call or write, that's great. If they can fax it, even better. Advertising on broadcast media cannot offer those options. Generally, one is about all you can clearly offer (though some 2-minute ads successfully feature both a mailing address and an 800 number). The problem with most broadcast media, at least before the advent of videotape, is that the audience never has a chance to go back to review the telephone number if it goes by before they get a pencil. In such cases, their response options are effectively zero.

- **More testable/lots of options.** Direct mail and telemarketing allow many test options (A/B splits allow you to mail one offer to half a list and another offer or format to the other half of the list). A/B splits with card packs or magazine ads also give you room to test. Broadcast media, because of their brief selling times and sometimes costly productions, limit flexibility in testing many different items.

- **Lots of room to state your message.**   Most broadcast media, other than long-form television offer very little room. Direct mail does.

- **Lots of creative flexibility.**   How much can you play with the look and feel of your offer? You have lots of room with direct mail and less room with newspapers (because most ads are black and white) and telemarketing (you are limited to a fairly one-dimensional progression with the sales script and have little room to expand the message). If you have the money, you can do almost anything you want with television and radio, but you are limited by available time.

- **Excellent reproduction.**   Reproduction can be important when you are selling fashion and art or when making a life-style statement. Newspapers are still a long way from offering the reproduction quality of magazines or direct mail. Radio can offer excellent reproduction, but the message could be blocked by poor reception, honking horns (during drive time), electrical storms, and home computers.

- **High graphic impact.**   Television offers the greatest graphic impact, but direct mail and magazines also do well in this category. I rated magazines as only three stars, however, because you have less control over the reproduction of the ad since the magazine does the printing. It's true that some radio commercials can also be amazingly graphic, but most aren't; that's why I rated radio as only one star.

- **Involves all senses.**   Since television has the greatest impact on the two main senses (sight and sound), it is rated highly. Direct mail, however, can beat television in a dozen different ways. It can offer scents, sound via tape or sound sheets, tastes via samples, all sorts of tactile sensations from raspy to sticky to slick (and lots of involvement devices), and, to beat television at its own game, videos of any length as well as interactive computer simulations. Magazines, via inserts, can also offer many of these senses. Most other media involve only one sense.

- **Highly participatory.**   Direct mail wins hands down. While telemarketing can also involve the listener, it doesn't always do so. Some long-form cable television shows have also involved various degrees of participation from their audiences (via toll-free response lines, various demonstrations, and lots of questions and answers).

- **Intrusive.**   Can people avoid your message if they are involved with the medium? If not, the medium is considered intrusive. Television commercials, especially before the age of video zapping, were intrusive. Long-form television, however, is not intrusive since the viewer can readily switch channels without missing a favorite show. Telemarketing is highly intrusive since it's almost impossible for anyone not to answer the telephone when it rings. Direct mail is more intrusive than magazine ads because a person has to make a conscious decision to open or toss the mailing, while in reading he or she can readily overlook an advertisement.

Radio commercials are not as intrusive as television commercials because the audience is rarely as involved.

• **Compatible editorial environment.** Specialty magazines clearly offer the most compatible editorial environment.

• **More flexibility in making changes.** Due to high production costs, television offers the least flexibility. Telemarketing is the most flexible: You can change a script in 5 minutes if need be. Because of their long lead times, magazines are limited. On the other hand, because of their short lead times, newspapers and spot radio offer lots of flexibility.

• **A long life-span.** Because they are retained, sometimes for years, magazines offer the longest life-span for your message. Billboards, on the other hand, flash by. Broadcast messages disappear with the wind. Since some people (I'm one of them) often save mailings, card packs, and newspapers for weeks or months before responding, these media have some longevity.

• **Great pass-along rate.** Magazines win hands down, but many newspapers also enjoy a pass-along readership. It's not uncommon, for instance, for three or four people in an office to share the same newspaper. I've also seen similar newspaper pass-along rates in eateries, airports, and waiting rooms. Direct mail and card packs, if they meet a need, are also passed along in some office environments. But how do you pass along a billboard or radio commercial? True, if your commercial contains a great story or joke, that might get passed along, but will your name and address go with it? Not likely.

• **Repeated exposure.** Because a person might take several days or weeks to read a magazine, he or she might easily pass by your ad three or four times. That's repeated exposure. You don't get that on television or radio. Only if a person tears your ad out of the newspaper or saves the direct mail piece will you get any repeated exposure from these media. As far as direct marketing is concerned, the best thing outdoor billboards have going for them is their ability to generate repeat exposures along regularly traveled routes.

• **Reach audience where you want to.** Card packs are the winner here. You wouldn't use a card pack if you want to reach your prospect at home. Few are mailed to home addresses. Direct mail and telemarketing can often give you this same accessibility (if the appropriate lists are available). If you want to reach your audience while they are at home, television is a good bet. If you want to reach them while they are driving home from work, radio drive time can be effective. If you want to reach them at work, use a trade magazine.

• **No wasted circulation.** Newspapers are rated low here because many newspaper readers are not mail order buyers. The same holds true for television and radio. Long-form television is rated higher because people who watch such shows do so by choice.

• **Media help in preparing ads.** If you want to cut some costs, this help could come in handy. But, as the saying goes, you get what you pay for. I would not trust a newspaper ad person accustomed to retail sales to design a direct response ad. On the other hand, production help from a radio station (as long as I control the copy) would be fine.

These 33 points cover the most important criteria to consider when making media buying decisions. Some factors, of course, will be more important to your promotion than others. That's why you should use the master copy of this competitive media analyzer to draw up a custom chart that will help you to focus on which media are truly right for your product.

HOW TO RESEARCH THE MEDIA

Once you've selected which media to use, research the choices within those media. For instance, if you choose to market your product through magazines, which magazines should you use? If you are close to your market (for instance, if you are an avid reader or hobbyist), you will know most of the major magazines without doing any research. But you will still have to research the costs, deadlines, and material requirements for your ads. And if you are on a limited budget, you will have to choose among the available magazines.

In this section, I describe some of the ways you can research the media to locate the best choices—the ones most likely to produce the greatest response to your ads. While I will make most of my points using magazines as an example, you can apply the same principles to researching other media.

How to Query Media

One of the first things to do when planning an advertising campaign is to obtain sample copies and advertising rate cards from all publications you are considering. Use a form letter similar to the advertising query letter shown as Figure 6-1. Be sure to request the information you need. First, you need to know the **advertising rates** so you can budget your money accordingly and determine which publications offer the best value for your money. The **circulation figures** will help you calculate the costs per thousand readers, which is one way of comparing the cost effectiveness of various publications.

If there are any **special upcoming issues** (crafts, gardening, decorating, Christmas, computers, etc.), you will want to know about these. If the special topic applies to your product, you can count on a better response to your ad if you place it in that special issue.

You will need to review several **sample copies** of the publication not only to determine the best size and placement of your ad but also because you need to get an understanding of the publication and its readers. Is the

---

Your Letterhead Here

(or that of your advertising agency)

June 6, 1992

XYZ Magazine
David Smith, Advertising Manager
123 Front Street
New York, NY 10022

Dear Mr. Smith:

We are considering advertising some of our products in your magazine. Please send us your media kit., including the following information:

* Advertising rate card (both display and classified),
* Audited circulation figures with readership demographics,
* Schedule of upcoming special editions, and
* 2 to 3 sample copies (to allow us to determine the best size and placement of our advertisements).

If you offer special rates for first-time advertisers or mail order advertisers, please include that information as well.

Also, please place us on file to be notified of any future rate or policy changes. Thank you.

Sincerely,
YOUR COMPANY NAME

Your Signature

Figure 6-1   Advertising query letter.

publication's editorial emphasis appropriate for your product? Will your ad fit in with the publication's graphic style? Are there similar ads already running in the publication? Is your competitor advertising in this publication? If not, why not?

Some publications offer a **special discount to new advertisers** (not many publications but some). Quite a few publications offer a discount to mail order advertisers and to other publishers. Be sure to use these discounts if they are available; they can save you hundreds of dollars.

Finally, ask them to **put you on file.** You might not advertise right away, but later, when planning another promotion or rolling out the current promotion, you might want to. You don't want to plan your advertising with outdated rate cards. It would distort your break-even analysis and profit projections.

For other media, ask similar questions. For instance, for radio, you want a rate card, programming schedule, Arbitron or Birch listenership ratings, audience demographics, and any special programming, such as weekend music roundups or sports call-in shows.

How to Keep Track of Media Information

As you begin receiving sample copies and advertising rate cards, file them according to one of two systems: all alphabetically or alphabetically but separated by categories (e.g., crafts, home and garden, general, men's, women's). If you have only one product that appeals to the general market, you can file all publications together. But if you have several products appealing to different interest groups, separate your publications file by categories. If a publication seems to fit two or more categories, file it under the most appropriate category, and place notes (about its location) in the files for the other categories.

Keep all the information you receive for each publication in its own file folder. As you run ads and get reviews in a publication, add copies of these into the file as well. Also keep your ad response records (see the next chapter) for that magazine in its file. In this way you will have all information concerning a publication in one place for easy reference.

On the outside of the folder, staple the publication data record (Exhibit 6-2) for that magazine. This form gives you a quick glance at all relevant information regarding the publication without having to sort through the folder. Update the data as they change, and make notes of the responses and costs per order for each ad you place.

The publication data record is easy to fill out. For a master copy to use for your own business, see Appendix II.

• **Publication.** Fill in the publication name, address, contact person, telephone number, and fax number.

• **Key Code.** Be sure to assign a key code to each publication (see p. 116 for details).

• **Frequency.** Make a note of how often the magazine or newspaper is published. Daily? Weekly? Monthly? 15 times per year?

• **Circulation** The circulation figures are the actual number of copies sold through subscriptions and newsstand sales.

• **Readership.** Most magazines claim a larger readership made up of pass-along readers. Readership numbers are usually anywhere from 1.5 to 3 times circulation.

Publication Data Record

Publication:	XYZ Magazine	Key Code: XYZ	Space Deadline: June 15
Address:	234 Fifth Avenue	Frequency: 12/year	Art Deadline: June 30
City/State/Zip:	New York NY 10020	Circulation: 350,000	Cover Date: September
Contact Person:	Jane Doe, Advertising Director	Readership: 560,000	On Sale Date: August 5
Phone:	212-123-4567	Subjects: Health, self-help, nutrition, exercise, psychology, fashion, relationships, women's issues	
Fax Number:	212-123-8901		

Size and/or Description of Ad Space	Cost of Ad	CPM (cost per thousand)
Full page (8 x 10)	$6,500.00	$18.57
Full page (8x10) Full-color	$9,545.00	$27.27
1/2 page (8 x 5)	$3,500.00	$10.00
Display classified ad — 1 inch	$235.00	$0.67
Classified ad -- 30 words ($4.65/word)	$139.50	$0.40

Date	Cost	Ad Size & Position	Ad Contents	Response	CPI/CPO
3/90	$6,500.00	Full right page	Widget for two	450 orders	$14.45
5/90	$3,500.00	1/2 page, bottom right	Widget for two	320 orders	$10.94
6/90	$3,500.00	1/2 page, bottom right	Widget for two	270 orders	$12.96
7/90	$3,500.00	1/2 page, bottom right	Widget for two	220 orders	$15.91

Exhibit 6-2   Publication data record.

- **Space Deadline.** This is the last day you can submit insertion orders for a specific issue (e.g., the fifteenth of the second month preceding the month of issue: May 15 for a July cover date). If it is easier for you, name an actual date for each of these four dates, just as I have done in the sample.

- **Art Deadline.** This is the last day you can send in camera-ready copy, negatives, separations, or whatever art you are providing.

- **Cover Date.** The date on the cover of the magazine is the cover date.

- **On-Sale Date.** This is the actual date the magazine is put on the newsstands. For a monthly, it is usually two to four weeks before the cover date.

- **Size and/or Description of Ad Space.** List some sample ad rates from the magazine's rate card. List the full-page rate plus the display and classified rates you would be most likely to use.

- **Cost of Ad.** List the one-time rate for each size ad you describe. If you want to compare costs on one-time rates versus three-time rates, list the same size ad twice under "Size and/or Description," and note that one is one time and the other is three time; then list the corresponding rates under "Cost of Ad."

- **CPM.** Note the cost per thousand. You will use the CPM of a full-page ad when comparing the costs of advertising in different publications. How do you calculate CPM? Easy. Divide the cost of the ad by the circulation and then multiply by 1,000. Here are two examples to show you how it is done.

> Cost of half-page ad in magazine 1 = $3,985.00
> Circulation = 312,000
> $3,985.00 ÷ 312,000 = $.01277 × 1,000 = $12.77/M
>
> Cost of half-page ad in magazine 2 = $2,770.00
> Circulation = 173,600
> $2,770.00 ÷ 173,600 = $.01596 × 1,000 = $15.96/M

Once you have calculated the CPM for each magazine, you can compare the costs of advertising in each of them: $12.77 versus $15.96 per thousand. The ad in magazine 2 will have to produce 1.25 times as many orders as the ad in magazine 1 if it is to be as profitable. Can it produce that many more? That is your decision, based on your experience with the magazines and your tests.

- **Date.** These lines help you to keep track of each ad you place in this particular publication. List the cover date for each ad run.

- **Cost.** List the total cost of each ad you place.

- **Ad Size and Position.** What size did you use? Full page? Half-page? Classified ad? For partial-page ads, indicate the position of the ad—for instance, top right on a right-hand page or bottom left on a left-hand page or bottom one-third on a left-hand page.

- **Ad Contents.** What product and offer were you advertising?

- **Response.** When most of the responses have been tallied, make a note of the response to the ad. How many units were sold, or how many people inquired?

- **CPI/CPO.** What was your final **CPO** (cost per order) or **CPI** (cost per inquiry)? Note one or the other depending on whether you were going for a sale or prospecting for inquiries.

To calculate CPO, divide the cost of the ad by the total number of orders. If you were going for inquiries rather than orders, calculate the CPI by dividing the cost of the ad by the total number of inquiries received.

Cost of display ad = $3,500.00
Number of orders received = 320
$3,500.00 ÷ 320= $10.94

You would need to have a fairly high-priced product and a contribution margin of $10.94 for this ad to break even.

You can also calculate CPI as a way of checking to see if it pays to get inquiries.

Cost of display ad = $3,500.00
Number of inquiries received = 576
$3,500.00 ÷ 576 = $6.08

That's a fairly high cost for an inquiry, but if you have a higher priced product, it could certainly pay off. You would have to decide if an inquiry were worth that much to you. If it were, then you would repeat the ad.

CPM, CPI, and CPO are indispensable for comparing the value of advertising in various media. Because CPM provides direct cost comparisons, it is useful in deciding which magazines to use in the beginning. But when you need to know which magazines are actually paying off, look at CPOs or CPIs.

You can design a variation of the publication data record to research and keep track of your advertisements in other media as well. For instance, if you were advertising on radio, you could indicate the Arbitron ratings for each station, as well as estimated audience size. Under "Costs," you could indicate rates for various day parts (morning drive time, afternoon drive time, overnight, etc.) and lengths of commercials (30 seconds, 1 minute, 2 minutes).

However you organize your media data—whether you use the publication data record, forms of your own design, or a computer database—be sure to keep records. Records are essential for making effective comparisons of various media and for determining which ads are paying off.

How to Key Your Ads

A **key code** is an identifying abbreviation used in ads and direct mail to indicate from what source a response originated. For example, you might use PM to indicate *Popular Mechanics* magazine. In an ad, this key might read as follows: Your company name, Dept. PM, your company address. Any responses addressed to Dept. PM would then be from the ad in *Popular Mechanics.* If you want to be less obvious, you can direct those responding to the ad to write to different people in your company each time you run an ad.

Key codes allow you to track the responses to an ad and calculate CPI and CPO figures, which, in turn, allow you to determine the profitability of an ad. If the ad is profitable, of course, you repeat it.

When advertising in more than one issue of the same magazine, use variations of the same key. For example, PM103 could be used to indicate the October 1993 issue of *Popular Mechanics,* and PM113 could be used to refer to the November 1993 issue. Since responses to magazine ads can come many months later, these codes are the only way to know for sure which of the ads produced the response.

Keep a record of these key codes. If you are computerized, these key codes can be entered into your customer database as source codes. But you might want to make a paper record of these key codes too. A simple way to keep track of these codes is to record them on 3″ X 5″ file cards.

At the top of the key codes file card (Figure 6-2) write the name of the publication and its key. Put the key in the top left-hand corner so you can file the keys alphabetically in a small file box.

This key file will allow you and your order processing or marketing personnel to check which keys refer to what publication. This key file is especially valuable in tracking orders that come in a year or two after the ad was placed—and it is not at all unusual to get such orders. About 1% of all orders from ads in monthly magazines come a year or more after the original ad appeared.

Remember to note each new variation of a key used. The sample file card in Figure 6-2 contains an example of how to indicate the variations.

Asking Your Customers

Besides writing letters to the media and keeping track of the information you receive via publication data records, there are two other steps you can take to research media more thoroughly before selecting which ones you will use to advertise.

One of the steps is to ask potential customers to tell you which media

PM
Popular Mechanics

Key	Issue	Product Offered
PM 109	October 1991	woodworking book
PM 119	November 1991	woodworking book
PM 119x	November 1991	catalog (in catalog showcase)
PM 129	December 1991	woodworking book
PM 010	January 1992	woodworking book
PM 030x	March 1992	catalog (in catalog showcase)

Open Horizons, P. O. Box 1102, Fairfield IA 52556

Figure 6-2 Key codes file cards.

you should use for advertising. How do you get them to tell you? The simplest way is to write a brief letter asking them to tell you which magazines they read regularly and then to rate the magazines according to which ones are more helpful for their job (if you are researching business magazines) or more useful to their hobby or active interests (if you are researching consumer magazines).

Figure 6-3 contains a sample customer query letter that you can use as a model for writing your own letters. Unlike this sample, though, you might want the letter to appear to come from an outside research agency. If so, begin the letter by saying something like the following: "One of our clients in the catalog business needs your help. This firm wants to communicate important developments to you in the best way possible. That is why they would like to know which direct marketing magazines you read regularly."

You might also want your potential customers to rate the magazines rather than check off only the most important one.

Who should receive this letter? First, select some previous customers who have bought similar products. You might mail to a few names from some of the lists you intend to use or have used in the past. The key element is to target people who are most likely to be interested in buying your product.

You could make this a rigorous test mailing by selecting random names and controlling all the variables, or you can do a more informal survey to get a feeling for the best way to reach potential customers. How formal you make this survey should be determined primarily by how certain you want to be about the media you select to use.

If you know your target market well and keep up with all the magazines on a regular basis, chances are that you will be able to select

**Open Horizons Publishing Company
P.O. Box 1102
Fairfield, IA 52556-1102**

March 6, 1992

Ken Smith, Marketing Director
ABC Company
123 Fourth Street
Ann Arbor, MI 45990

Dear Mr. Smith:

Because we want to know the best way to communicate important developments to you, we would like your help in answering a few short questions. We need to know which direct marketing publications you read regularly and which are most helpful to you in your job.

Please take a minute to review the list of the magazines listed below. In column 1, check which magazines you read regularly. In column 2, check the one magazine you find most helpful in doing your job.

Then just slip this letter into the enclosed business reply envelope and drop it in the mail. Thank you for helping us to serve you better.

Sincerely

John Kremer
Publisher

1		2
[ ]	Catalog Age	[ ]
[ ]	Catalog Business	[ ]
[ ]	Direct Magazine	[ ]
[ ]	Direct Marketing	[ ]
[ ]	DM News	[ ]
[ ]	Target Marketing	[ ]

Figure 6-3   Customer query letter.

the right media to reach customers without doing this survey. The less you know about the media, however, the more important it becomes to do some sort of survey of potential customers.

Analyzing the Competition

If you want an even better idea of which publications to use for ads, check out which ones are being used by your competition. Read at least three or four recent issues of each magazine you are considering. As you read, make notes about which competitors are advertising in that magazine, how much space they are using, and an estimate of how much it is costing them to run the ad. To make it easier to take down these notes in an organized way, use the competition ad analysis worksheet in Exhibit 6-3 (a master copy is included in Appendix II).

You are looking for magazines in which your competition advertises over and over again. No good direct marketer would ever continue advertising in a publication that was not producing profit-making results. Review magazines from at least six months ago. If your competition is currently advertising and was also advertising at least six months ago, chances are that the company is doing well and making money hand over fist.

The competition ad analysis worksheet is easy to use. First make a note of the product and promotion you are researching (for example, the product could be widgets and the promotion could be an ad for your catalog). Then note the time period during which you reviewed magazines. You should review at least three months' worth. If you do not have time to do this research, hire a freelancer to do it for you.

The worksheet allows room to list 29 issues of various magazines plus 3 of your competitors. If you need more room for magazines or competitors, add another worksheet.

Under the "Magazines" heading, list the magazines and the cover dates of the issues you reviewed. Then note the name of each competitor whose ads appear in one of the magazines you reviewed. Finally, under each competitor, note the description of the ad placed and an approximation of what it might have cost to place that ad.

The sample worksheet in Exhibit 6-3 illustrates what your analysis might look like. As you look over the sample, see what conclusions you can draw. Why, for instance, doesn't Humdingers advertise in *Woodworking* when other competitors consistently do so? It may well be that humdingers don't appeal to woodworkers but do appeal to mechanically minded individuals. Note that the Humdinger company is apparently doing very well with its ads in *Popular Mechanics* since it continued to use full-page ads for five months. But note also that it is cutting back on its use of two other magazines.

By reviewing your own competition ad analysis worksheet, you should be able to come up with a good picture of what is working for your

Competition Ad Analysis Worksheet

Product: Widgets		Promotion: Catalog Ad		Time Period: 3/91 to 6/91	

Magazines	Competitor: Humdingers		Competitor: Toodles		Competitor: Doodads	
	Space	Cost	Space	Cost	Space	Cost
Popular Mechanics 2/91	FP B/W CP	$17,500.00	1/2 B/W CP	$9,350.00	1/2 B/W CP	$9,350.00
Popular Mechanics 3/91	FP B/W CP	$17,500.00			1/2 B/W CP	$9,350.00
Popular Mechanics 4/91	FP B/W CP	$17,500.00	1/2 B/W CP	$9,350.00	1/3 B/W CP	$6,950.00
Popular Mechanics 5/91	FP B/W CP	$17,500.00			1/3 B/W CP	$6,950.00
Popular Mechanics 6/91	FP B/W CP	$17,500.00	1/2 B/W CP	$9,350.00	1/4 B/W CP	$5,350.00
Mechanix Illustrated 3/91	1/2 B/W CP	$9,800.00				
Mechanix Illustrated 4/91	1/2 B/W CP	$9,800.00	1/2 B/W CP	$9,800.00		
Mechanix Illustrated 5/91	1/3 B/W CP	$7,250.00				
Mechanix Illustrated 6/91	1/3 B/W CP	$7,250.00	1/2 B/W CP	$9,800.00		
Woodworking 2/91			1/2 B/W CP	$3,500.00	1/2 B/W CP	$3,500.00
Woodworking 4/91			1/2 B/W CP	$3,500.00	1/2 B/W CP	$3,500.00
Woodworking 6/91			1/2 B/W CP	$3,500.00	1/2 B/W CP	$3,500.00
Popular Science 3/91	FP B/W CP	$16,950.00				
Popular Science 4/91	FP B/W CP	$16,950.00				
Popular Science 5/91	1/2 B/W CP	$9,925.00				

Descriptive Codes:	FP — full page ad	1/3 — 1/3 page ad	IN — inserts	B/W — black & white	BL — bleed
	2/3 — 2/3 page ad	1/4 — 1/4 page ad	2P — 2-page spread	2C — two colors	SE — special effects
	1/2 — 1/2 page ad	1/6 — 1/6 page ad	PC — bind-in card	4C — full color	CP — coupon in ad
	IS — island ad	1" — 1 inch by 1 col.	CA — classified ad	SP — special	PH — phone # in ad

Exhibit 6-3   Competition ad analysis worksheet.

competitors. Once you do, you should test the same sort of ads for your products in the same magazines. Chances are, your ad will be successful.

SCHEDULING YOUR ADS

Once you have completed all the research you need to do, begin to plan your own media advertising schedule. This schedule, like the sample media schedule in Exhibit 6-4, should list all the media you intend to use with notes on how and when you intend to use them. Lay out a schedule for the coming 12 months. Such a schedule will give you a good overview of your advertising, as well as help you to remember when to make placements.

In making up such a schedule, of course, keep your budget in mind. Don't set up a schedule you know you cannot afford. Rather, set up a realistic schedule and then modify it later if you find that your ads are doing well and you can afford to expand the schedule to include more magazines or more frequent ads.

In the sample media schedule, ads are scheduled for four magazines and one newsletter. Since the newsletter has a small circulation and does not allow display ads, the company chose to use a classified ad each month. The ad for XYZ *Magazine* is a test ad for a marginal magazine. The rest of the ads are full-page rollouts.

Here are the items that should be covered in any media schedule you draw up (a master copy of this schedule is included in Appendix II):

- **Product/Promotion.**   Enter the name of the product being advertised or the offer you are making.
- **Period.**   Enter the dates that this schedule covers.
- **Name.**   List the magazines or other media you will be using for your advertisements.
- **Circulation.**   Note the circulation. You can take this information from the publication data records.
- **Frequency.**   Enter frequency of publication.
- **Rate.**   If your ads earn a discounted rate, make note of the cost in the space provided. Also note what that rate is, whether a 6X, 12X, or other rate (6X is the rate earned if you commit to running an ad 6 times during a year; 12X for 12 times a year).
- **Contract Period.**   If you have signed on for a discounted rate, indicate the period of time covered by the contract.
- **Key.**   For each ad placed, list the key code for the ad.
- **Size.**   Make note of the size of the ad.
- **Color.**   Note the color (black and white, two color, or full color) of the ad.
- **Closing.**   Enter the closing date for that ad (the date when you have to reserve the space).
- **Cost.**   Enter the cost for each ad.

Media Schedule

Product/Promotion: Machetes **Period:** January 1992 **to** December 1992

Media Name	Items	January	February	March	April	May	June	July	August	Sept.	October	November	Dec.
Name: Popular Machetes	Key:		PM2	PM3	PM4	PM5	PM6	PM7					
Circulation: 1,600,000	Size:		Full page	Full page	Full page	Full page	Full page	Full page					
Frequency: monthly	Color:		B/W	B/W	B/W	B/W	B/W	B/W					
Rate (6 x): $16,900.00	Closing:		Dec 15	Jan 12	Feb 10	March 11	April 12	May 15					
Contract Period: one year	Cost:		$16,900	$16,900	$16,900	$16,900	$16,900	$16,900					
	Note:												
Name: Machetes Illustrated	Key:		MI2		MI4		MI6		MI8		MI10		MI12
Circulation: 800,000	Size:		Full page		Full page		Full page		Full page		Full page		Full page
Frequency: monthly	Color:		B/W		B/W		B/W		B/W		B/W		B/W
Rate (6 x): $7,500.00	Closing:		Dec 10		Feb 10		April 10		June 10		August 10		Oct 10
Contract Period: one year	Cost:		$7,500		$7,500		$7,500		$7,500		$7,500		$7,500
	Note:												
Name: Machete World	Key:				MW4	MW5	MW6	MW7					
Circulation: 350,000	Size:				Full page	Full page	Full page	Full page					
Frequency: monthly	Color:				B/W	B/W	B/W	B/W					
Rate (4 x): $4,500.00	Closing:				Feb 15	March 15	April 15	May 15					
Contract Period: 1/2 year	Cost:				$4,500	$4,500	$4,500	$4,500					
	Note:												
Name: Machete Hotline	Key:		MH2	MH3	MH4	MH5	MH6	MH7	MH8	MH9	MH10	MH11	MH12
Circulation: 3,000	Size:		35-word	35-word	35-word	35-word	35-word	35-word	35-word	35-word	35-word	35-word	35-word
Frequency: biweekly newsletter	Color:												
Rate (x): $3.50 / word	Closing:		Jan 10	Feb 10	March 10	April 10	May 10	June 10	July 10	August 10	Sept 10	Oct 10	Nov 10
Contract Period: none	Cost:		$122.50	$122.50	$122.50	$122.50	$122.50	$122.50	$122.50	$122.50	$122.50	$122.50	$122.50
	Note:												
Name: XYZ Magazine	Key:			X3									
Circulation: 350,000	Size:			1/2 page									
Frequency: bimonthly	Color:			B/W									
Rate (x): ...	Closing:			Jan 5									
Contract Period: none	Cost:			$3,500									
	Note:												
Name:	Key:												
Circulation:	Size:												
Frequency:	Color:												
Rate (x):	Closing:												
Contract Period:	Cost:												
	Note:												

Exhibit 6-4 Media schedule.

- **Note.** Make any notes here. For instance, if you are advertising in a special edition such as a trade show issue, indicate that information here.

If you are placing ads in more than six publications, draw up a second media schedule. After you have noted all the ads you intend to place for this promotion, add up all the costs for each magazine and then total the costs for all magazines. This total will give you a way to double-check that you haven't overspent your advertising budget.

HOW TO PLACE YOUR OWN ADVERTISING

When you are placing lots of ads in many media, you will have ad agencies bidding for your business. If you are starting small, however, you will probably have to design and place your own ads until you are billing $50,000 in ads. Since ad agencies earn their keep by getting agency discounts from media in which they place ads, you need to be billing at least $50,000 to get a major ad agency even to look at you. Until then, you have two alternatives: place your own ads, or pay a smaller ad agency for each service it provides.

You can save up to 17% of your advertising costs by forming your own in-house ad agency. You can save that much by keeping the 15% agency discount for placing your own ads and by paying for your ads within 10 days of billing to earn a 2% discount from media that offer such a discount for prompt payment.

Some magazine and newspaper publishers frown on giving these discounts to in-house ad agencies. One way to get around this restriction is to form a separate ad agency with a different name, checking account, check signer, and telephone number.

Placing an ad in a publication is quite simple. Just complete an ad insertion order like the one in Exhibit 6-5 and send it to the publication. Until you have established credit, you will generally have to send a check with the insertion order. Once you have established credit, you can wait for the bill to arrive before paying for the ad. Since most bills are sent about 3 to 7 days *after* the ad has appeared in the publication, you will be able to keep your money an additional one to three months. Plus, you could actually begin receiving returns from the ad before having to pay for it.

A master copy of an ad insertion order can be found in Appendix II. To use it, first enlarge it and then paste in a copy of your letterhead for the ad agency. Then fill out the following information.

- **To the Publisher of.** Type in the name of the publication and its address.
- **Order No.** This order number will be used by the publication to keep track of your order. You can use your key code for that particular publication, thereby keeping your references consistent.

Your Letterhead Here

To the Publisher of:

XYZ Magazine
Jane Doe, Advertising Manager
234 West 42nd Street
New York NY 10010

Order No. 435

Date April 2, 1992

Advertiser ABC Company

Product Widgets

☐ This is a SPACE RESERVATION.

☒ This is an INSERTION ORDER.

☐ This ia a CANCELLATION or CHANGE of _____

Insertion Dates	Space	Position	Key	Caption / Description	Ad Rate
June 1990	Full Page B/W	Right Hand Page	XY6	A New Way to Do Whatever You Want in Only 21 Minutes — Wonder Widgets!	$3,475.00

Additional Instructions:

This ad will have two half-tones; negatives will be supplied.

Send invoices and proof of insertion to this office.
Also furnish checking copies to the advertiser.

Total Ad Cost	$3,475.00
Agency Discount	521.25
Subtotal	2,953.75
Cash Discount (2 %)	59.08
Net Amount This Order	$2,894.67

Ad copy and materials   ☒ Enclosed   ☐ To Follow

Name John Smith

Phone 212-472-6310

Signature

Exhibit 6-5   Ad insertion order.

- **Date.** Enter the date you placed the insertion order.
- **Advertiser.** Type in the name of the company for which you are placing the advertisement. If you are an in-house agency, the advertiser is your company.
- **Product.** Enter the name of the product to be advertised.
- **Space Reservation.** Check this box if you are only reserving space for an upcoming issue.
- **Insertion Order.** Check this box if you are placing an order for space. The order is binding unless you cancel it before the closing date for that issue's ads.
- **Cancellation.** Check this box if you are canceling an insertion order or changing part of the ad copy already submitted. Specify the order number of the canceled or changed insertion order.
- **Insertion Dates.** List the issue date or dates in which you want the ad to appear. You have space to list three different ads or dates. If you want the ad to continue running in the magazine indefinitely until you cancel it, write "till forbid."
- **Space.** Specify the size of the ad—full page, half-page, half-page island, classified, or something else. If the publication is a newspaper, enter the line count. If the ad is a classified ad, make a note of the number of words in the ad, then type the copy in the "Caption/Description" box.
- **Position.** If you want a special position (e.g., back cover, right-hand page, no coupon on back), specify your request here. For a classified ad, state the heading you want it to run under (e.g., books and publications, crafts, personals, consulting services, or whatever else is appropriate for your product).
- **Key.** Make a note of your key for that ad. If the ad is to continue running, specify a change in the key each time (e.g., "change key from PM103 to PM113 for second insertion").
- **Caption/Description.** Enter the headline of the ad or some other means of identifying it.
- **Ad Rate.** List the cost of the ad, including any frequency discounts you have earned.
- **Additional Instructions.** If you want the ad to run in only certain regional editions, if you want the copy to bleed, or if you want color, specify those additional instructions in this space.
- **Total Ad Cost.** Add up the costs of the advertisements you have entered above.
- **Agency Discount.** Subtract your agency discount of 15%. Note that classified ads rarely qualify for a discount.
- **Subtotal.** Subtract the agency discount from the total ad cost.
- **Cash Discount.** If you intend to pay for the ad within 10 days of the bill, deduct the prompt payment discount offered by the publication.
- **Net Amount This Order.** Subtract the cash discount (if one is available) from the subtotal.
- **Ad Copy and Materials.** Check the "Enclosed" box if you are

enclosing the ad copy and any other materials (color separations, photos, negatives) with the insertion order. If you will be sending the ad copy later, check the "To Follow" box, and specify what you will be sending later.

Finally, sign and date the ad insertion order.

7

Advertising in Different Media: Some Tips

This chapter is not a comprehensive guide to advertising. It couldn't begin to cover the topic in its few short pages. What it does offer, though, are some basic tips on how to get the most from your various media advertisements.

If you want to know more, read some of the books listed in the Bibliography at the end of this book, and subscribe to some of the magazines that focus on advertising and direct marketing, including *Advertising Age, Adweek, Catalog Age, Direct, Direct Marketing, DM News, Sales and Marketing Management,* and *Target Marketing.* The addresses for these magazines and others of interest to direct marketers are featured in the resource listings in Appendix III.

MAGAZINES FOR EVERY TASTE

Magazines offer something most other mass media cannot offer: targeted readership. There are magazines aimed at almost any audience you'd ever want to reach. Here's a checklist of a few samples:

[ ] animals (*Cats, Horseman, Ranger Rick*)
[ ] art (*Art and Auction, North Light, HOW*)
[ ] business (*Business Week, Forbes, Inc., Income Plus*)
[ ] children (*Highlights for Children, Humpty Dumpty, Parents*)
[ ] clubs (*American Legion, Rotarian, Kiwanis, National 4-H News*)
[ ] computers (*Byte, PC, Macworld, Windows/OS*)
[ ] crafts (*Crafts, Workbasket, Woodworkers Journal*)
[ ] ethnic/minorities (*Ebony, Jet, Scandinavian Times*)

[ ] farm (*Successful Farming, Ohio Farmer, Farm Journal*)
[ ] fashion (*Glamour, Mademoiselle, Vogue*)
[ ] food (*Bon Appetit, Gourmet, Cuisine, Cooking Light*)
[ ] health (*Prevention, Bestways, Longevity, In Health*)
[ ] home (*Better Homes & Gardens, House Beautiful*)
[ ] homemaking (*Good Housekeeping, Family Circle, Woman's Day*)
[ ] life-style (*Interview, Playboy, Cosmopolitan, Seventeen*)
[ ] literary (*New Yorker, Grand Street, Pig Iron*)
[ ] marketing (*Bank Marketing, Catalog Age, Potentials in Marketing*)
[ ] news (*Newsweek, Time, U.S. News and World Report*)
[ ] people (*People, Us, National Enquirer, Star*)
[ ] regional (*Mpls, New York Magazine, Houston Living*)
[ ] science (*Omni, Discover, Scientific American*)
[ ] sports (*Golf, Running, Sports Illustrated, Sports Afield*)
[ ] trade (*Gift & Decorative Accessories, Lawn and Garden*)
[ ] women (*First for Women, New Women, Working Woman*)

And there are many more: alumni magazines, religious magazines, company publications, in-flight magazines, scholarly journals, entertainment guides, Sunday magazine sections of local newspapers, gossip tabloids, and professional journals.

For a complete list of magazines focusing on a specific subject, see one of the following directories: *Standard Periodical Directory, Gale's Directory of Publications and Broadcast Media, SRDS Business Publication Rates and Data,* or *Ulrich's International Periodicals Directory.* You should be able to find one or more of these directories at your local library.

ADVERTISING IN MAGAZINES: SOME TIPS

Here are a few tips on getting the most for your money through magazine advertising:

Advertise in regional editions of national magazines. You can buy space in regional editions for much less than the cost of the entire national edition. One company ran a single ad in a regional edition of *Time* magazine and then used reprints of that ad for its window displays and direct mailings for the next five years. By advertising in the regional edition of such a well-known and respected magazine, the company was able to gain a level of credibility with its customers it could not have gained in any other way.

Arrange per-order ads. Some magazines accept a per-inquiry or per-order arrangement for products that they feel will interest their readers. Similarly, some magazines will run an ad for free if you will drop-ship the orders for them. In this case, orders are sent to the magazine; the magazine processes the order, takes its cut, and sends the order on to you (with their check) for drop-shipping. In such cases you will be expected to give a discount of anywhere from 40% to 60% to the magazine.

Globe Pequot Press provides ad slicks to special interest magazines for them to use when they have unsold ad space. These full-page ads and two-page spreads offer Globe's books for sale through the magazine publisher on a per-order basis. Not only does Globe get free advertising, but they are also able to go to bookstores and tell them that full-page ads appear regularly in major magazines.

Buy remnant space. Ask the magazine to let you know when they have unsold space, which can be bought at a fraction of the usual cost. Of course, when you rely on remnant space, you have no way of controlling when and if your ads will appear. Hence, remnant ads are best used for products that are not time sensitive.

Use classified ads. Classified ads are an inexpensive way to compare the pulling power of different magazines, and they often outpull display ads costing 10 times as much.

The main disadvantage of classified ads is that it is tough to sell products costing more than $5 through the classifieds, for two basic reasons: (1) the space limitation of classifieds may not allow a complete description of your product, and (2) classifieds do not attract as affluent an audience as normal display ads.

There are, however, apparent exceptions to the rule. Jay Levinson used classified ads for many years to sell his self-published book, *Secrets of Successful Free-Lancing*, for $10. His ad worked where others didn't because he avoided the two main limitations of classified ads (1) by writing a long ad that described the benefits of his book in a clear and appealing way and (2) by placing his ads in upscale periodicals such as the *Wall Street Journal* and several professional artists' and writers' magazines.

Use Selectronic printing to target readers. Some magazines (including *American Baby, Farm Journal*, and *Medicine*) are now offering Selectronic printing and binding that allows an advertiser to target individual readers with personalized ads or messages. This personalization costs more money, so test its pulling power before committing a major budget to it.

Use their support services. Some trade journals provide advertisers with a variety of other marketing programs. Be sure to ask. Here, for example, are a few of the support services provided by *Target Marketing*:

- **List rental.** You may mail to their entire list of 42,000 direct marketers (free one-time use of their list).
- **Market research.** They will prepare a survey of 1,000 of their readers for your company. They print, mail, and tabulate the survey at no charge.
- **Research studies.** All half-page or larger ads in certain issues are analyzed and studied for their effectiveness and recall by an independent research company.
- **Purchasing reports.** They send confidential reports on their readers' projected buying plans.
- **Reader service.** They forward leads to you when readers request

more information about your ad by using the reader service cards in each issue.

- **Ad display mounts.** They will mount up to five of your ads for greater visibility at trade shows and exhibits.
- **Bonus distribution.** Besides its regular subscriber mailings, *Target Marketing* is also distributed free at nearly 40 trade shows each year, giving you additional exposure to new buyers.
- **Special catalog ad rates.** If you'd like to insert a four-page or eight-page catalog, you can do so for half of the regular cost.
- **Editorial support.** When space is available, *Target Marketing's* editors make every effort to support your advertising with free publicity.

Other services that magazines might provide (either at cost or for free) include the following: reprints of articles, product sampling to prospective buyers, convention promotions, ad design and layout, typesetting, and free directory listings.

HOW TO DESIGN AN AD THAT SELLS

Many of the tips given in the chapter on direct marketing also apply to any print advertising, but here are a few additional suggestions for improving the response to your ads:

The most important element of most newspaper and magazine ads is the headline. The headline must offer a strong benefit—one strong enough or dramatic enough to get the attention of readers.

Consider using a second color. A number of tests conducted over a period of 20 years in the *Long Beach Press-Telegram* showed that two-color ads (one color plus black) outsold noncolor ads by 64%.

Use illustrations or other graphic elements. According to some studies conducted by McGraw-Hill, illustrations increase readership of ads and increased readership usually results in increased sales.

Testimonials in the ad copy usually increase response. They are more believable than straight ad copy.

Create a sense of urgency by putting a time limit on the offer.

With smaller ads, the border becomes more important. It should clearly set the ad off from surrounding editorial matter or other ads and yet not distract readers' attention from the ad's message.

Advertisements that look like editorial copy have often proved to be effective in producing sales.

Put a coupon in the ad. Make it easy for the reader to order your product. In general, ads with coupons pull better readership than ads without coupons. If you use coupons, place them on the lower outside corner, where readers can cut out the coupon without having to ruin the entire page.

Make sure your address and telephone number are printed several times in the ad—once outside the coupon and once in the coupon itself. If someone has already clipped the order coupon, other readers can still find out where to send their order. For that same reason, your basic offer (the name of the product, the cost, and any special conditions) should also be repeated outside the coupon.

For newspapers, advertise on Sundays. Since Sunday newspapers usually have a higher circulation and a longer life, it's generally better to advertise in the Sunday editions as opposed to any daily editions. The new larger Saturday editions put out by some major newspapers might also be effective.

If you are using classified ads, make every word count. Don't be penny wise and pound foolish. If you need more words to describe your product adequately, use more words. At the same time, don't waste words. You need to strike a balance between minimum word count (and, hence, minimum cost) and an adequate description of your product (and, hence, maximum sales results).

Start small. Use smaller display ads before you place larger display ads. Indeed, many companies have found that a series of smaller display ads often outpulls one large ad. Not only do smaller ads cost less, but a series of smaller ads can create multiple impressions that one larger ad cannot.

Maintain a swipe file. Whenever you see an ad with a good headline, an attractive layout, well-written copy, or something else that attracts your attention, save that ad. Then when you write your own ads, borrow the best ideas from the ads in your "swipe file." Pay special attention to the ads for competitive or related products.

THIRTY-ONE WAYS TO GET MORE INQUIRIES FROM YOUR ADS

Here are 31 more ways to increase response to your ads, especially if you are seeking inquiries or catalog requests. These 31 ways are taken from a *Bank Marketing* article written by Bob Bly, a freelance copywriter specializing in business-to-business and direct response advertising (for more information, see his listing under Copywriters in Appendix III). The following is reprinted by his permission.

1. **Ask for action.** Tell the reader to telephone, write, contact the sales rep, request technical literature, or place an order.
2. **Offer free information, such as a color brochure or catalog.**
3. **Describe your brochure or catalog.** Tell about its special features, such as a selection chart, planning guide, installation tips, or other useful information it contains.

4. **Show a picture of your brochure or catalog.**
5. **Give your literature a title that implies value.** "Product Guide" is better than "catalog." "Planning Kit" is better than "sales brochure."
6. **Include your address in the last paragraph of copy and beneath your logo, in type that is easy to read.** Also place it inside the coupon, if you use one.
7. **Include a toll-free number in your ad.**
8. **Print the toll-free number in extra-large boldface type.**
9. **Put a small sketch of a telephone next to the telephone number.** Also use the phrase, "Call toll-free."
10. **Create a hotline.** For example, a filter manufacturer might have a toll-free hotline with the numbers 1-800-FILTERS. Customers can call the hotline to place an order or to get more information on the manufacturer's product.
11. **For a full-page ad, use a coupon.** It will increase response 25% to 100%.
12. **Make the coupon large enough** so that readers have plenty of room to write in their name and address.
13. **Give the coupon a headline that affirms positive action**—"Yes, I'd like to cut my energy costs by 50% or more."
14. **Give the reader multiple response options**—"I'd like to see a demonstration," "Have a salesperson call," or "Send me a free planning kit by return mail."
15. **Put a heavy dashed border around fractional ads of one-half page or less.** This border creates the appearance of a coupon, which, in turn, stimulates response.
16. **"Clip this ad."** In the closing copy for fractional ads, say, "To receive more information, clip this ad and mail it to us with your business card [or name and address]."
17. **Use a bound-in business reply card.** Such a card, appearing opposite your ad, can increase response by a factor of two or more.
18. **Use a direct headline that promises a benefit or stresses the offer of free information rather than a headline that is cute or clever.**
19. **Put your offer in the headline.** To get more inquiries, offer a free booklet, selection guide, or other item in the headline of your ad.
20. **Offer a free gift, such as a slide rule, metric conversion table, or pocket ruler.**
21. **Offer a free product sample.**
22. **Offer a free consultation, analysis, recommendation, study, cost estimate, computer printout, or something similar.**
23. **Talk about the value and benefits of your free offer.** The more you stress the offer, the better your response will be.
24. **Highlight the free offer in a copy subhead.** The last subhead of your ad could read, "Get the facts—free."
25. **Run your offer in a sidebar if you are using a two-page ad.**
26. **Be sure the magazine includes a reader service number in your ad.**
27. **Use copy and graphics that specifically point the reader toward using the reader service number.** For example, an arrow can point to

the number, with copy that says, "For more information, circle the reader service number below."

28. **Consider using more than one reader service number.** For example, use one number for people who want literature and another for people who want an immediate response from a salesperson.
29. **Have a separate reader service number for each product or piece of literature featured in a full-page ad for multiple products.**
30. **Test different ads.** Keep track of how many inquiries each ad pulls. Then run only those ads that pull best.
31. **Look for a sales appeal, key benefit, or theme that might be common to all of your best-pulling ads.** Highlight that theme in subsequent ads.

HOW TO ADVERTISE ON RADIO

Radio is not used often by direct response advertisers for at least two reasons: (1) it is difficult to target the audience, and (2) the times when people are truly listening to the radio (morning and afternoon drive time) are not times when they can effectively respond.

True, if your product has a specific life-style target audience, you might find it effective to advertise on the radio stations or shows that target that audience. For instance, you might advertise a rock biography during a syndicated top-40 show or on local rock stations or sell subscriptions to a new charismatic magazine on a religious station.

Rex Publishing of Clearwater, Florida, has sold more than 140,000 copies of their $99.95 book, *Action Guide to Government Auctions*, via hundreds of spots on cable television and radio. Most of the sales come from spots during talk shows on AM radio stations. They have found that such shows target their best customers: people with middle incomes who have at least one credit card.

If you decide to advertise your products and offers on radio, here are a few guidelines to follow. As with all other media, be sure to test your ads before rolling out with a major campaign.

Match your product with the format and, hence, audience profile of any radio stations you intend to use for advertising. All of the following formats target different demographics and psychographics: country music, all news, easy listening, sports, urban contemporary, new age contemporary, album-oriented rock, golden oldies, classical, big band, and CHR (contemporary-hit radio).

For the lowest cost and widest reach, advertise on a syndicated radio show. A 30-second spot, for instance, on *"Live from Gilley's,"* costs only $250. This show, which airs on 256 stations, has an estimated audience of 335,000 listeners.

Advertise on a network. Note that some of the major radio networks offer several possible divisions that enable you to target your audience more specifically. For instance, ABC radio at one time offered the following networks:

ABC Contemporary—262 affiliates (CHR and AC [adult contemporary] formats)
ABC Direction—362 affiliates (AC and country formats)
ABC Entertainment—555 affiliates (country and AC formats)
ABC FM—133 affiliates (CHR and urban contemporary)
ABC Information—622 affiliates (news, sports, and talk)
ABC Rock—80 affiliates (AOR [album-oriented rock], rock, CHR)
ABC Talk—116 affiliates (talk and call-in formats)

Buy time through a media rep network. By working with such reps (see Appendix III for the names of some major ones), you can buy spot time on local radio stations across the country without having to contact each station individually.

Try per-inquiry ads. Per-inquiry (PI) ads are still available in some radio markets, but they are not easy to find. If you'd like to try offering products direct to consumers via per-inquiry radio advertising, work with a media rep group. For instance, about 90% of Katz's direct response advertising placements are done on a PI basis.

Radio and television rate cards are negotiable. Remember, if they don't sell the time, it is gone forever. Generally if they have open time, they will be willing to negotiate a lower rate than the one stated on their rate cards.

The best times for running most ads on radio are during its prime-time hours—the morning and afternoon drive times. Afternoon drive time has one plus over the morning drive time: as a rule, people are more relaxed and happier as they head home for the evening. Hence, they may be in a better mood for buying. For direct marketers, however, the far less expensive late evening and overnight day parts can often be more effective selling times.

Radio requires frequent repetition for maximum effect. Hence, you're better off concentrating ads during a short period of time rather than stretching them out over a longer period.

As repetition of the commercial makes radio spots more effective, so does repetition within the commercial. Repeat your main message at least three times in different ways. Repeat the name of your product and your company name at least twice.

Thirty-second spots can sometimes work as well as 60-second spots and are less expensive. Indeed, some studies indicate that people listen more attentively when an announcer speaks more quickly. Thus, you may find it more effective, as well as cheaper, to squeeze your message into 30-second spots.

Use an 800 number that's memorable, such as 1-800-FLOWERS. That way, even if the listener doesn't have time or opportunity to write the ordering information down, he or she might at least remember your telephone number. There's a good chance, then, that a listener would call for more information or to place an order.

Take time to make your lead-in effective. With radio, you have about 3 seconds to attract the attention of listeners.

If you are asking for a direct order, repeat the ordering information at least twice. Don't try for a direct order unless you use a 60-second or 2-minute spot. You would not have time to repeat your basic message and the essential ordering information in less than 60 seconds.

Listen to the tape of your commercial on your car audio system. The closer you can get to simulating how it will actually sound on ordinary car radio speakers, the more accurately you will be able to judge its effectiveness.

Use professional announcers and studio equipment to make commercials. Don't skimp on production.

Since radio is an audio medium, consider using appropriate music to heighten the impact of your commercial. Or use other audio effects to enliven the presentation.

Don't get stuck. You can make changes to the content of any radio commercial far more easily, more quickly, and less expensively than with almost any other medium. Make use of that flexibility to fine tune your commercials so they are truly effective in selling your product.

HOW TO ADVERTISE ON TELEVISION

Television has a great advantage over radio: not only can it be heard, it can be seen. Studies have shown that people's memories improve as much as 68% when they have a visual element to help them remember something. Hence, if your product lends itself to a visual presentation, you might find that television commercials will produce greater sales than radio commercials or print advertisements.

On the down side, television costs more. To make it worth your while, then, your television commercials must be effective. Here are a number of ways to increase the effectiveness of television promotions.

Offer a toll-free number. Hal Lindsey's book *Countdown to Armageddon* was advertised via 2-minute commercials asking viewers to order through a toll-free telephone number. Within 90 days, over 370,000 copies of the book were sold via television ads.

Use long-form ads outside of prime time. More and more companies are using such ads on independent stations, local network affiliates, and many cable networks. Such shows dominate the late evening and overnights on many cable systems. The Beckley Group marketed its

"Millionaire Maker Course" through one-hour shows in major and minor markets all over the country. They purchased the entire hour and presented an informative seminar on how to get rich in real estate. Interspersed throughout the hour were commercials that presented the hard sell for the course. The advantage of this format is that the hour-long shows, which were packed with information of interest to the potential buyers of the course, presented the soft sell while the commercials closed the sale. Their courses sold for $295, and orders were taken via credit card, COD, or check either by telephone or through the mail. Using this method, they sold as many as 20,000 courses in one week.

That sounds like lots of sales, and it is, but note that this is a high-risk way to sell anything. The Beckley Group had COD refusal rates as high as 30%. And when they offered a later course on credit cards, they were hit with a blizzard of returns. They ended up bankrupt.

Negotiate rates. The secret to success in long-form advertising is to get the best times at the lowest rates. If you have never negotiated television time before, sign up with a broker who specializes in buying such time. If you don't know of any, ask a local cable system to put you in touch with a reputable buyer.

Don't overlook local cable TV stations when planning your television promotions. Local cable TV is still quite inexpensive as compared to local network TV. If your product can be linked in any way with a popular cable feature, you have a good chance of making the commercial pay for itself.

Advertise on a satellite channel.

Try per-inquiry ads. While WTBS and some other major cable networks rarely accept per-inquiry or per-order ads anymore, local cable companies still accept them. When WTBS was accepting per-inquiry ads, they required an advance payment of $50,000 to be placed in an escrow account (to ensure payment of all monies due them and to ensure fulfillment of all direct sales to viewers).

Give away your product on game shows such as "The Price Is Right" **or** "Wheel of Fortune." Even if your product isn't all that expensive, it might still be appropriate as an addition to a larger prize. For instance, a game show might give away a year's supply of macaroni and cheese dinners with a new stove. Here are two companies that, for a fee, will help you get your products featured on television shows:

Game Show Placements, 7011 Willoughby Avenue, Hollywood, CA 90038; (213) 874-7818; fax: (213) 874-0643.
Video Enterprises, 11340 Olympic Boulevard #365, Los Angeles, CA 90064; (310) 312-1500; fax: (310) 312-1568.

Use videotapes as your direct marketing package. The advantages of video direct mail are twofold. First, it is perceived as something of value, so it is not likely to be tossed out until the recipient has viewed the beginning of the tape. Second, because recipients are involved with sight, sound, and action when viewing the tape, they are more likely to get involved with your message (as compared to print promotions).

Remember that television is a mass medium. If you are planning major television exposure for direct sales via your own toll-free number, make sure you have enough operators to handle the response. According to one television advertiser, you will need at least five lines to handle most local campaigns and even more to handle a larger regional or national campaign. If you are not prepared to hire and train operators and lease adequate telephone lines to handle any response, hire a professional telemarketing agency to organize and staff your telephone orders.

Many of the rules of print and radio advertising also apply to television ads. Be sure you have a good offer, well-written copy, and an easy way for people to respond.

TIPS ON PRODUCING TELEVISION SPOTS

While major television commercials currently cost as much as $70,000 per 30 seconds to produce, it is possible to create an effective television commercial for much less. While you balance budgetary constraints against your need for a quality production, don't try to do it all yourself. Use your in-house staff where your expertise is strong (for example, in the area of copywriting), but hire professionals where your expertise is weak (for example, in video production). As a guideline, remember that your audience is accustomed to high-quality production values and will notice any commercials that are not carefully produced and edited.

To help you in designing and producing your own television commercials, here are a few guidelines:

• The key to television success, according to a number of regular advertisers, is your media buying skills. If you do not have knowledgeable media buyers, don't try to do the buying yourself. Use a professional agency. Radio and television rate cards are essentially works of fiction; they are highly negotiable. Hence, make sure your buyers are highly skilled negotiators; the money you save could make the difference between profit and loss. The Beckley Group had as many as 20 buyers negotiating for media time whenever they rolled out one of their national television campaigns.

• If you are working with a local station, let them provide all the technical production assistance (equipment, camera operators, lighting technicians, directors). Often they provide such assistance for a minimum cost as long as you are buying time on their station. In most cases, however, don't let them write your commercial unless you want it to sound exactly like every other commercial on the station.

• Although many ad agencies use storyboards to lay out the story line of a commercial, you may not need one, especially if your commercial is well written, with all the action clearly described in the script. Storyboards can add from $200 to $500 to the cost of a commercial.

• Perhaps the best way to save money is to do most of your work at the preproduction stage rather than during the actual taping when costs can skyrocket if you have to stop to work out a problem. Hold preproduction meetings to make sure everyone understands the script and knows what to do. Check the scripting details, the lighting, and the timing. Hold a dress rehearsal. Never go before a camera crew until you are sure that the production will go smoothly.

• Tape more than one commercial at a time. Since in most cases you will have to pay for a minimum amount of production time regardless of how much time you actually use (as well as travel and setup time), make the best use of the time by taping two or more commercials or variations at the same time.

• When you plan the taping of your commercial, try to arrange the segments so that editing costs are kept to a minimum. Editing can cost anywhere from $250 per hour on up.

• Remember that television is a visual medium, so be sure to create a strong visual message in your commercial. If the commercial can make its point even with the sound turned off, you have a winner. Use music, sound effects, and words to enhance the visual impact, not to replace it.

• If possible, show your product in use. If it is a cookbook, show someone using it to create a scrumptious meal. If it's a mystery, tease the viewers with a look at the unsolved crime.

• As with radio, commercials on television must gain the attention of the viewer within the first few seconds. Make sure your commercials have a captivating lead-in.

• Don't be afraid to repeat.

MARKETING VIA TELEPHONE

Within the next couple of years, almost all companies will be offering toll-free telephone service for orders and customer service. The cost is now so low and the potential results so great that few companies can afford not to offer the service.

While the installation of a toll-free number can have a great impact on sales, you should not limit telemarketing to passive order taking. As long as you have the customer on the telephone, take the opportunity to make additional sales or to ask questions of the buyers (to discover how they found out about your product and why they decided to order it). If you prepare a standard script for order takers, they can easily increase sales without any additional cost to you.

After you have organized an effective system for handling incoming orders, consider establishing an outgoing telemarketing effort as well. While some consumers resent the invasion of telephone sales calls into their homes (and rightly so), outbound telemarketing can still be an effective sales tool. Here are a few ways to use outbound telemarketing to your advantage:

Test a list fast. You can test a list of a thousand names within a few days by using the telephone. If the results are good, you have reason to expect a follow-up mailing to a larger portion of the same list to produce good results. Such a test is clearly not as reliable as a test mailing, but it can provide quick feedback on which of two or more possible lists is likely to produce the best results. According to one telemarketing expert, calls to 100 people will give a response equivalent to a direct mailing to 1,000 people.

Test an offer fast. You can use telephone calls to test two alternative offers (for example, to test which of two premium offers will produce more sales).

Follow up inquiries and leads. Try responding to an inquiry with a telephone call rather than a letter. It could easily increase response.

Research your market. For example, you might make telephone calls to a sampling of doctors to see if they'd be interested in a book on gallbladder operations. Or, perhaps better, you could use the same calls to ask open-ended questions that encourage the doctors to tell you what kind of information or services they do need. Then you can produce products designed to fill that need.

Increase sales. Telemarketing can increase the response to an offer by as much as five times. For example, if a list would normally yield a 5% response to direct mail, telemarketing might increase the response to 20% or 25%. Such increases may be attributed to the more personal nature of telephone calls, to the greater opportunity for give and take in a telephone conversation, and/or to the greater immediacy of telephone calls.

Upsell. When customers call to order one item, take that opportunity to sell them additional items or a higher-priced product in the same line.

Sell new products to your in-house list. Your in-house list is your best prospect for any new products, especially ones related to the products previously bought by your customers. With a proper computer order entry and tracking system, you should be able to sort out those previous customers who are most likely to buy new products.

Cut sales costs. Telemarketing can be an inexpensive substitute for direct sales visits. Indeed, for retailers located out in the boondocks, telephone calls may be the only practical way to keep in touch with them. For smaller companies unable to set up sales representatives (for whatever reason), telemarketing offers a viable alternative, especially if it is used to supplement direct mail offers.

Create publicity. Outbound telephone calls are an essential element in any aggressive publicity campaign. They are often the only practical way to follow up previous contacts. Also, since they allow a certain give and take, negotiations for interviews and appearances are much easier to conduct over the telephone rather than through the mail.

Build goodwill. A toll-free telephone number demonstrates that you are responsive to the needs of customers and open to their feedback. Answer your telephone. Be open to calls from customers.

Answer questions. You can answer questions over the telephone that you could never answer in a print ad or catalog.

Provide customer service. You can provide better customer service via the telephone than you can by mail.

TIPS FOR MORE EFFECTIVE TELEMARKETING

Telemarketing sales now exceed $200 billion a year. Because telemarketing costs run high (anywhere from $1,200 to $2,000 per thousand names), response rates must also be high. While response rates for consumer telemarketing can range up to 15% to 25%, you cannot expect such high rates unless your telemarketing campaign is carefully designed.

Telemarketing must be highly organized to be effective. You cannot play it by ear. Plan every step of the process if you hope to make efficient use of what is one of the most expensive and effective media for making sales. Here are a few tips to help you organize outbound telephone campaigns:

Use highly targeted lists. Don't waste your telephone time on general lists or random canvassing of telephone books. Your own in-house list of buyers and inquirers or outside lists of buyers are your best prospects. Of all factors in any telephone marketing campaign, the list is the most important. Again, the offer and the audience must match.

Make a clear, specific offer—one that can be easily stated in a few sentences. Make it easy for the listener to say yes or no.

Have a definite script that your callers must follow. Be sure to spend time training callers to handle any customer questions or other responses. Anticipate most questions in the script and have clear answers prepared for the most prevalent ones.

Hire only callers who can handle rejection, who can terminate a call politely, and who can proceed right away with the next call. The best callers are those who can be casual in their tone and presentation while sticking to the script.

Accept purchase orders, COD, or credit card sales. Don't expect people to send checks in response to telephone sales calls.

Prepare a simple but complete order form that allows the caller to record the order easily while continuing to talk with the customer.

Record responses. With outside lists, you might want your operators to check off a simple form recording the number of responses for each general category (orders, requests for more information, simple rejection, vehement rejection, hang-ups, no answers).

Outbound sales calls can be more effective as follow-ups to previous mailings than as cold calls. Such a one-two punch can be more effective than telephone calls or mailings made independent of each other. Enterprise Publishing uses outbound telemarketing to solicit feedback from previous customers. These outbound calls often result in sales; about 10% of their sales come via outbound telemarketing.

Don't telemarket to any customer you have called within the previous three months. For its encyclopedias, book clubs, and continuity programs, Grolier has a policy of not telemarketing anyone who has been called within the past three months. They also make an effort never to call anyone twice about the same product.

Make it as easy as possible for potential customers to reach you. While continuing your outbound telemarketing, also work to make it easy for people to call you. Advertise your inbound numbers—both regular and toll-free numbers.

Offer a special service. To increase incoming telephone traffic, offer a special service for customers who are not ready to order anything. Then when they call, offer them a limited-time special or some tie-in merchandise. Banana Republic offered catalog customers a climate desk telephone service. Customers could call this toll-free number to find out the weather for their travel destinations. Information included high and low temperatures for various seasons, average rainfall, political situations that might affect travel in that area, medical requirements, health precautions, State Department regulations, and clothing needs. Where appropriate, Banana Republic also suggested clothing or travel books that might be useful. Of course, any clothing or travel books that they recommended, they also sold. Customers could order right away.

Use call processing. If you receive lots of incoming calls, consider using the call processing technology that functions like an automated receptionist. These machines automatically answer every call and, when the caller presses the appropriate touch-tone number, transfer the call to the right person or to another message. Here are just a few of the benefits this technology can offer you:

- Answers all calls without intervention, thus saving on the number of people you need to hire to answer telephones. All calls are answered by human voices (taped by you).

- Automatically routes calls to the right department.
- Can take orders right over the telephone, with the callers leaving all required information by voice message or by punching the appropriate touch-tone numbers on their telephone pads.
- Allows callers to leave messages for various people (so those people can always get their messages by just checking their telephone mailbox).

You can program various sales messages that callers can access by pressing the right touch-tone number. Hence, you can have separate sales messages for each product you make. And you don't have to provide a separate line for your fax or modem. Callers can access those machines by sending the correct touch-tone numbers to reach the appropriate extensions.

HOW TO MAKE THE BEST USE OF CARD PACKS

Card packs, those ubiquitous collections of loose postcards advertising from 30 to 150 offers, are one of the fastest-growing areas of direct marketing. You can choose from over 650 card packs—at least one for almost any audience you want to target (from engineers to doctors, from sales managers to craft store owners).

Before you decide to use card packs, be aware of the disadvantages as well as the advantages of advertising in them.

Disadvantages of Card Packs

- Since they are cooperative advertising vehicles, it is quite possible to have several of your competitors also advertising in the same pack. Actually, this could be an advantage or a disadvantage depending on how your product measures up to the others in price, offer, and benefits.
- Because of the small size of the cards, it is often difficult to sell products that require detailed explanation or extensive copy.
- Because of the size limitation, it is sometimes not possible to offer multiple order or payment options.
- You can't offer a business reply envelope, though you can offer a business reply card.
- Returns and bad debts tend to be higher among card pack buyers as compared to magazine advertising or regular direct mail.
- Since many packs are mailed only two or three times a year, they may not allow the best timing for your promotions.
- Since card pack advertising may be more widely distributed than your own direct mail package, such advertising can tip off your competitors to your new offers.
- Response rates are low; anywhere from .1% to 1% is common.

Advantages of Card Packs

- Card packs offer one of the lowest costs for direct mail advertising ($17 to $20 per thousand as compared to $400 to $600 per thousand for your own packages).
- They are easy to use.
- Per-inquiry or per-order insertions are quite easy to arrange in many of the packs, especially with the recent oversaturation of the market.
- Card packs are superb lead generators.
- Card packs offer fast response. You can expect to receive half the response from your ad within 12 days of receiving the first response.

Before using packs, consider the following questions:

- **What is the source of the list?** Make sure it's a reputable source.
- **Is the list made up of buyers?** Mail responsive lists are better than compiled lists.
- **How often is the list cleaned?** The more often it is cleaned, the better the list is.
- **How much did the buyer spend on the product?** The price must be at least as high as the price of your product offer.
- **How often is the pack mailed?** The better packs are mailed four to six times a year, thus allowing you more opportunities to follow up on the success of a card placement.
- **Is it mailed to the same people each time or to different lists?** Different lists are often better since they allow your offer to reach new prospects each mailing.
- **Does the pack offer an A/B split for testing?** A/B splits allow you to mail one offer to half the list and another offer or format to the other half. Such splits enable you to test which offers or formats produce the best results.

Tips on Using Card Packs

Companies that use card packs have discovered some basic rules on how to use them most effectively:

- Use packs that are sent to mail-responsive names rather than to compiled lists. However, avoid hotline names if they represent current respondents only rather than paid buyers.

- Position is important. Some studies have shown that cards in the first half of the pack produce twice the results of cards in the second half of the pack. Hence, if you have to pay a premium for position, it may well be worth the extra payment.

- Free trial offers work better than direct credit card sales. McGraw-Hill has consistently found that 10-day free trial offers work the best for their books. If you do use free trial offers, expect some debt collection problems and some returns (up to 13% or more of all orders). Factor these considerations into your calculations when figuring whether participation in the pack will pay off.

• Card packs are best for generating inquiries or leads that can be followed up with sales letters, telemarketing, or direct sales visits. As a result, offers for higher-priced products are more likely to pay off as compared to lower-priced products.

• State the price of your product in the ad. Card pack recipients tend to be more price conscious than magazine readers. You will get more qualified buyers and inquirers by stating the price up front.

• Ask for a business card rather than having buyers fill out an order blank. Buyers with business cards are more qualified buyers. Also you can learn more about a buyer from a business card than you can from any information in an order blank. Many card pack participants now print a light line saying, "Tape Business Card Here," over the coupon area.

• Use graphics or a photo of your product in the ad.

• Multiple colors work better than a single color. Many card pack publishers throw in a second color free to encourage you to test their pack.

• Lay out your offer in a horizontal format. Customers read the pack this way.

• Use headlines that compel casual browsers to read on: FREE CATALOG! or FREE SAMPLE! or 50% OFF! or SAVE $10.00!

• Cards are 1-second billboards. Most cards receive no more than a 1-second glance from recipients as they flip through the deck. That 1 second is all you have to gain the attention of the recipient and earn a second chance to make a sale. Design your card with this rule in mind.

• Many card packs accept per-inquiry or per-order advertising. In many packs, up to 30% of the cards are PI or PO ads. When requesting a PI or PO deal, make it clear to the pack publisher that if the results are good, you will be placing more ads.

• Buy remnant space. Some pack publishers sell on a space-available basis, which could save you up to 50% of the pack cost. If you choose this option, you run the risk that the pack will fill up and your ad won't run.

• Other packs offer a 15% agency discount to advertising agencies and card brokers. Many, however, also offer such a discount for direct placement. Main Deck, for example, allows such a discount on the first placement.

• Many card pack publishers typeset, design, and even write the copy for your card. Many offer this service free to first-time users (in the hope that you will become a regular participant in their pack).

• Business card packs, according to many direct mailers, have a huge pass-along readership. Consumer packs don't.

• Large packs work as well as smaller ones. Many direct marketers report no fall-off of orders with larger packs (when packs go from 40 to 60 cards).

Card Pack Directories

To locate the card decks that are be most appropriate for your products, refer to the following directories:

SRDS Card Decks Rates & Data Directory, SRDS, 3004 Glenview Road, Wilmette, IL 60091; (708) 256-6067; fax: (708) 441-2252. $95.00. Lists 650 card packs with rates, frequencies, circulation, and more.

Book Publishing Resource Guide, Ad-Lib Publications, 51-1/2 W. Adams, Fairfield, IA 52556; (515) 472-6617; fax: (515) 472-3186; (800) 669-0773. $25.00. Among other marketing opportunities, this directory lists over 350 card packs. Includes circulation figures, target audiences, and subject categories.

8

How to Track Responses
to Promotions

One of the great advantages of any kind of direct marketing is that you can track the results of your promotions. But this advantage won't benefit you one bit if you don't keep records of those results. If you have a computer, such records are easy to maintain as long as you have at least one field in the order entry database that indicates the source of the order.

Having the information in the computer is not enough. As a direct marketer, you need to output that information as printed reports so you can actually *see* the results. Each day print out a daily record of responses (Exhibit 8-1), and, at least once a week, print an advertisement response record (Exhibit 8-2). By reviewing these printed records, you will be able to verify which of your promotions are paying off.

KEEPING TRACK OF RESPONSES

Keep a daily record of all responses to any promotions that are active. For each promotion, separate the responses by the source of the order (which you should be able to track from the key codes in your ads). If you are carrying out more than one promotion, use a separate daily record of responses for each active promotion. (See Exhibit 8-1.)

If you don't have a computer, record these responses as you sort the day's incoming mail. Once you have completed the daily record, you can transfer the information concerning each individual ad or mailing to its advertisement response record.

Daily Record of Responses

Product: 1001 Ways to Market Your Books   **Date:** September 10, 1991

Key	Number of Inquiries	Number of Orders	Cash Received
A1	25	36	$620.00
A2	51	31	542.50
BMU20	13	16	278.00
GMA9	104	34	593.00
HOT29	24	10	170.98
HOT30	47	32	539.95
HOT31	14	25	437.50
NW25	56	78	1,179.90
PMA8	96	32	557.78
PW831	127	58	1,012.50
S&M8	142	60	1,049.95
SP8	33	67	1,167.50
TT14	10	14	240.90
WD8	42	31	527.50
WH7	23	37	647.50
No Key	23	3	44.85
Total	830	564	$9,610.31
Refunds	- - -	15	224.25
Net	830	549	$9,386.06

Exhibit 8-1   Daily record of responses.

Advertisement Response Record

Publication	XYZ Magazine	Issue	July 1992	Key	XY7
Proposition	Widgets for Two	Page No.	235	On Sale Date	June 7, 1992
Version	Trampoline Version	Size	Full Page	Cost of Ad	$15,600.00
Circulation	1,800,000	Position	Right Page	CPM	$8.67

	DATE	INQUIRIES		ORDERS		CASH SALES	
		Number Received	Total To Date	Number Received	Total To Date	Today's Sales	Total Sales
1	June 15	4	4	6	6	$120.00	$120.00
2	June 16	6	10	10	16	200.00	320.00
3							
4	June 18	7	17	12	28	240.00	560.00
5	June 19	12	29	16	44	320.00	880.00
6	June 20	14	43	19	63	380.00	1,260.00
7	June 21	19	62	25	88	500.00	1,760.00
8	June 22	18	80	29	117	580.00	2,340.00
9	June 23	15	95	35	152	700.00	3,040.00
10							
11	June 25	17	112	39	191	780.00	3,820.00
12	June 26	16	128	53	244	1,060.00	4,880.00
13	June 27	21	149	54	298	1,080.00	5,960.00
14	June 28	25	174	39	337	780.00	6,740.00
15	June 29	23	197	57	394	1,140.00	7,880.00
16	June 30	29	226	47	441	940.00	8,820.00
17							
18	July 2	31	257	68	509	1,360.00	10,180.00
19	July 3	30	287	66	575	1,320.00	11,500.00
20							
21	July 5	29	316	67	642	1,340.00	12,840.00
22	July 6	25	341	46	688	920.00	13,760.00
23	July 7	23	364	52	740	1,020.00	14,780.00
24							
25	July 9	15	379	48	788	960.00	15,740.00
26	July 10	17	396	46	834	920.00	16,660.00
27	July 11	13	409	41	875	820.00	17,480.00
28	July 12	12	421	37	912	740.00	18,220.00
29	July 13	11	432	31	943	620.00	18,840.00
30	July 14	9	441	24	967	480.00	19,320.00

Exhibit 8-2   Advertisement response record.

The daily record of responses provides you with a quick glance at the day's returns from all advertisements; more important, it provides a record of all orders and cash receipts. This record forms the basis for all your financial records. File your printed daily records by date in a separate folder with your other financial records.

• **Product.**   Keep a separate daily record for each product you are actively promoting.

• **Date.**   Enter the date that these responses were received.

• **Key.**   Record the inquiries, orders, and total cash receipts for each ad or mailing. Separate results by key codes.

• **No Key.**   Most orders will be keyed to a specific ad or mailing list. Those that are not keyed may be recorded in the "No Key" line.

• **Number of Inquiries.**   Enter the number of inquiries from each ad.

• **Number of Orders.**   Enter the number of orders resulting from each ad. If your ad is designed to get orders, the number of orders for that ad should generally be more than the number of inquiries.

• **Cash Received.**   Indicate the dollar volume of the orders—whether in the form of cash, checks, credit cards, CODs, or billings. If you want to track the form of payment, you will need to have separate columns for each (and, if you are using a computer, you will need a separate field that records the form of payment). Why record the form of payment? Here are a couple of reasons. First, if you are using a computer to enter orders and have noted the form of payment, you can later track which forms of payment result in the most requests for refunds and which result in additional orders. If one form of payment stands out, you can adjust your promotions to eliminate that option (if it results in too many refund requests or bad debts) or feature that option (if it encourages the customer to order more often). Second, if your target audience clearly favors one form of payment over all the others, you might be able to eliminate some payment options. For instance, if you are selling to other businesses and 90% of them request to be billed, consider eliminating the credit card option from your order forms. Why? Because some businesses might hesitate ordering from you if you place too much emphasis on the credit card option as compared to the billing option that they would prefer to use.

• **Total.**   For each of the three columns, add up the total inquiries, orders, and cash receipts for that day.

•**Refunds.**   Any refund requests received that day are subtracted from the total cash receipts for that day.

• **Net.**   This is the total number of orders and cash receipts after any refunds have been subtracted.

A quick review of the daily record of responses should show which advertisements and mailings are producing the kind of results you want.

It will also give a clear picture of how much money is coming in each day. If money is tight, this daily record can help you keep better control over cash flow.

KEEPING TRACK OF YOUR ADS

Each day, after you complete the daily record of responses, transfer the results to the advertisement response record for each individual advertisement or mailing. The master copy of the advertisement response record (which can be found in Appendix II) allows room for 30 days of returns.

Write in the following information at the top of each ad response record, and then enter each day's returns as they come in.

- **Publication.** The name of publication, mailing list, broadcast station, or other medium.
- **Issue.**   For magazines, this is the issue date. For most other media, this box can be left blank.
- **Key.**   The key code for that particular advertisement or mailing.
- **Proposition.**   The product and offer being promoted through the ad or mailing.
- **Page No.**   The page number on which the ad appears (does not apply for mailings). For broadcast media, you might enter the time of day that the commercial was aired.
- **On-Sale Date.**   The date the publication went on sale, the date the mailing was sent out, or the date the commercial was broadcast.
- **Version.**   The version used in this publication if you are using several versions of an ad or mailing package.
- **Size.**   The size of the ad for magazines and newspapers or the length of the commercial for broadcast media.
- **Cost of Ad.**   The cost of the ad or commercial, less any frequency discounts. If a mailing package, enter the total cost of that particular mailing.
- **Circulation.**   The actual audited circulation of publication, not the claimed readership. For mailings, enter the size of the mailing list. For broadcast media, enter the average audience size.
- **Position.**   For publications, where the ad is located on the page; for broadcast media, the time of the commercial.
- **CPM.**   The cost per thousand. Divide the cost of the ad or mailing by the circulation; then multiply by 1,000.

Once the responses start coming in, note the date as well as the number of inquiries, orders, and cash sales for each day. Day 1 in this form should be the first day you receive any responses, not the day you send out the mailing or the on-sale date of the magazine.

- **Date.**   The date of the first and subsequent responses.

- **Inquiries.**   The number of inquiries received that day from that ad. Add up the total number of inquiries received to date (you need not total the receipts every day). You can use the running totals to estimate your expected returns by referring to the average rates of response chart shown as Figure 8-1.
- **Orders.**   The number of orders received that day and the total received to date.
- **Cash Sales.**   Cash receipts for that day and the total cash receipts to date from that particular ad or mailing.

Once the returns have dropped to a trickle, close the record for that publication and file the advertisement response record in your publications file for that particular medium. Before filing, however, add up the total number of inquiries, orders, and cash receipts. Then calculate your CPI (the cost of the ad divided by the total number of inquiries), CPO (the cost of the ad divided by the total number of orders), and net income (the total cash receipts minus the cost of the ad). These figures should be inserted into your ad comparisons form for that promotion (see Exhibit 8-3).

HOW TO ESTIMATE RESULTS QUICKLY

The average rates of response chart (Figure 8-1) displays the average rates of response for various advertising media. The rates can vary depending on the product, the offer, the time of year, and the media. You can, however, use this chart as a general guide for estimating results before all the replies have come in (the longer you wait to make your projection, the more reliable it will be). As you advertise more, you will be able to rely on your own advertising records to set up a more reliable response chart for your products.

To use the chart to estimate your potential response, note the average percentage of responses for the medium and time period in question. Then invert that percentage (for example, 7% inverted equals 100 divided by 7, or 14.276). Multiply the inverted percentage by the number of responses you have received thus far. For example, if you have received 51 replies to a display ad in a general monthly magazine by the end of four weeks (from the time you received the first response), you can expect to receive 102 total replies from the ad:

$$(100 \div 50) \times 51 = 102 \text{ total expected replies.}$$

Or if you have received 129 responses to a third-class bulk mailing to a consumer list after one week (again, from the time you received the first response), you can expect to receive as many as 391 total replies from the mailing:

$$(100 \div 33) \times 129 = 391 \text{ total expected replies.}$$

Average Rates of Response Chart

Media	1 wks.	2 wks.	4 wks.	8 wks.	1/2 yr.	1 year
Magazines — Monthly General	5%	20%	50%	75%	95%	100%
Magazines — Monthly Newsstand	4%	15%	35%	60%	90%	100%
Magazines — Weekly	30%	50%	65%	82%	96%	100%
Newspapers — Daily Run of Press	75%	90%	96%	100%		
Newspapers — Sunday Run of Press		+90%				
Newspapers — Sunday Preprints		+50%	+90%			
Newspapers — Comics	+50%	+90%				
Newspapers — Supplements	40%	65%	90%	95%	99%	100%
Direct Mail — First Class to Consumers	50% within 10 days					
Direct Mail — Bulk Rate to Consumers	33%	66%	84%	95%	99%	100%
Direct Mail — Bulk Rate High Ticket	1%	2%	30%	84%	99%	100%
Direct Mail — Bulk Rate to Businesses	50%	80%	90%			
Mail Order Catalogs	50% within 90 days					
Television Direct Response Ads	82%	96%	99%	100%		
Radio Direct Response Ads	80%	94%	99%	100%		

Note: The elapsed time in this chart refers to the number of weeks since the day the first response arrives. It does not refer to the first day the advertisement appeared or the day your direct mail was sent out.

The rates of response listed in this chart are average rates. Use this chart only as a general guide. Note that responses from magazines in newsstands are slower than from those sold by subscription, simply because all subscription copies are received by subscribers within a few days while newsstand sales occur over an entire month or more.

Publications which are intended to be saved (such as shelter magazines, do-it-yourself magazines, and gardening magazines) have a longer response curve than magazines which only cover current topics.

Figure 8-1   Average rates of response chart.

Product/Promotion: Widgets for Two   **Date:** November 10, 1991

Key	Publication / List	Cost of the Ad	# of Inquiries	CPI	# of Orders	CPO	I/O %	Order Income	Refunds	Gross Income	Net Income
A1	ABC Magazine, January	$4,900	25		221	$22.17		$11,050	$450	$10,600	$5,700
A2	ABC Magazine, February	4,900	14		213	23.00		10,650	350	10,300	5,400
BM20	Bxxx Magazine	3,400	13		135	25.19		6,750	200	6,550	3,150
GM9	Good Morning Magazine	7,800	10		345	22.61		17,250	750	16,500	8,700
HT20	Hot Tips Newsletter #20	400	20	20.00	17	23.53	85%	850	0	850	450
HT21	Hot Tips Newsletter #21	400	19	21.05	14	28.57	73.7%	700	50	650	250
HT22	Hot Tips Newsletter #22	400	16	25.00	12	33.33	75%	600	0	600	200
NW25	New Widgets Magazine	6,500	14		314	20.70		15,700	550	15,150	8,650
PM8	Pxxx Magazine	7,800	15		298	26.17		14,900	250	14,650	6,850
PM83	Pxxx Magazine, classified ad	134	45	2.98	9	14.89	20%	450	0	450	316
SW8	Special Widgets Magazine	2,900	127	22.83	**						
SP8	Such Priorities Magazine	8,500	25		322	26.40		16,100	500	15,600	7,100
TT14	Tried & True Magazine	6,300	34		245	25.71		12,250	200	12,050	5,750
WD8	Widgets Deluxe	3,600	63		212	16.98		10,600	50	10,550	6,950
WH7	Widgets Hotline	400	72	5.56	15	26.67		750	0	750	350
TOTALS		$58,334	512	$15.50	2,372	$23.37	52%	$118,600	$3,350	$115,250	$56,916

Exhibit 8-3   Ad comparisons form.

The response chart is not the only way you can project the final response to your ads or mailings. Indeed, direct mail professionals have used at least five ways to project responses. None of the following rules of thumb is foolproof, but they can be used to give you an idea of how your promotion is working.

1. **Fifty percent of the total response will come within four weeks of the drop date.** This method is probably the least reliable way to project response rates to mailings. In an actual test of these five rules of thumb described by Deborah Gallagher in the February 5, 1990, issue of *Magazine Week,* this rule of thumb projected a response rate way over the actual response of the test mailing (242,644 orders versus the actual number of 138,606).

2. **Sixty percent of the total response will come two weeks after the first response comes in.** This rule of thumb is similar to the method used by the average rates of return chart. The percentages are different because the time periods are different. In the test described in *Magazine Week,* this method would have predicted 184,898 total responses (60% of the orders coming in the first two weeks). At 50% in the first 10 days, this method would have predicted 191,858 responses.

3. **You will receive half as many orders each week as the previous week.** For example, if you received 10,000 orders the first week, you would receive 5,000 the second week, 2,500 the third week, 1,250 the fourth week, 625 the fifth week, and so on, until response dropped to zero. In the test, here are the actual responses received each week:

Week 1	78,444
Week 2	32,495
Week 3	10,383
Week 4	5,177
Week 5	4,166
Week 6	3,858
Week 7	3,572

This rule of thumb was fairly accurate from week 1 to week 2 and highly accurate from week 3 to week 4, but it doesn't adequately predict the response for the other weeks.

4. **You will have half of your total response on the day you receive the highest number of orders.** In other words, if you graph your responses each day, you will have received half your orders when the curve of the graph has peaked. This method assumes that the responses will follow a normal probability distribution curve. In the test noted, the greatest response (21,863 orders) was received six days after the first response. As of that day, 71,045 orders had been received. When multiplied by two, this gives a predicted total response of 142,090, or about 3,500 more than the actual results.

5.   **The response pattern for this mailing will be similar to the historical response pattern from previous mailings that are similar.** This method will generally provide the best prediction, but it is not one that is available to a new direct marketer or that will be very useful when you are promoting a new product. This historical method also has flaws. It presumes that you are using the same class postage, that seasonal patterns won't have any effect on the results, that the audience is similar, and so on.

In the test described in *Magazine Week*, this historical method produced the best results but only if you looked at the responses after 25 days had elapsed since the mailing had been sent out. The response during the first three weeks of the current mailing varied widely from the historical pattern.

The key lesson to learn in reviewing these five rules of thumb is that the rules are not absolutely reliable. They can provide a suggestion of what the final response will be but only that. If you must have some sort of prediction because you want to roll out to the entire list or you want to advertise again in a magazine, try using more than one of the rules of thumb. That way you will not be totally misled by the inadequacies of any one method.

HOW TO COMPARE THE EFFECTIVENESS OF ADS

At the end of a special promotion or at some point in the middle when you want to compare the effectiveness of various publications, use the ad comparisons form in Exhibit 8-3. It allows you to compare the results of all publications in a glance and select those that will probably be most effective for continuing ads or a new promotion.

The information for this form can be taken from the advertisement response records for each individual publication or list. To complete the form, fill in the following information:

• **Product/Promotion.**   It is best to compare only one promotion at a time if you want a fair comparison between publications. Comparing a full-page ad in one publication versus a quarter-page ad in another does not enable you to say what caused the difference. Was it the size or substance of the ad? Or was it the publication? How can you know if you try to compare apples with oranges?

• **Date.**   Enter the date on which you do the comparisons.

• **Key.**   List the keys used for the various publications and lists, including the keys used for ads in different issues of the same publication.

• **Publication/List.**   Enter the name and issue date (if applicable) of the publication in which the ad appeared or the name and drop date of the list you mailed to.

- **Cost of the Ad.** Enter the cost of the ad less any frequency discounts. If a mailing, enter the total cost of the mailing.

- **# of Inquiries.** Enter the total number of inquiries received as of the date this form is prepared.

- **CPI.** For each ad where you were prospecting for inquiries rather than orders, calculate the cost per inquiry. Divide the cost of the ad by the number of inquiries.

- **# of Orders.** For each publication or mailing, enter the total number of orders received as of the date this form is prepared. In the sample, I did not list the number of orders received from the ad in *Special Widgets* magazine because that ad was targeted at widget retailers.

- **CPO.** Calculate the cost per order by dividing the cost of the ad by the number of orders you received.

- **I/O %.** This inquiry to sales conversion percentage is obtained by dividing the number of orders by the number of inquiries. The result will be the I/O% in decimal form. Calculate this percentage for each ad where you are seeking inquiries that you later hope to convert to orders. This I/O percentage indicates whether your ads are producing serious or frivolous inquiries. The lower the percentage is, the more frivolous or the less serious the inquiries are. A low percentage could also indicate that the mailing package you send to inquirers needs improvement.

- **Order Income.** Enter the total cash receipts from each ad. You can take this number from your advertisement response record. It is your total cash sales from that ad.

- **Refunds.** Enter the total cash refunds sent to customers who ordered from that particular ad or mailing.

- **Gross Income.** To calculate the gross income, subtract the refunds from the order income.

- **Net Income.** To calculate your net income, subtract the cost of the ad from the gross income.

Total the ad costs, number of inquiries, CPI, number of orders, and so on for all the ads, and enter these on the bottom line of the ad comparisons form. These totals indicate how well the entire ad campaign or promotion is working.

Net income is not net profit. Net income indicates the money left over from sales receipts after the ad has been paid for. An advertisement can produce net income and yet be a losing proposition because net income still has to cover the product and fulfillment costs. Nevertheless, net income figures do aid in comparing the cost effectiveness of various advertisements.

Compared to the net income listed in the ad comparisons form, the cost per order (CPO) is a much better indicator of the net profitability of an ad. If the CPO is less than your contribution margin (see details on page 41), then your ad will show a profit. The ad with the lowest CPO will produce the most profit per order.

The ad with the lowest CPO will not, however, necessarily produce the greatest total net profit, since total net profit depends on both the profit per order *and* the number of orders. You will get your greatest total net profit from that advertisement that combines a relatively low cost per order with a large number of orders. For instance, in the sample in Exhibit 8-3, the two lowest CPOs were for the classified ad in *Pxxx Magazine* and the display ad in *Widgets Deluxe*. Although *Widgets Deluxe* has a higher CPO, it will produce a greater total net profit because it drew significantly more orders. If you work out the numbers, you will see that this is true.

If the product and fulfillment costs for these widgets were $17.50 per order, the *Pxxx* classified ad would produce a net profit of $158.50 (attained by multiplying the product and fulfillment costs times the number of orders and then subtracting the resulting number from the net income). On the other hand, the *Widgets Deluxe* ad would produce a net profit of $3,240.00 (again attained by multiplying $17.50 times 212, which equals $3,710.00, and then subtracting that number from the net income of $6,950.00).

If you wanted to know the total net profit produced by each ad in the ad comparisons form, you would have to add several columns to the form, including one for total product and fulfillment costs and one for the total net profit. The effectiveness of most ads, however, can be reasonably compared by simply looking at the "Net Income" column in the form.

9

Selling through Catalogs

When selling your products by catalogs, analyze the catalog by product and page to verify that all products are carrying their share of the costs. Get rid of any losers, or give them less space. Push winners even harder.

HOW TO ANALYZE YOUR CATALOG'S SALES

In reviewing your catalog sales, treat every page and every item as a separate paid advertisement, which should earn back its costs and make a profit. Every inch you use in your catalog costs you money and should be accounted for. For example, if your 32-page catalog costs $64,000 to prepare, print, and mail, then each page should be viewed as a $2,000 advertisement. Similarly, if an item's photo and description occupy half the page, that item should be assigned an advertising cost of $1,000.

You can analyze your catalog's individual sales by using a worksheet like the catalog sales analysis shown in Exhibit 9-1. You may use the master copy of this form (in Appendix II) to analyze your catalog's sales. Here's how to use the form:

- **Catalog.** Write in the name of the catalog and indicate if it is a special issue (spring catalog, fall catalog, special sale catalog).
- **Data of Analysis.** Enter the date that you analyze your catalog's sales.
- **Page Number.** Analyze each page in the catalog. The sample worksheet in Exhibit 9-1 analyzes pages 7 through 12. If you had a 32-page catalog, you would need to use six of these worksheets to complete the analysis.

Catalog Sales Analysis

Catalog: XYZ Spring Catalog to Customers   **Date of Analysis:**   6 / 10 / 92

Page Number	Item Number	Space Taken	Dollar Volume	Product Cost	Contribution Margin	Ad Cost	CM / AC Ratio	Item Profit / Loss
7	23	1/2 page	$5,428	$1,946	$3,482	$1,000	3.48	$2,482
	24	1/4 page	1,094	431	663	500	1.33	163
	25	1/4 page	776	353	423	500	.85	- 77
Totals for Page 7			$7,298	$2,730	$4,568	$2,000	2.28	$2,568
8	26	1/4 page	679	309	370	500	.74	- 130
	27	1/4 page	750	323	427	500	.85	- 73
	28	1/4 page	943	300	643	500	1.29	143
	29	1/4 page	621	268	353	500	.71	- 147
Totals for Page 8			$2,993	$1,200	$1,793	$2,000	.90	- 207
9	30	1/3 page	1,075	376	699	667	1.05	32
	31	1/3 page	1,923	831	1092	667	1.64	425
	32	1/6 page	845	279	566	333	1.70	233
	33	1/6 page	767	360	407	333	1.22	74
Totals for Page 9			$4,610	$1,846	$2,764	$2,000	1.38	$764
10	34	1/4 page	950	456	494	500	.97	- 6
	35	1/4 page	1,452	531	921	500	1.84	421
	36	3/8 page	846	234	612	750	.82	- 138
	37	1/8 page	326	97	229	250	.92	- 21
Totals for Page 10			$3,574	$1,318	$2,256	$2,000	1.13	$256
11	38	1 page	8,341	3,459	4,882	2,000	2.44	2,882
Totals for Page 11			$8,341	$3,459	$4,882	$2,000	2.44	$2,882
12	39	2/3 page	4,229	2,013	2,216	1,333	1.66	883
	40	1/3 page	3,635	1,549	2,086	667	3.13	1,419
Totals for Page 12			$7,864	$3,562	$4,302	$2,000	2.15	$2,302
Total Sales for Pages			$34,680	$14,115	$20,565	$12,000	1.71	$8,565

Exhibit 9-1   Catalog sales analysis.

- **Item Number.** Identify each item in your catalog by item number, product name, order number, or something else.
- **Space Taken.** Note how much space was allocated to each item (whether a full page, half-page, one-sixth page, etc.).
- **Dollar Volume.** Enter the amount of sales generated by each item.
- **Product Cost.** Enter the total variable costs for each item, taken from your break-even worksheet (see Exhibit 3-4).
- **Contribution Margin.** Subtract the product costs from the dollar volume to obtain the contribution margin.
- **Ad Cost.** Divide the cost of designing, printing, and mailing the catalog by the number of pages. In the sample, the ad costs were $2,000 ($64,000 divided by 32 pages). Each item on the page is assigned its portion of the ad costs for that page.
- **CM/AC Ratio.** Divide the contribution margin (CM) by the ad cost (AC) to get this ratio. If the ratio is above 1.00, the item or page is making a profit. If the ratio equals 1.00 exactly, the item or page is breaking even. If it is less than 1.00, the item or page is losing money.
- **Item Profit/Loss.** To find out if the page or item is making money, subtract the ad costs from the contribution margin.

After calculating these columns for each item on the page, do the same for the page. Once the pages have been analyzed, do the same for the catalog as a whole.

To see how this works, look closely at the sample worksheet in Exhibit 9-1. The catalog as a whole is probably producing a profit, but page 8 is a definite loser—something you could not know unless you did a detailed analysis like this. Of the 18 items on the six pages analyzed on this worksheet, 7 are losing money and 11 are making money.

Once you have an analysis for every item and every page, you can begin to make reasoned decisions about what items to drop and to keep. The basic principle of successful catalog sales management is to allocate more space to those items producing a profit and less space (or no space) to those losing money.

One way to calculate how much space to give each item is to allocate space so that the CM/AC ratio is the same (or nearly the same) for each item in the catalog. If, for example, the overall CM/AC ratio of your catalog is 1.71, then you could allocate space in your next catalog so that each item has approximately the same CM/AC ratio of 1.71. By doing this, it might be possible to turn a losing item into a winner.

Here's how this space allocation method might work in the catalog just analyzed. To reach the target CM/AC ratio of 1.71 for item 36, we would decrease the size of its space to one-sixth page. If the item still produced the same amount of sales as the current catalog, it would turn into a winner with a CM/AC ratio of 1.84 (the current contribution margin of $612 divided by the ad cost of $333). The 1.84 ratio is far closer to the catalog average of 1.71 than the current ratio of .82. If we can decrease the amount of space given to an item and still get the same amount of sales, we can turn any loser into a winner.

Conversely, you would assign more space to items that are big winners in your current catalog. That is, for items producing a CM/AC ratio greater than the catalog average, you would assign more space in the next catalog. For instance, we would give item 23 a full page in the next catalog. If the sales remained the same, the CM/AC ratio for that item would then be 1.74 (the current contribution margin of $3,482 divided by $2,000, the ad cost for a full page).

Of course, in the case of a big winner, we hope that the sales do not remain the same but actually increase significantly because of the added space given to the item. If we found that sales did not increase much at all, we would go back to giving that item only half a page in any future catalogs since that is where it produces the best CM/AC ratio.

In this example, some items from the current catalog would have to be dropped because we cannot assign any smaller space that would be effective in selling the item. For instance, item 37 is losing money, and that situation is not likely to improve if we were to decrease the space to one-sixteenth of a page. Items 26 and 29 are also marginal. All three items would likely be dropped.

By doing such an extended item-by-item analysis of sales, you can begin to weed out the poor producers and highlight products that are winners. In this way, not only does the catalog make more money for you, but there is also a good chance that you will be serving your customers better by providing the kind of products they truly want.

Here are a few other suggestions regarding the value of a catalog sales analysis and how to apply it to your catalog:

• The amount of space given to an item must be determined to some extent by the minimum amount of space necessary to illustrate and describe the item.

• Note the big winners. Are there similar products or accessories that could be added to the catalog to build on the existing winners (for example, a leather handbag to go with a fast-selling pair of shoes)?

• Remember that any change in the size of the ad will cost money in preparing new copy and other materials. Will the additional preparation costs be worth the possible increase in profit?

• Not all positions in a catalog are equally productive. The back cover, the pages opposite the order form, and the first few pages of a catalog usually produce larger sales than other pages. You might want to charge a higher advertising cost for these pages (just like many magazines do) so that items on these pages are compared fairly with items on other pages.

• The analysis assumes that the sales pattern in the current catalog will carry over into the next catalog. Yet consumer tastes and buying habits do change. If you have reason to believe that some trend will affect sales, either up or down, adjust your figures accordingly when planning future catalogs.

• Some items might lose money and yet be worth keeping in the catalog because they complement another item. For example, the Edmund Scientific catalog has carried books about metal detecting along with their metal detectors. The metal detectors have produced a nice profit, but the books have been losers. Yet Edmund continues to carry the books because they feel the books get people interested in the hobby of metal detecting and help to sell more metal detectors.

• Other marginal items might be kept because they allow you to offer a complete selection of kitchen utensils, or office supplies, or whatever it is that you sell. Some customers will buy from your catalog simply because you offer a complete line.

HOW TO SELL TO MAIL ORDER CATALOGS

Many companies that use direct marketing to sell their products also offer their products to other mail order companies. For instance, the books published by Open Horizons are also carried by *Adweek Books*, the *Whole Work* catalog, the *Sure-Fire Success Business* catalog, *Big Books from Small Presses*, and a good number of other relatively small catalogs. We sell our books through them because they often reach markets we don't, and they give our books added exposure. And, finally, they don't cut into our own sales in any significant way.

What is the best way to sell to other catalogs? First and foremost, prepare a merchandise data sheet that provides all the details any prospective buyer would want to know. Then read my special report *How to Sell to Mail Order Catalogs* (for details, see the Bibliography). This report details every step you need to follow to sell your products to other catalogs, and it includes listings of 550 catalogs (with names, addresses, telephone numbers, buyer names, fields of interest, and more).

I have included two formats for a merchandise data sheet—one that is rather simple and the other that is more complex but also more complete. The simple form (Figure 9-1) is one I used to sell one of my books, *Tinseltowns, U.S.A.*, to catalogs. This simple format provides all the basic information: the name of the item, a description, price, size, weight of one item, carton quantity, shipping details, discounts, and terms. Use this format when you want to get information out quickly.

Use a more complex format, like the one in Exhibit 9-2, when you want to present complete details about your product. To complete the merchandise data sheet, answer the following points:

• **Manufacturer's Name.** Enter the name of your company, if you are the manufacturer or owner of the rights to the item.

• **Contact Person.** Enter the name of the person in your company who handles special sales.

Open Horizons Publishing Company
P. O. Box 1102, Fairfield IA 52556-1102

(515) 472-6130 / Fax: (515) 472-3186

Catalog Merchandise Data Sheet

Item:	Tinseltowns, U.S.A.
Description:	Tinseltowns, U.S.A. is a trivia quiz book about towns and cities featured in movies and TV shows. Over 400 cities are mentioned, from Los Angeles, California, to New York, New York; from Ottumwa, Iowa, to Monroe, Louisiana; from Seattle, Washington, to Key West, Florida. The book features over 350 movies and 200 TV shows!
	144 pages, including 10 pages of photographs
Retail Price:	$6.95 (softcover) / $13.95 (hardcover)
Size of 1 Book:	5.5" x 8.5" x 0.4"
Weight of 1 Book:	0.4 pound
Carton Quantity	44 books per carton
Shipping:	F.O.B. Fairfield, Iowa Dropshipping of individual orders is available. Call for details.

Discounts:			
	1 carton	50%	[We offered percent
	2 to 9 cartons	55%	discounts because
	10 to 25 cartons	60%	of the two bindings
	25 or more cartons	65%	and prices.]

All sales are final. No returns.

Payment Terms:	Net 30 with approved credit; otherwise, payment with order.

Figure 9-1   Catalog merchandise data sheet: Simple format.

• **Address, etc.**   Enter the street address, city, state, zip code, and telephone number for your company. Enter your fax number if you have one.

• **Sales Agent.**   If you have hired an agent to handle your special sales, provide the company name, contact person, address, telephone number, and fax number for the sales agent. Otherwise, type in "Not Applicable".

• **Name of Product.**   Provide the name of your product.

Merchandise Data Sheet

Manufacturer's Name	Sales Agent (if any)
ABC Company	Not applicable

Contact Person	Contact Person
John Doe	

Address	Address
123 Fourth Street	

City	State	Zip	City	State	Zip
Anytown	MN	56573			

Phone Number	Phone Number
(218) 346-0000	

Fax Number	Fax Number
(218) 346-0001	

Name of Product	Discount Schedule
Widgets for two	$9.98 1 carton

Item Number

#W234

$8.98   2 - 10 cartons
$7.98   11 - 20 cartons
$6.98   20+ cartons

Description of Product

Widgets are simply the most wonderful and delightful thingamabobs available anywhere at anytime. They are yellow or blue or white or whatever. And they can spin tales and create magic in the hearts of little kids everywhere.

Size of Item	Weight of Item	# of Items Per Shipping Carton	Weight of Shipping Carton
3" x 11" x 4"	2 lb. 3 oz.	20 per carton	48 lb.

Suggested Retail Price	Terms	F.O.B. Point	Shipping Point
$19.95	2% 10/EOM Net 30	Anytown, MN	Anytown, MN

Time required to ship merchandise after receipt of order

3 weeks

Items are packed as follows

packed in own boxes and then shipped in cartons

The following are the major selling features of the product:

1. Widgets are wonderfully stupid.
2. Widgets offer more fun per minute than any videos priced at $20.00 or more.
3. Widgets come in many colors to match any decor.
4. Widgets love company.

[X] The item is prepriced.

[X] We can remove the price from the item.

[X] The item is available for immediate delivery.

[X] The item will be available for at least one year.

[X] We guarantee no changes in price for one year.

[X] The item itself is guaranteed.

[ ] We carry product liability insurance.

[ ] The item can be dropshipped.

[X] The item can be modified per buyer's request.

[X] Line art or photos are enclosed.

[X] Descriptive literature is enclosed.

[X] Samples of the product are enclosed.

John Doe	April 15, 1992
Signature	Date

Exhibit 9-2   Merchandise data sheet: Complex format.

- **Item Number.** If you have a specific item number, model number, or other identifying number for this product, note it here.

- **Description of Product.** Describe the product as completely as possible within the space given. Note any special features that make the product unique or causes it to stand out above the crowd.

- **Discount Schedule.** List your quantity discounts. Enter these either as a percentage (50% discount, 55% discount, etc.) or in terms of dollars.

- **Size of Item.** Indicate the size of the item. If more than one size is available, attach a separate sheet of paper outlining all the available sizes. The availability of different sizes, of course, is essential for clothing. The size of the item can be important to a mail order company because it affects how items are packed together for customers who order more than one item from the catalog. The size of the item might also have some impact on the warehousing of the product.

- **Weight of Item.** The weight of the item can affect the shipping costs and perhaps the handling costs as well.

- **# of Items per Shipping Carton.** If you have quoted your discount schedule in carton quantities, this number is essential. Otherwise, its main value is for inventory purposes once the items arrive at the cataloger's warehouse.

- **Weight of Shipping Carton.** If the carton is too heavy, it will limit the number of people who can handle it in the warehouse. Most catalogers prefer carton weights under 50 pounds since that is the upper comfort level for most people (especially if the cartons need to be handled often).

- **Suggested Retail Price.** Indicate the normal selling price for the product.

- **Terms.** Most mail order catalogs pay much better than most retail stores. If you offer catalogs a 2% discount for prompt payment, many will take it. Most pay within 30 days.

- **FOB Point.** This point determines who pays the shipping. If FOB destination, the manufacturer pays the freight. If FOB origin, the catalog pays the freight.

- **Shipping Point.** From what point will the product be shipped? Since this place could be different from the company address, this information is important to the cataloger.

- **Time required to ship merchandise after receipt of order.** For mail order catalogs, this timing is vital. Most catalog companies wait until they are about to mail their catalog before they place orders for the items in the catalog. They try to time it so the items arrive at their warehouse just in time to fulfill the orders generated by the catalog. That way, they can use the cash income from the sales to pay for the items.

- **Items are packed as follows.**   Describe how the items are packaged. This point can be important, especially for perishable or breakable items.

- **The following are the major selling features of the product.**   List the main selling features of the product. Think in terms of benefits to the catalog's customers.

Once you have entered the basic information that every catalog needs to know before placing an order, answer the questions in the checklist on the lower left. These points answer most of the questions a catalog might ask of you.

[ ] *The item is prepriced.*   Some catalogs prefer items that have no price on them. If the items are not priced, they have leverage to raise the price without causing their customers to think they've been gypped.

[ ] *We can remove the price from the item.*   If the item is prepriced, can you remove the price? Or if the quantities are great enough, can you provide a special edition just for the catalog?

[ ] *The item is available for immediate delivery.*   Is it available right now, or will it be available in time for the catalog to fulfill its orders?

[ ] *The item will be available for at least one year.*   Since the catalog companies will be investing a lot of space and money in promoting your product, they need to be assured that the product will be available long enough to allow them to fulfill all the orders received.

[ ] *We guarantee no changes in price for one year.*   Because the catalog is investing so much in promoting your product, they do not want to be surprised by a series of price increases that could easily affect their profit margin.

[ ] *The item itself is guaranteed.*   Do you stand by your product or provide some sort of guarantee? Will you service the item after the customer buys it?

[ ] *We carry product liability insurance.*   If your product could be considered dangerous or is susceptible to being used improperly, you should carry product liability insurance.

[ ] *The item can be drop-shipped.*   If your product is large or heavy, the catalog company might want you to drop-ship it. Drop-shipping also allows catalogs to test new items without committing themselves to a warehouse full of products they cannot sell.

[ ] *The item can be modified per buyer's request.*   Catalog companies like to have exclusives. If your product can be customized to the needs of the catalog, you'll have an easier sell.

[ ] *Line art or photos are enclosed.*   Enclose photos or line art of the product with the data sheet, or let the catalog know that such art does exist.

[ ] *Descriptive literature is enclosed.*   Enclose any brochures, fact sheets, and other literature that describes the product in greater detail.

[ ] *Samples of the product are enclosed.*   Without at least one sample, most catalog companies will not buy a product. If the item is clothing, enclose several sizes. If the item might be perceived as breakable,

hard to assemble, or difficult to use, enclose more than one sample so the catalog can feel free to put the item through its paces and test it thoroughly.

When you have completed the data sheet, sign and date it. A master copy of the sample merchandise data sheet is included in Appendix II. You may use the master copy to submit your products for review by other mail order companies.

BUYING PRODUCTS FOR YOUR CATALOG

If you operate your own mail order catalog, you can use the merchandise data sheet to winnow out products submitted for your review. Send a data sheet to every company that submits a product or idea for your catalog. Be sure to have your return address, telephone number, and fax number printed somewhere on the data sheet so the sheet can be easily returned to your company.

Catalog companies can also use this form as a checklist to verify that a submission has covered all the important points. A merchandise data sheet really systemizes the screening process for a company. If you've been buying products for your catalog without using a data sheet, seriously consider formulating one that works for your catalog and the products you carry.

10

Serving Your Customers

Perhaps the biggest mistake many direct marketers make is to fail to follow through. They design a great direct mail promotion, make an enticing offer, target the best list, and mail at the right time—but they fail to organize a fast and effective fulfillment system. That can be fatal.

Your customers are the key to any long-term success you might have in direct marketing. Serve your customers well, and they will come back to you again and again. Indeed, the major asset of any direct marketing firm is its customer list.

FAST, FRIENDLY SERVICE (WITH A SMILE)

To retain customers, always respond to any orders, inquiries, or complaints with fast, friendly service. Here are a few ways to keep customers happy (a detailed plan for processing inquiries and orders follows these basic points):

Process orders as fast as possible. My company has a policy of shipping all orders within 24 hours. We don't always make that deadline, but we do ship 90% of orders within one day. Because we offer such fast response time, we have customers who will order from us before they'd go to a neighborhood bookstore. We are fast, reliable, and friendly.

Respond to inquiries the same day you receive them. The faster you respond (whether by telephone, mail, or a sales representative), the greater your chances will be that the inquirer will order from you. If you make inquirers wait more than two weeks, you've lost the order.

Immediately acknowledge any back orders, out-of-stock products, or other products that cannot be shipped right away. Be as specific as possible about the date you will ship the order.

Answer complaints right away. In fact, don't just answer the complaints; resolve them. Remember, no matter how petty or ill conceived the complaint, the customer is always right. Don't take that statement as just another platitude; make it a working philosophy that all your personnel adhere to without question.

Send refunds as soon as they are requested. Stand by your guarantee, and your customers will stand by you.

Never fulfill an order without going for an additional sale. Include bounceback offers in every outgoing package. Don't feel shy about letting your customers know about other products or services that might interest them. Such notices should be an integral part of your service to them.

The value your company puts on customer service must permeate the entire company, from top management down to the mailroom. Only then will your company truly be able to create and maintain satisfied customers. Why should that matter to you? First and foremost, satisfied customers are repeat buyers. But they are even more than that: they are also your best advertisements. When you create satisfied customers, you are also creating walking/talking billboards for your products.

OFFER SATISFACTION GUARANTEED

To keep customers once you have them, offer a firm guarantee of satisfaction and then stand by it. Sears, the largest retailer in the world, built its business on its unconditional guarantee of satisfaction. Why should you offer less?

No company can survive for long if it does not stand by its products. I won't buy from a company that doesn't believe enough in its products to offer a strong guarantee. And I would certainly never buy again from a company that did not quickly follow through on its guarantee if I had to return the product.

Here are a few direct marketing companies that offer guarantees that truly show how much they value their customers (and also how strongly they feel about their products).

Enterprise Publishing offers the following four-point risk-free, postage-free, 100% money-back guarantee for its *Basic Book of Business Agreements:*

(1) The *Basic Book of Business Agreements* must save you at least $695 (10 times what you paid for it) within 6 months of purchase!

(2) You will recover the full cost of the book in saved legal fees the first one or two times you use it.

(3) Regardless of how much money it saves you, you must be completely satisfied. Look it over at our risk for 30 days. If you don't think it lives up to our claims, we'll refund your money.

(4) You may return the book using the postage-free return label on the reverse [of their guarantee].

Boardroom Books offers a $100,000 guarantee good for a whole year: "If the *Book of Inside Information* doesn't give you at least $100,000 worth of money-making/money-saving ideas, return it at any time up to a full year from the date you receive the book. We'll promptly refund the money you paid, no questions asked."

Guarantees can also be used to state your company's philosophy of doing business. Sierra Club offers the following guarantee on all items in its catalog: "*Lifetime Guarantee*—At Sierra Club, our work spans lifetimes. So in the spirit of the Club, we offer you a lifetime guarantee on any merchandise you purchase from our catalog. If you are not unconditionally satisfied with your selection, you may return it for a prompt refund, repair or replacement."

The following guarantee is printed on the inside front cover of *Marketing Without Advertising* by Michael Phillips and Salli Rasberry:

Nolo Press, the publisher of *Marketing Without Advertising*, is confident that you will find this unique small business book to be worth far more than your purchase price. If for any reason you do not agree, we will refund your full purchase price, no questions asked, no reasons requested. (We thought about asking for a copy of your financial statements before and after reading this book to make sure your business didn't in fact improve, but decided what the heck, if you trust us, we trust you.)

The reason we make this unusual offer is that we firmly believe *Marketing Without Advertising* authors Phillips and Rasberry when they write that for any small business to successfully market goods and services over the long term, they not only need a quality product, but must also go out of their way to provide excellent customer service. This is done by assuring customers in advance that if they are dissatisfied with the product they have easy to understand rights to effective recourse. One of these is to be able to ask for and promptly receive a full refund. So, while we look forward to not hearing from you, we will promptly and cheerfully refund your money if we do.

Jerome K. Miller of Copyright Information Services offers a personal guarantee at the end of his sales letters: "I am very enthusiastic about this book. If you buy it and don't like it, I will immediately refund your money."

A SIMPLE SYSTEM FOR HANDLING ORDERS AND INQUIRIES

The following section outlines one system for processing inquiries and orders. This system is adequate for handling small volumes of mail order

(50 or fewer inquiries and orders per day). As your volume grows, switch your list files and order processing routines to a computer. Nevertheless, even if you switch to a computer or already are using one, the basic procedures outlined will still be applicable.

If you are not using a computer, you should switch to one as soon as you can afford to do so. Why? Here are four good reasons:

1. You can save money by switching a manual list file over to a computer while the list is still small.
2. The computer will give you far more flexibility in storing and retrieving data, which will allow you to serve customers better.
3. Given the proper software, a computer allows you to input orders in such a way that all records, lists, and other information required to operate your business can be generated from the data in your order entry database. Not only will you be able to print labels and invoices, but you will also be able to print out some of the essential worksheets described in this book, including a daily record of responses and the ad response record.
4. If your customer list is in the computer, you can add, delete, and update customer information far more easily. Not only will this allow you to target your customers more readily, but it will also make your list more attractive for rental by outside companies.

How to Handle Inquiries

The first step in handling inquiries and orders is to sort incoming mail by key codes. Refer to the inquiries/order flowchart (Figure 10-1) as we discuss how to handle inquiries.

  1. Open each inquiry. Staple the letter and envelope together (in case the complete address is not on the letter).

  2. Type up five address labels for each inquiry. You can obtain gummed label sets with carbon paper between each page from any office supply store, or you can type a master list and photocopy it onto sheets of pressure-sensitive labels. In this way, you can type all five labels at once. Type all inquiries received each day on the same sheet.

```
031690   WD9
JOHN DOE
123 MAIN ST
ANYTOWN NY 10026
```

Type the customer's full name, address, and zip code on the label as indicated in the sample shown here. Also type the date of the inquiry and

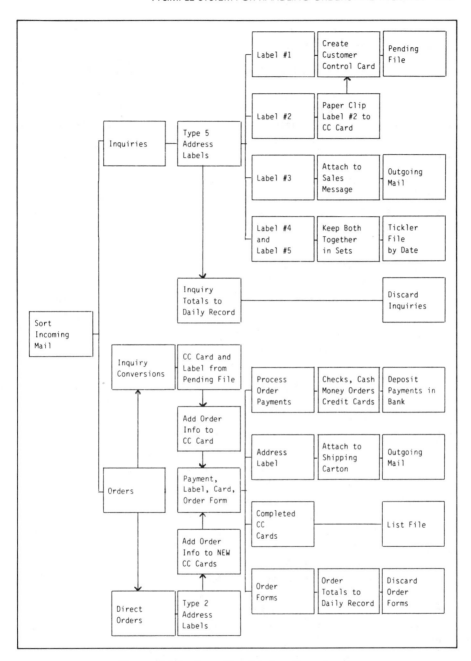

Figure 10-1 Inquiries/orders flowchart.

the key indicating the source of the inquiry. Type the date and key above the name, not below the address.

3. Paste label 1 on a 3" × 5" card for your "pending" file. This card will eventually become your customer control card (refer to Figure 10-3).

4. Use a paper clip to attach label 2 to the customer control card.

5. File both the customer control card and the attached label 2 alphabetically in your "pending" file.

6. Paste label 3 to an envelope, insert the sales message, add postage, and mail.

7. Labels 4 and 5 remain with the sheets they were typed on. These sheets should be filed by date (dates 1 through 31) in your "tickler" file (See pp. 179–181 to learn how to use the tickler file to generate more sales.)

8. After typing the five labels, use the original inquiries to complete your daily record of responses if you have not already done so. Once the labels are typed and the daily record is filled out, the original inquiries and envelopes may be discarded.

> Some companies retain the written inquiries and orders for a few months in case they have to track down a customer question about the inquiry or order. At mine, we retain the original correspondence for one year.

For businesses with a computer, keep a file of all inquiries. At the very least, the database of inquiries should include the following fields:

- **Customer name.** If you intend to personalize letters in the future, you should have three fields: First Name, Last Name, and Salutation (Mr., Mrs., Ms., etc.). The index for the customer file should be built upon the last name of the customer.
- **Company name.** If your customers are businesses, have a separate field for the company name. The main index for your customer file should be built on the company name rather than the name of the individual contact.
- **Address.** Have at least one line (28 to 32 characters) for the address. Some companies maintain two address lines—one for the post office box and the other for the street address.
- **City.** Allow 15 to 18 spaces for the city name. If you must abbreviate the city name, follow the conventions outlined by the post office. See your postmaster for details.
- **State.** Enter the two-character abbreviation for the state (for instance, MN for Minnesota or CA for California).
- **Zip code.** Enter the five-digit zip code. If you want to set up the system for even greater postal savings, begin with a 10-character field so you can enter the entire nine-digit zip code when it is provided to you by the customer.
- **Telephone number.** Whenever possible, get the customer's telephone number. While you might never use the number for telemarketing, it comes in handy when you are trying to track down new addresses or

following up on an order. Never accept a credit card payment, COD, or billing request without getting a telephone number.

- **Customer code.** To ensure that each customer record is unique, assign a customer code to each new customer. Since it is quite possible to receive orders from two customers with the same first and last names (or the same company name), a customer code is the only way you will be able to differentiate between them.

These eight fields are the basic ones you need for almost any type of customer file. At my company, we include three other fields in the customer file portion of the order entry database:

- **I/O/L.** This field indicates whether the customer is the result of an inquiry, an order, or a name we've entered from an outside list as a good prospect for our products.
- **Type of customer.** This code allows us to segment customers by type of company—publisher, self-publisher, printing company, direct marketer, writer, or PR firm. We can then target promotions to any one of these groups.
- **Update code.** This field indicates the month a customer was added to our database or the month the address changed. Most customer files might not require this field, but it is important to us because some companies that rent our lists want only addresses that have been added or changed.

What other fields might you put in a customer file? With the growth of fax numbers in business, you might want a fax number field. If you use first name, last name, and salutation fields for customer names, you might also want to add a title field that will allow you to target only sales managers, presidents, health directors, or some other designation.

Some companies also have a field that indicates the original source of the customer. At mine, the original source field is entered in our orders data file, which is related to the customer file by the customer code field. Here are some other fields we include in the orders file:

- **Date.** Each time you receive an order, enter the date the order was received or entered into the database.
- **Source code.** Enter the source of the order (a display ad, a company mailing, or something else). This source code is essential if you want to track the results of your promotions.
- **Total amount.** Enter the total amount of the sale. This field might actually be a calculated field derived from the sum total cost of all the products ordered, plus shipping and handling, sales tax, and any discounts offered to the customer. If this field is a calculated field, you need to have separate fields for the other data (shipping and handling, sales tax, etc.).
- **Method of payment.** Is this a cash order, payment by check, credit card sale, COD shipment, or a billing? Along with this field, you might

also have fields for noting the check number, credit card number, or invoice number.
- **Line item.** Somewhere in your order entry data file (in the file itself or in a related file), record what items were bought. At the very least, note the name of the items ordered, the quantity of each item, and the dollar value of each item. If you want to track sales by item, you need this information.

Most direct marketing companies want to store at least this information. Many also track other data, which detail the demographics or psychographics of their customers. Not only do these details help them in targeting their own promotions, but they also make their list far more valuable for rental by other companies.

Companies that are just starting out and still processing orders by hand should decide which details to keep on customer control cards (see Figure 10-3). The more information you keep now, the more you will be able to transfer to computer when you are ready to upgrade your order processing system.

How to Handle Orders

Here is a simple system for handling orders (refer to the inquiries/orders flowchart in Figure 10-1):

1. Open each order. Then paper clip the order form, envelope, and check or money order together.
2. Sort incoming orders into two piles: orders resulting from inquiries (inquiry conversion) and direct orders from ads and mailings. You should recognize the source of orders from their key codes.
3. Pull the customer control card from the "pending" file, and add the order information to the card. Paper clip the card and its accompanying label to the order.
   For direct orders, type two address labels (like the ones you typed in step 2 of handling inquiries). Paste one of the address labels to a 3" X 5" card to create a customer control card. Add the order information to the card. Paper clip the card and its accompanying label to the order form.
4. Take the extra address label and paste it to your shipping carton. Insert your product, add postage, and mail.
5. File the completed customer control card in your list file (which for start-up companies may be nothing more than a file box).
6. Process the payments. Endorse checks, process credit card payments, make up a deposit slip, and deposit all payments in the bank. If an order comes in without a payment, send a letter requesting payment and file the order in a folder marked "Hold for Payment." You may use a form letter like the one in Figure 10-2 (printed on your letterhead and signed by your customer service representative).

Your Letterhead Here

Date

Dear Customer:

Thank you for your recent order for <u>name of product</u> which we received on <u>such and such a date</u>. Unfortunately, no payment was found with your order. Perhaps you forgot to enclose the check?

If you would send us a check for $_____, we will be most happy to send your order to you the day we receive payment. If you have any questions about this letter, please call me at 123-456-7890.

Again, thank you for your interest in our products.

Sincerely

Customer Service

Figure 10-2   Hold-for-payment letter.

HOW TO MAINTAIN YOUR MAILING LIST

Your customer control card (or, if you have a computer database, the customer data file) is the basic unit of the mailing list you will develop as you get more orders and inquiries. Hence, you need to keep it up-to-date and complete. The customer control cards serve five important functions:

1. Verify that you received and sent orders (for tax records).
2. Allow you to process refund requests quickly and surely.
3. Enable you to follow up on inquiries.
4. Serve as the basis for your own in-house mailing list so you can announce new products and services to customers.
5. Make your mailing list more precise and, hence, more valuable to potential renters because of their detailed record of your customers' responses.

The customer control card should contain the following information: name, address, a key identifying the source of the customer, and the date of first customer contact (inquiry or order). If you followed the system for handling inquiries and orders, all four of these items will have been typed on the original mailing label made when the first inquiry or order came in. One copy of the label should be pasted on a card to create the customer control card. Store the cards in your list file.

Your customer control card might look like the card in Figure 10-3. You could paste the label over the top part of the card.

Any other information you can decipher about the customer should also be included on the card—for example, the customer's telephone number (often on the check), whether the customer is male or female, the customer's age, and whatever other information you think might help you to target customers more effectively.

Also add the order information as it comes in. Note the date of the order, the item ordered, amount of payment, check number (or money order or credit card), and how the item was shipped (UPS, fourth class, third class, first class, etc.).

Anytime you correspond with the customer, make a notation on the card. For example, if you mail out an announcement of a new product, note the date, the offer, and how it was sent. If you receive a testimonial, note the date received and indicate that a testimonial was received under the item heading.

Using all these data, you can select your most active or most satisfied customers for special mailings. You can also charge more to other companies interested in renting hotline names or special selections from your list.

If you have a computer, store most of the information in your order entry database and update it as required.

Name________________ Date________

Address________________ Key________

________________ Phone________

Other data________________

Date	Item	Amount	Ck No.	Shipped

Figure 10-3 Customer control card.

HOW TO GET MORE ORDERS FROM INQUIRERS

The main purpose of the tickler file is to ensure that all inquiries are followed up not once but twice (or more). In the simple system for handling inquiries already outlined, when you mail out your first sales message to an inquirer, you also file two extra sets of labels by date in the tickler file (step 7 of handling inquiries). Check these sets of labels 30 days later to see whether the inquirers have bought your product. If not, do a second mailing to the inquirers to draw in more orders.

Check the tickler file every day, acting on all sets of labels that have been in the file for 30 or 60 days. For example, on May 12 check all sets of labels filed on April 12 or March 12 (both of which should be filed under the twelfth).

Following are directions for processing the sets of labels from the tickler file. Refer to Figure 10-4 as these steps are discussed.

1. If both sets of labels (4 and 5) are still in the tickler file, check the order section of your list file. (Note that the list file should have two sections: one for names of people who have ordered [the order section] and one for those who have inquired but not ordered [the no order section].)

2. If there is a matching customer control card in the list file, you know that the inquirer has ordered. Once you have verified that the inquirer has ordered, discard the extra sets of labels and refile the customer control card in the list file. If there is no matching customer control card in the list file, check the hold-for-payment folder to see if the order is there.

3. If there is an order in the hold-for-payment folder, discard label 4 and make a note on label 5 that an order is awaiting payment. Refile the sheet of labels with label 5 in the tickler file.

If there is no order in the hold-for-payment folder, the inquirer has not yet ordered. In that case, it is time to send another mailing to encourage him or her to buy your product. To send another mailing, paste label 4 to the second-chance mailing envelope, insert your sales message, add postage, and mail. Then return the sheet with label 5 to the tickler file under the same date as before (to be checked again in 30 days).

4. If label 4 is no longer in the tickler file, you have already sent out a second-chance mailing and have given the inquirer 60 days and two chances to respond with an order. Now you must decide if it is worthwhile to continue mailing more sales announcements regarding this product to that particular inquirer or to file the inquirer's name in your list file under the "no order" section.

5. If you decide to send out more mailings, make up more address labels, send out your sales message, and refile the inquiry in the tickler file again (so it can be followed up in another 30 days). If you decide not to

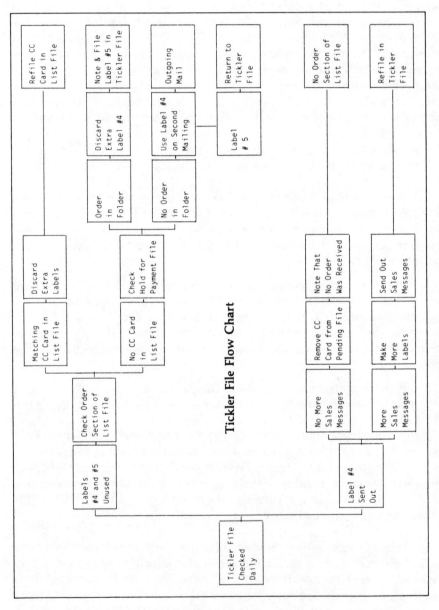

Figure 10-4 Tickler file flowchart.

mail any further sales announcements, remove the customer control card from the pending file, note on the card that no order was received, and file the card in the "no order" section of your list file.

> The inquiry names you place in the "no order" section of the list file are still valuable to you; do not discard them. You can send them announcements of other products that you sell. You can also rent these names to other companies.

If you use this simple system to fulfill orders and inquiries by hand, you will be keeping five separate file boxes or folders:

1. Pending file. All inquiries are originally placed in the pending file until they either place an order (step 3 for handling orders) or are filed in the "no order" section of your list file (step 5).

2. Hold-for-payment file. File any orders you receive that do not include some form of payment alphabetically in this folder or box. Every three or four months, clean out all orders held for payment more than six months. Chances are not very good that you will receive payment after that amount of time.

3. List file (order section). File all customer control cards that result from orders alphabetically (by last name, if a consumer, or by company name, if a business).

4. List file (no order section). File all inquiries that have never resulted in an order alphabetically in this section of the list file. You can still mail future announcements to these people and rent out their names to other companies. Inquirers' names get transferred from the pending file to this section when you decide that they merit no more mailings concerning the product for which they initially inquired.

5. Tickler file. File sets of labels from each day's inquiries in this folder by date (days 1 through 31). Use this file to follow up the inquiries with additional mailings. Continue mailing to inquiries as long as such mailings produce enough orders to pay for the cost of the mailings.

This simple system will get you started. As you stay in business longer and develop a line of products, you will have to refine and expand the system to suit your needs. Once you are computerized, most of the steps outlined in this system will be taken care of automatically by a good software program. Appendix III lists a few off-the-shelf software programs available for small to mid-size mail order companies.

CUSTOMER SERVICE LETTERS

To speed up the handling of customer queries, complaints, shipping delays, refund requests, and order discrepancies, it is efficient and effective to have some form letters already prepared. While it's not practical for you to respond personally to every customer, you can at least respond quickly.

Refund Letter

If you offer a good product, you will get few refund requests. When, however, you do get such a request, always send the refund right away. Never delay a refund. If you stand by your guarantees and process refunds quickly and without question, you will maintain customer goodwill—and a chance to sell another product to that person.

Besides customer dissatisfaction, there are a number of other reasons you might have to send a refund to a customer. For instance, the product may no longer be available, especially if an order comes a year or more after the original offer; or you may be out of stock but expecting delivery soon; or the customer overpaid.

To make refunds easier to process, use a refund letter such as the one illustrated in Figure 10-5. All you have to do to process a refund is to check the appropriate response, fill in the blank with the date or amount, sign the letter, and mail it with the refund check. You might also want to make a copy for your records.

Shipping Delay Letter

Sometimes you will have to delay shipping an order—perhaps because your supplier cannot keep up with the unexpected volume of orders or because of a strike or natural disaster. Whenever you cannot ship right away, send your customers a postcard or a letter advising them of the delay.

If the delay will be 30 days or longer, Federal Trade Commission regulations require that you notify the customer and give the option of canceling the order and receiving an immediate refund or agreeing to wait for a later shipping date (which must be named).

You can use a shipping delay letter similar to the one in Figure 10-6. Fill in the blanks, sign the letter, insert a reply postcard, and mail.

Discrepancy Memo

Besides refunds and shipping delays, there are a number of other things that can cause problems with an order. Some people forget to enclose checks with their orders. Others forget to sign their checks. Still others use the wrong prices or neglect to include the postage and handling fee.

To cover the most common order discrepancies that we come across here at Open Horizons, we developed a standard discrepancy memo (see

---

Use Your Letterhead

Date:

To:

Dear Customer:

   We are enclosing a refund check in the amount of $_____.
This refund is being made for the reason checked below:

   [ ] As per your request, letter dated _____.
   [ ] The product is no longer available.
   [ ] We are out of stock. Please reorder on _____.
   [ ] The item you ordered is not our product.
   [ ] Price discrepancy.
   [ ] You overpaid. The product costs $_____. You sent $_____.
   [ ] Duplicate payment of your payment dated: _____.
   [ ] Cancellation of prepaid order, dated: _____.
   [ ] Credit memo #_____.
   [ ] Other reason:

   Please feel free to contact us if you have any questions
regarding this refund, or if we can be of any further assistance.
We appreciate your interest in our products.

                          Sincerely,

                          Your Signature

Enclosure: Refund Check

Figure 10-5   Refund letter.

Figure 10-7). Develop a similar letter or memo for your business; it will
make it easier for you to serve your customers quickly.

Testimonial Letters

Nothing helps to promote your products more than the testimonials of
satisfied customers. That's why you should encourage the buyers of your
products to send you comments about the product—how it has helped

---

Use Your Letterhead

Date:

To:

Dear Customer:

Thank you for your recent order. However, due to unforeseen circumstances [you might name the reason for the delay; the more specific you are, the more your customers will trust you], we are unable to ship your order to you at this time. We apologize for this delay. Your order will be sent to you as soon as our new supplies come in. Please bear with us.

Product:

Reason for delay:

Expected shipping date:

We will not cash your check until we ship your order. If, because of this delay, you wish to cancel your order, please notify us via the enclosed postcard. We will return your check to you immediately upon your request.

Again, we appreciate your business. Thank you for your patience.

Sincerely,

Your Signature

Enclosure: Reply postcard

Figure 10-6   Shipping delay letter.

them, how much they've enjoyed it, how much money it has saved them, or what a bargain it is.

Whenever you receive unsolicited testimonials or reviews, send a letter to the person asking for permission to use the testimonial in your promotional literature. Also verify whether you can use any other information with the testimonial—for instance, the person's name,

```
YOUR LETTERHEAD HERE




                              Date _____



                        DISCREPANCY MEMO

To:

Re: Your recent order received for_____.

[ ] There was no check enclosed.
[ ] Your check was not signed.  Please sign it, and return
      immediately to expedite your shipment.
[ ] Incorrect prices were used on the order.
[ ] Please check our catalog for the current pricing.
[ ] The proper postage and handling fee was not included.
[ ] There was an error in addition on the order.
[ ] Your remittance was not sufficient to cover the cost of
      the item(s) you ordered plus the postage.
[ ] You have an outstanding invoice.
[ ] We no longer stock this title.
[ ] One of the books you ordered is currently out of stock.
[ ] We have a problem with your credit card number. Please check
      your card number and submit the order again.

OUR ACTION

[ ] We have shipped what your remittance would cover.
[ ] We have shipped all items to you.  Balance due_____
[ ] We are withholding release of shipment pending your remittance
      of_____.
[ ] We are withholding release of shipment pending verification
      of your credit card number.
[ ] We have shipped the item(s) you ordered. An invoice is enclosed.
[ ] A copy of our current catalog is enclosed.
[ ] One or more titles on your order are temporarily out of stock.
      Missing item(s) _____
      will follow in approximately 10 days.
[ ] A credit memo is enclosed.

                              Sincerely,
```

Figure 10-7 Discrepancy memo.

address, occupation, and whatever other details might be appropriate. Use a letter similar to the request for permission to quote letter in Figure 10-8.

You can solicit testimonials or comments from customers. When you send them their order, send out a warranty form, comment card, or research questionnaire that solicits their response. Make sure you give

Open Horizons Publishing Company
P. O. Box 1102
Fairfield, IA 52556-1102

Date

Reader's Name
Address
City, State Zip

Dear Reader:

Thank you for your wonderful comments regarding our new book, *1001 Ways to Market Your Books*. May we quote you in our promotional literature? Here are the parts of your letter which we would like to quote:

Just picked up a paperback copy of *1001 Ways to Market Your Books*. It's great! The only problem is that I am sure I am going to "reference" it to death. Send me a hardcover edition! Thanks for the valuable information.

If it's all right for us to quote these words, please sign below and return this letter to us. If you'd rather we didn't use your name and/or address, just say so. Thank you for your help.

Sincerely

John Kremer, publisher

[ ] Check here if we may quote your comments.

_____   _____
Signature   Date

Figure 10-8   Request for permission to quote.

them a good enough reason to take the time to fill out the form. You could, for instance, send a research poll. People like to give their opinions, especially if they feel that their opinions will have some impact. Such a poll could not only give you valuable testimonials, but it could also provide more life-style data about your customers (data that will make your customer list more valuable to you and to others).

If you don't send a questionnaire with the original order, perhaps send one later, one similar to the letter in Figure 10-9. Note that the letter asks for your feedback regarding this book. It is authentic as I would like

**John Wiley & Sons
605 Third Avenue
New York, NY 10158-0012**

Date

Reader's Name
Address
City, State Zip

Dear Reader:

Thank you for reading *The Complete Direct Marketing Sourcebook*. I hope it will help you to market your products more effectively by direct mail.

I will be revising this book periodically, both to update its information and to improve it contents. To do so effectively, I need feedback from the users of this book. Could you help me by commenting on both the strengths and weaknesses of *The Complete Direct Marketing Sourcebook* as it is now? Does it fulfill its purpose? How can it be made better?

Please use the space below to make your comments. If you need more room, write on the back side of this letter.

May I quote you in a testimonial for the book? If so, please check the space below. If you'd rather I did not use your name and/or address, just say so. Thank you for your help.

Sincerely

John Kremer,
Author

_____

_____

_____

[ ] Check here if I may quote your comments.

_____   _____
Signature   Date

Figure 10-9   Request for feedback.

feedback from you. Please send me your comments, both good and bad. Thanks for your help.

Even if you don't use the feedback from your customers in promotional literature, you should definitely use it to help you revise your product and service so they better suit the needs of your customers. Customer service is the key to any long-term success in direct marketing.

11

How to Control Your Inventory

HOW TO KEEP TRACK OF YOUR SUPPLIES

Keep an accurate record of the inventory for each product you sell and for each item or raw material that goes into manufacturing your products. Once a week, count the stock you have on hand. Then fill in an inventory record like the one in Exhibit 11-1. This worksheet will provide you with a record of your weekly usage rate and alert you far enough in advance so you have time to reorder before you run out of stock.

- **Item.** Enter the name or description of the item to be inventoried.

- **Product.** List the name of the product of which the item is a part (or a whole). If you are manufacturing the product yourself, inventory all the parts that will be assembled into the product.

- **Reorder Point.** List the stock level at which you need to reorder from suppliers. Take into account your average weekly usage, the lead times of your suppliers, the shipping times, plus at least two to four weeks as a safety factor. For instance, if your average weekly usage is 500 units and the lead time from your supplier is four weeks plus one week shipping, then you need to reorder when your stock level reaches 3,500 or 4,500, depending on the safety period you have chosen to use.

- **Reorder Quantity.** List the amount you need to reorder. Take into account the quantity price breaks, how sure you are that you can sell what you order, your cash flow, any planned promotions, and so forth.

- **Vendors.** List your prime sources for the item.

- **Date.** Enter the date that the inventory is taken. Take inventory

Inventory Record

Item: Widget Handle			Reorder Point: 9000			
Product: Widgets for Two			Reorder Quantity: 8000			

Vendors for This Item —>	ABC Company		DEF Company		GHI Company	

Date	Carry-over	Received	In Stock	Usage	On Order	Total
1/12/90	5,500	4,000	8,000	1,500	0	8,000
1/19/90	8,000	0	6,700	1,300	8,000	14,700
1/26/90	6,700	0	5,350	1,350	8,000	13,350
2/2/90	5,350	0	3,700	1,650	8,000	11,700
2/9/90	3,700	4,000	6,200	1,500	4,000	10,200
2/16/90	6,200	0	4,800	1,400	4,000	8,800
2/23/90	4,800	4,000	7,300	1,500	8,000	15,300
3/2/90	7,300	0	5,900	1,400	8,000	13,900
3/9/90	5,900	0	4,300	1,600	8,000	12,300
3/16/90	4,300	0	2,900	1,400	8,000	10,900
3/23/90	2,900	4,000	5,100	1,800	4,000	9,100
3/30/90	5,100	0	3,800	1,300	4,000	7,800
4/6/90	3,800	4,000	6,200	1,600	8,000	14,200
4/13/90	6,200	0	4,900	1,300	8,000	12,900

Exhibit 11-1   Inventory record.

on a regular basis—at least once a week when you are heavily promoting a product.

- **Carry-over.** This is the number of items in stock from the previous time the inventory was taken.

- **Received.** Enter the number of new items received from suppliers since the previous inventory.

- **In Stock.** Count the number of items you have in stock, and enter that number here. You will have to establish a quick but sure way to count inventory. If you have a well-designed computerized order entry system, you should be able to get this number from the database. If you do rely on the inventory number from the computer, do a hand count of the inventory at least once every three months to be sure that all items are being accounted for.

- **Usage.** Usage = Carry-over + Received − In Stock. This usage number should equal the number of items sold (plus those given away, used, or rejected) since inventory was last taken. If this number increases dramatically and stays up for several weeks in a row, you might need to establish a new reorder point.

- **On Order.** Enter the number of items on order from vendors but not yet received.

- **Total.** Total = In Stock + On Order. This total provides the number of items "available" for sale to expected customers. When this total falls below your reorder point, it is time to reorder.

HOW TO KEEP TABS ON YOUR SUPPLIERS

Besides keeping track of the items in stock, track the performance of your suppliers by inspecting everything received from them. As you unload the items, open several cartons and inspect the items inside. Also, note any shipping cartons that might have been damaged in shipment.

As you complete the inspection, fill out a receiving inspection report like the one in Exhibit 11-2. This report details all the points to cover during the inspection.

- **Received from.** Where did the shipment come from? Who was the vendor? If the vendor's address and the source of the shipment are different, list both.
- **Carrier Name.** Check the box indicating how the shipment came. Also indicate the name of the carrier if other than UPS or USPO.
- **Prepaid/Collect.** Check whether the shipment was sent prepaid or collect. If collect, enter how much was paid.
- **Our Order Number.** Enter your purchase order number or numbers for the items in this shipment.
- **Date Shipped.** Note the date the shipment was sent out.

Receiving Inspection Report

RECEIVED FROM

XYZ Company

1234 Timberwolf Lane

Newtown MN 55432

Carrier Name __ABC Carriers__

☐ UPS   ☐ Air Express
☐ Parcel Post   ☐ Express Mail USPO
☒ Truck   ☐ Rail
☐ Shipper's Truck   ☐ Other _____

☒ Prepaid   ☐ Collect $ _____

Our Order Number	Date Shipped	Date Received	Date Inspected	Inspected by
N2345	4/5/92	4/10/92	4/10/92	Jane Doe

Quantity	Description of Item	Number of Cartons	Weight of Each	Total Weight	Condition of Carton	Condition of Items
2,300	Widget handles	92	44 lb.	4,048	2 bad	okay
1,000	Widget feet	78	26 lb.	2,028	okay	okay
1,200	Widget boppers	55	36 lb.	1,980	okay	okay
	Total No. of Cartons	225	**Total Weight**	8,056		

Shipment
☒ Complete Shipment
☐ Partial Shipment

Number of Cartons
☒ Received O.K. __223__
☒ Received Damaged __2__

Number of Items
☒ Received O.K. __all__
☐ Received Damaged _____

Exhibit 11-2   Receiving inspection report.

- **Date Received.** Enter the date the shipment is received at your warehouse.
- **Date Inspected.** Enter the date the shipment is inspected, especially if the date is different from the date that the shipment was received.
- **Inspected by.** The person who does the inspection should sign the report.
- **Quantity.** Note how many items were received.
- **Description of Item.** Describe each item in the shipment. Enter a separate line for each item.
- **Number of Cartons.** Enter the number of cartons for each item in the shipment.
- **Weight of Each.** Note the weight of one carton for each item.
- **Total Weight.** Multiply the number of cartons times the weight of one carton to obtain the total weight.
- **Condition of Carton.** Note the condition of the cartons. If any are damaged, note the number and, if necessary, the extent of the damage.
- **Condition of Items.** If any items are damaged, note how many and the extent of the damage.
- **Total No. of Cartons.** Enter the total number of cartons from the shipment. To calculate the total, add up the number of cartons for each item in the shipment.
- **Total Weight.** Add up the total weight for each item in the shipment.
- **Shipment.** Check whether this shipment is complete or partial.
- **Number of Cartons.** Enter the number of cartons received in good condition and the number of cartons that were damaged (whether at the plant or in shipment).
- **Number of Items.** Enter the number of items received intact and the number of items that were damaged.

File this receiving inspection report with the vendor record for the manufacturer of the items included in the report. Also file a copy with the inventory record for each item in the report.

POSTAGE RATES COMPARISON CHART

Since you will be selling and shipping your products via direct mail, be aware of any changes in shipping rates. To give you a start in this direction, I have prepared a handy postage rates comparison chart, which lists the various rates as of December 1, 1991 (it is in Appendix I).

A comparison chart makes it easy to handle unusual shipments such as odd lots, special orders, or packages that have to get there faster than usual. The chart can be a money saver and, more important, a time saver. If you use other carriers, customize such a chart for your own use and update it as the rates change.

A FEW FINAL WORDS

I hope this book will help you to organize and carry out your direct marketing programs more effectively. But it will do so only if you actually put the principles outlined in this book into action. If I were writing a direct mail letter to you right now, I would ask you to act on this today. The longer you wait, the less you will get out of this book. Do it today.

Appendix I

How to Reduce Rising Postage Costs

One of the harsh realities of direct marketing is rising shipping costs. During the past 20 years, postal rates have risen far faster than inflation—and there is no end in sight. Within two months of the 1991 postal rate increase, the post office was already announcing the need for another rate hike before the end of the year.

To survive as a direct marketing company, you need to reduce postage costs. To help you decide what measures to take, this appendix lists more than a dozen techniques that other direct marketers are using to cut their postage costs. If you incorporate three or four of these techniques into the day-to-day operations of your company, you should be able to keep your postage costs in check. Indeed, with a little vigilance, you could use many of these techniques to cut your postage costs so much that you will actually pay *less* than you were before the last rate hike.

Here, then, are a few of the many ways that direct marketers just like you are reducing their postage costs:

Work with the post office. When the post office raised its rates in early 1991, it also provided many new incentives to encourage companies to work with it to help cut costs. To obtain the details concerning these added incentives, talk with the person at your local post office who is responsible for working with businesses. Ask for the rate schedules, sorting and handling requirements, and the new discount options that are available.

Mail bulk rate. When bulk mailing, there are three ways to affix the postage: (1) by printing the bulk rate notice on the envelope, (2) by metering, or (3) by affixing precanceled third-class stamps. A printed indicia is the least expensive option, but it is also the most obvious

Postage Rates Comparison Chart — As of December 1, 1991

Parcel Weight	Book Rate	Library Rate	Third Class / Parcel Post			First Class Mail			U.P.S. to Businesses		
			Zone 3	Zone 5	Zone 7	Zone 3	Zone 5	Zone 7	Zone 3	Zone 5	Zone 7
1 oz.	1.05	0.65	0.29	0.29	0.29	0.29	0.29	0.29	2.01	2.25	2.41
2 oz.	1.05	0.65	0.52	0.52	0.52	0.52	0.52	0.52	2.01	2.25	2.41
3 oz.	1.05	0.65	0.75	0.75	0.75	0.75	0.75	0.75	2.01	2.25	2.41
4 oz.	1.05	0.65	0.98	0.98	0.98	0.98	0.98	0.98	2.01	2.25	2.41
5 oz.	1.05	0.65	1.21	1.21	1.21	1.21	1.21	1.21	2.01	2.25	2.41
6 oz.	1.05	0.65	1.33	1.33	1.33	1.44	1.44	1.44	2.01	2.25	2.41
7 oz.	1.05	0.65	1.33	1.33	1.33	1.67	1.67	1.67	2.01	2.25	2.41
8 oz.	1.05	0.65	1.44	1.44	1.44	1.90	1.90	1.90	2.01	2.25	2.41
9 oz.	1.05	0.65	1.44	1.44	1.44	2.13	2.13	2.13	2.01	2.25	2.41
10 oz.	1.05	0.65	1.56	1.56	1.56	2.36	2.36	2.36	2.01	2.25	2.41
11 oz.	1.05	0.65	1.56	1.56	1.56	2.59	2.59	2.59	2.01	2.25	2.41
12 oz.	1.05	0.65	1.67	1.67	1.67	2.90	2.90	2.90	2.01	2.25	2.41
14 oz.	1.05	0.65	1.79	1.79	1.79	2.90	2.90	2.90	2.01	2.25	2.41
1 lb.	1.05	0.65	1.79	1.79	1.79	2.90	2.90	2.90	2.01	2.25	2.41
2 lb.	1.48	0.89	2.32	2.74	2.85	2.90	2.90	2.90	2.02	2.51	2.80
3 lb.	1.91	1.13	2.49	3.12	4.00	4.10	4.10	4.10	2.18	2.73	3.18
4 lb.	2.34	1.37	2.65	3.50	4.35	4.65	4.65	4.65	2.34	2.91	3.45
5 lb.	2.77	1.61	2.81	3.88	5.20	5.45	5.45	5.45	2.43	2.97	3.61
6 lb.	3.20	1.85	2.98	4.26	6.33	5.55	6.10	7.65	2.48	2.99	3.77
7 lb.	3.63	2.09	3.14	4.64	7.06	5.70	6.70	8.50	2.51	3.02	3.97
8 lb.	3.88	2.21	3.31	5.02	7.78	5.90	7.30	9.40	2.55	3.21	4.29
9 lb.	4.13	2.33	3.47	5.40	8.51	6.10	7.95	10.25	2.64	3.39	4.61
10 lb.	4.38	2.45	3.63	5.78	9.24	6.35	8.55	11.15	2.71	3.56	4.93
11 lb.	4.63	2.57	3.80	6.16	9.97	6.75	9.20	12.05	2.80	3.78	5.27
12 lb.	4.88	2.69	3.96	6.54	10.69	7.15	9.80	12.90	2.92	3.99	5.62
13 lb.	5.13	2.81	4.08	6.79	11.17	7.50	10.40	13.80	3.00	4.21	5.99
14 lb.	5.38	2.93	4.19	7.04	11.65	7.90	11.05	14.65	3.13	4.42	6.33
15 lb.	5.63	3.05	4.28	7.23	11.99	8.30	11.65	15.55	3.26	4.65	6.70
16 lb.	5.88	3.17	4.36	7.40	12.31	8.70	12.30	16.45	3.39	4.88	7.05
17 lb.	6.13	3.29	4.44	7.56	12.61	9.10	12.90	17.30	3.52	5.09	7.40
18 lb.	6.38	3.41	4.51	7.72	12.90	9.50	13.55	18.20	3.64	5.31	7.76
19 lb.	6.63	3.53	4.59	7.87	13.17	9.90	14.15	19.05	3.80	5.52	8.12
20 lb.	6.88	3.65	4.65	8.01	13.43	10.30	15.40	19.95	3.93	5.75	8.46
21 lb.	7.13	3.77	4.72	8.15	13.68	10.70	16.00	20.85	4.06	5.98	8.83
22 lb.	7.38	3.89	4.79	8.28	13.91	11.10	16.65	21.70	4.19	6.19	9.18
23 lb.	7.63	4.01	4.85	8.40	14.14	11.50	17.25	22.60	4.31	6.41	9.53

indication that the mailing is bulk rate. Affixing precanceled stamps is more labor intensive and, hence, more expensive, but it does make the envelope look like first-class mail. A metered mailing, which looks much like a first-class metered stamp, is a good compromise since you can cut costs by metering the envelope at the same time it is sealed.

Presort to obtain greater discounts. By presorting bulk mail, you can obtain additional discounts. For example, if you have at least 125 pieces going to zip codes with the same first three digits, you can get a discount over the basic bulk rate. You can get further discounts by sorting to carrier route (the routes of individual postal carriers) or by saturation mailing, but these require hundreds of pieces going to relatively small areas.

Barcode your addresses. Earn an additional discount by barcoding your mailing pieces. The bar code (the little vertical bars at the bottom of an envelope) is a computer-readable duplicate of the nine-digit zip code. It allows the post office to machine read and sort the letters automatically. That speeds up your mail and ensures it gets to the right address.

Use san serif type on addresses. Typefaces without serifs can be recognized more reasily by the optical character readers used by the post office to process mail that has not been barcoded previously.

Use zip + 4. Whenever possible, use the full nine-digit zip code on all outgoing mail to increase the chances that your mail will get to the people you want to reach. If you keep the mailing list on computer, the post office will accept your tapes or diskettes and add the last four digits to your zip codes. At the same time, they will standardize your addresses and verify your five-digit zip codes. This service is free, but that might change.

Clean your lists regularly. At least twice a year, add an "Address Correction Requested" endorsement on the outside of your mailings. You might also want to have your house list processed by the National Change of Address system developed by the post office. About a dozen service bureaus are qualified by the post office to offer this service.

Merge/Purge. If you are renting other lists, merge all the lists to purge or eliminate duplicates.

Use a lettershop or mailing service to prepare your mail. If you are a small company with a large mailing, consider using a lettershop to collate, insert, seal, affix postage, sort, bag, and deliver your mailing direct to the post office. If you don't do mailings often, it could pay to have the experts help you wade through the postal regulations to gain the special presort discounts. Lettershops offer many other services as well. A few major lettershops are listed in Appendix III. If you want to work with a local lettershop, check the yellow pages.

Join with other mailers. Under certain limited conditions, the post office allows mailers to combine mailings to earn quantity discounts and/or the special presort discounts. Some larger lettershops and mailing houses can help you combine with other mailers to earn these higher discounts.

Explore other post office discounts. If you are a quantity mailer, you might qualify for discounts if you palletize or trailer load your mailings. Check with the post office for the other options available to large mailers.

Use an alternative delivery service. As postage rates rise, there will be more room for private companies to make a profit competing against the post office. Already, United Parcel Service and Federal Express compete with the post office for certain classes of mail. Other alternate delivery services, such as Alternate Postal Delivery and Publishers Express, serve the magazine and catalog industries by providing better and cheaper deliveries in major markets. By the time you read this book, these services will be reaching at least 32 major markets. By 1995, they will be servicing the top 100 major markets.

Use alternative media, such as television, newspapers, magazines, or radio. These media can often deliver greater response. At the very minimum, their costs per thousand are far less than direct mail. Look into telemarketing and fax marketing, telephone methods that have proved to be cost-effective in generating responses. In many cases, a fax message is cheaper to send than a first-class letter, especially if you fax during nonbusiness hours.

Cut down on marginal mailings. To cut down on mailings that bring you little profit, use list enhancement and computer modeling techniques to pinpoint those customers most likely to buy a specific product from you again. Use these techniques to select other lists to rent. Look for lists with the same demographics or psychographics to match your own house list. (For more information on selecting lists, see Chapter 5.)

Target your mailings. Target all your mailings so you are truly reaching real prospects rather than mere suspects.

Cut down the size of your mailing package. To decrease the weight of your mailing, consider cutting the size of the package. Leave out a component in the mailing package or cut down the size of the catalog. Indeed, many catalogers are already cutting down the size of their catalogs to offset the increased postage rates.

Remember: The most effective way to cut postage costs is to talk to and work with the post office, printer, service bureau, list broker, lettershop, and any other services involved in planning, preparing, and carrying out your mailing programs. It's in their best interest to help you succeed. It's also in your best interest, so don't be afraid to ask for help.

Appendix II

Master Copies of the Worksheets

Many of the worksheets in this book have two versions: one in the main body of the book that illustrates how the worksheet should be filled out and a second one (a master copy) that is not filled out. This appendix includes master copies of all worksheets that were used as exhibits in the main text.

If you would like to have full-size standard (8 ½" - 11") master copies, enlarge the following worksheets on a photocopier. You may have to adjust your placement of this book on the copier before you get the positioning just right—in other words, so your copier captures the complete master copy and centers it properly.

The worksheets in this book fall into four basic categories. All are easy to use. Just follow the directions in each case, as outlined below.

MASTER COPIES

You may use some worksheets just as they are without any modifications (except, perhaps, to enlarge them). Examples of such master copies include the advertising record worksheets, the inventory control form, the new products evaluation form, and the project log.

SAMPLE LETTERS

This book also includes many sample letters that you may use as guides in writing your own standard letters. Because they contain references to specific products or procedures, they are not appropriate for you to photocopy and are not included in this appendix. Examples of such letters include the testimonial request letters and the sample refund letter. To get an idea of how to adapt the letters to your own needs, read the instructions that accompany the sample letters.

LETTERHEAD REQUIRED

Some of the worksheets and sample letters should not be copied until you have added your letterhead to them. These include the request for printing quotation and the ad insertion order. Master copies of these worksheets and sample letters are included in this appendix.

To use these, first make a full-size master copy; then paste your letterhead (address and company logo) at the top and photocopy onto appropriate paper. Or you could white out the "Your Letterhead Here" statement on the full-size master copy and then photocopy directly to your printed letterhead stationery. Or, if you prefer, make up your own master copy using ours as an example.

CHARTS AND PROCEDURES

A number of the worksheets are designed to be used directly in your operations. Use them right out of the book or make copies to keep handy. For example, the test sample probability table might be kept near your computer terminal when you are projecting probable responses to your mailings.

Since the charts in the main body of this book are the master copies for these forms, I have not duplicated them in this appendix. You may copy them direct from the page on which they appear, enlarging as desired.

PROJECT PRIORITY WORKSHEET

Product	Promotion	Audience	1	2	3	4	5	6	7	Total

1 — Promotion Timing
2 — Product Timing
3 — Capital Requirements
4 — Profit Potential
5 — Back End Potential
6 — Ease of Operation
7 — Odds of Success

For each of the seven numbered columns, assign a value of 0 to 10. For the number assignments shown at the left, follow the guidelines in the text. If you want to assign other meanings to the numbers, you may do so. When you have completed filling in the numbers, add up the total for each project. Generally, the project with the highest total will allow you to make optimum use of your time and resources.

Exhibit 1-1 Project priority worksheet.

PROJECT LOG

Project Name:

Starting Date:

Target Completion Date:

Scheduled		Actual		Actions to Be Accomplished	Done
Start	Finish	Start	Finish		

Exhibit 1-2 Project log.

Production Schedule for		Week 1	Week 2	Week 3	Week 4	Week 5	Week 6	Week 7	Week 8	Week 9
Jobs or Actions to Be Accomplished										

Exhibit 1-3   Schedule-at-a-glance.

New Product Evaluation Worksheet

Product:

Date:

Description:

Selection Criteria	Relative Importance	Rating (1 thru 10)	Total (RI x RA)
Is the market for this product large enough?			
Is the audience or market easy to target?			
Is there any competition (potential or established)?			
Can it be competitively priced?			
Is the cost low enough to justify a high markup?			
Does it offer real value for the price asked?			
Is the product original? Unique?			
Does it fill a need?			
Is the product easy to use? To understand?			
How safe is the product?			
Is the product readily available or easy to manufacture?			
Does the product require any special packaging?			
Is the product suitable for shipping? Easy to ship?			
Does the product require any service or follow up?			
Does the product have a long life expectancy?			
Is the product exclusive? Patentable?			
Does the product encourage repeat business?			
Is it compatible with the current product lines?			
Is the expected return on investment high enough?			
Will it contribute to the long-range growth of company?			
Average Weight:		Total:	

Exhibit 2-1   New product evaluation worksheet.

Request for Quotation

Issued by:	This is a request for quotation, not an order. Please provide us with your best prices and delivery times for the following described products or services. Please sign and date this RFQ and return to us by the date noted below. Thank you.

Vendor:	RFQ Number:
	Date of RFQ:
	Reply Not Later Than:
	Delivery Required By:

Terms:	F.O.B.	Ship via	Ship Wgt.

Quantity	Item	Description	Unit Cost	Total

Special charges (dies, plates, set-up charges, etc.):

Shipment can be made within _____ days after the order is placed.

Prices quoted include all costs, except where noted. Prices firm until:

Date of Quotation	Authorized Signature
Telephone Number	Name and Title

Exhibit 2-2   Request for quotation.

Vendor Record

Item:	Product:

Vendor _____   Phone _____

Address _____   Fax No. _____

_____   Contact _____

Terms:	F.O.B.	Ship via	Ship Wgt.

Item	Description	Quantity	Unit Cost	Total

Special charges (dies, plates, set-up charges, etc.):

Lead Time:	Estimated Shipping Charges:

Special Ordering Instructions:

COMMENTS

Quality:

Cooperation:

Dependability:

Exhibit 2-3   Vendor record.

Product Costs Worksheet

Product:		Qty:	Qty:
Item	**Description of Part or Labor**	**Unit Cost**	**Unit Cost**
Part #1	Raw Material		
	Set-up Charges		
	Tooling Costs		
	Inbound Freight		
	Labor		
Part #2	Raw Material		
	Set-up Charges		
	Tooling Costs		
	Inbound Freight		
	Labor		
Part #3	Raw Material		
	Set-up Charges		
	Tooling Costs		
	Inbound Freight		
	Labor		
Part #4	Raw Material		
	Set-up Charges		
	Tooling Costs		
	Inbound Freight		
	Labor		
Labor	Assembly of product		
Labor	Finishing Labor		
Packaging	Package		
	Set-up Charges		
	Tooling Costs		
	Inbound Freight		
	Labor		
Royalty	Inventor:		
Overhead	Plant Overhead		
Misc.			
	Total Unit Cost		
	Quantity times total unit cost = **Total Product Cost**		

Exhibit 2-4   Product costs worksheet.

Your Letterhead Here

Request for Quotation

Contact:

Please quote by

To:

Please quote your best price and turnaround time for the following job:

Specifications:
  Title of Job:
  Quantity:
  Total Pages:
  Page Size:
  Text Paper:
  Text Ink:
  Cover Stock:
  Cover Ink:
  Bindery:
  Packing:

  Material Provided:
  Special Instructions:

Quote:
  Price: $_____

  Estimated Delivery: _____ working days from receipt of camera-ready copy.

  Terms:

  Remarks:

Signed:_____

Thank you for your quote. We look forward to working with you.

Exhibit 3-1   Request for printing quotation: Simple.

Request for Quotation

Company:

Contact:

Address:

Phone:

Please quote your best price and delivery on the following job. Please quote:

☐ as firm price   ☐ verbally

☐ as rough estimate   ☐ in writing

To:

Job Name:

Date of RFQ:

Date quote needed:

Date job to printer:

Date job needed:

This job is a: ☐ new job	☐ exact reprint	☐ reprint with changes _____	
Quality desired: ☐ basic	☐ good	☐ premium	☐ showcase
Quantity: 1) _____	2) _____	3) _____	☐ additional _____

Format

Product Description: _____

Trim Size: Flat: _____ x _____   Bound or folded: _____ x _____

No. of pages: _____   ☐ self cover   ☐ plus cover

Copy

Design features: ☐ bleeds   ☐ screen tints #___   ☐ reverses #___   ☐ comp enclosed

Art provided: ☐ camera-ready   ☐ negatives   ☐ printer to typeset and paste up

Extras: ☐ halftones #___   ☐ duotones #___   ☐ color separations #___

Proofs: ☐ galley   ☐ blueline   ☐ composite color   ☐ progressive

Paper

	weight	name	color	finish	grade
Cover					
Inside					
_____					

Printing

	ink colors / varnish		ink colors / varnish
Cover	side 1 _____		side 2 _____
Inside	side 1 _____		side 2 _____
_____	side 1 _____		side 2 _____

Bindery

Operations: ☐ deliver flat   ☐ trim   ☐ collate & gather   ☐ fold _____
               ☐ round corner   ☐ punch   ☐ drill   ☐ score / perforate

Bindings: ☐ saddle stitch   ☐ side stitch   ☐ perfect bind   ☐ case bind
            ☐ spiral bind   ☐ plastic comb   ☐ Wire-O   ☐ pad

Packing: ☐ band in #___ s   ☐ wrap in #___ s   ☐ bulk in cartons   ☐ skid pack

Shipping: ☐ will pick up   ☐ send UPS   ☐ ship via truck   ☐ deliver to _____

Comments: _____

Exhibit 3-2   **Request for printing quotation: Complex.**

Direct Mail Promotion Costs Worksheet

Product:		Promotion:	

Dept.	Description of Job	Cost/M	Total Costs
Creative	Writing copy		
	Design and layout		
	Artwork (mechanicals and finished art)		
	Photography (photos, models/talent, retouching)		
Prep	Typesetting (typography, proofing, corrections)		
	Paste up camera-ready copy		
	Halftones, color separations		
	Platemaking (camera work, proofs, negatives, stripping, plates)		
Printing	Letter		
	Outer envelope		
	Reply envelope		
	Order form, response vehicle, reply card		
	Brochure, catalog		
	Other inserts (lift letter, buck slip, etc.)		
Lists	List rental		
	List selects (zip code, hotline names, etc.)		
	Merge/purge		
Lettershop	Inserting		
	Addressing or labeling		
	Sorting, metering, and mailing		
Overhead	Percentage of overhead for advertising and mailing departments		
Misc.			
	Production Costs Subtotal		
Postage	First class, bulk rate, alternative delivery methods		
Notes:	Totals		

Exhibit 3-3   Direct mail promotion costs worksheet.

Break-Even Worksheet

Product:		Promotion:		

Item #	Description of Item	Formulas	Subtotals	Totals
1 - A	Price of product or service being sold			
B	Other charges (postage & handling, etc.)			
C	Adjusted price of product	(1A + 1B)		
2 - A	Cost of product or service			
B	Handling expense and order processing			
C	Package expenses (mailing carton, tape, etc.)			
D	Shipping (postage or UPS charges)			
E	Premium costs including handling (if premium offered)			
F	Sales or use tax, if any	(1C x _____%)		
G	Total costs of filling the order			
3 - A	Estimated percentage of returns (expressed as a decimal)			
B	Postage and handling of returns	(2B + 2D)		
C	Refurbishing returned merchandise	(10% of 2A)		
D	Total costs of handling returns	(3B + 3C)		
E	Chargeable costs of handling returns	(3A x 3D)		
4 - A	Estimated percentage of bad debts (expressed as a decimal)			
B	Chargeable costs of bad debts	(1C x 4A)		
5 - A	Estimated percentage of sales via credit cards (as a decimal)			
B	Credit card processing charge	(_____% of 1C)		
C	Chargeable cost of credit	(5A x 5B)		
6 - A	Administrative overhead	(_____% of 1A)		
7 - A	Miscellaneous costs			
8 - A	Total variable costs	(2G + 3E + 4B + 5C + 6A + 7A)		
9 - A	Unit profit after variable costs	(1C - 8A)		
10 - A	Percentage of final sales (expressed as a decimal)	(1.0 - 3A)		
11 - A	Net unit profit	(9A x 10A)		
12 - A	Credit for returned merchandise	(3A x 2A)		
13 - A	Contribution margin (net profit per order)	(11A + 12A)		
14 - A	Mailing or advertising cost per thousand			
B	Number of orders per M to break even	(14A / 13A)		

Notes:

Exhibit 3-4   Break-even worksheet.

Projected Profit and Return on Investment Worksheet

Product:		Promotion:			

No.	Profit Projections and ROI Calculations Formulas	Projected Rates of Response (Pull)			
		Rate 1	Rate 2	Rate 3	Rate 4
1	Estimated number of orders / M				
2	Break-even number of orders / M (line 14-B, B-E)				
3	Profit-producing orders (#1 - #2)				
4	Contribution margin (line 13-A, B-E Worksheet)				
5	Profit / M circulars (#3 x #4)				
6	Total number of circulars mailed divided by 1000				
7	Total net profit (#5 x #6)				

No.		Rate 1	Rate 2	Rate 3	Rate 4
8	Total variable costs (line 8-A, B-E Worksheet)				
9	Selling Costs / M circulars (line 14-A, B-E Worksheet)				
10	Investment / M circulars [(#8 x #1) + #9]				
11	Selling price (adjusted) (line 1-C, B-E Worksheet)				
12	Total Income / M circulars (#1 x #11)				
13	Net Income / M circulars (#12 - #10)				
14	Return on Investment (#13 / #10)				
15	Return on Investment as a % (100 x #14)				

Notes:

Exhibit 3-5   Projected profit and ROI worksheet.

Direct Mail Checklists

How to Improve Your Offer

☐ Offer a premium for buying your product.

☐ Set a time limit.

☐ Offer a discount.

☐ Offer payment options.

☐ Make it easy for the customer to order.

☐ Offer a free trial period.

☐ Offer a demo version.

☐ Buy one, get one free offer.

☐ Make your unique selling proposition stand out.

☐ Enhance your product.

☐ Offer several versions of your product.

☐ Make a special offer.

☐ Offer special benefits to repeat buyers.

☐ Guarantee satisfaction.

☐ Run a sweepstakes or contest.

☐ Offer rush service.

How to Improve Your Copy

☐ Sell the benefits of your product.

☐ Offer a benefit right away.

☐ Use "you" copy.

☐ Remember the classic formula: AIDA.

☐ Ask for the order.

☐ Repeat important points.

☐ Use key words that people respond to.

☐ Include testimonials and success stories.

☐ Direct your offer to the recipients.

☐ Use details and specifics.

☐ Offer free information.

☐ Personalize your letter.

☐ Personalize your salutations.

☐ Change your style to suit your audience.

☐ Be honest.

☐ Write as much copy as you need to tell your story. No more, no less.

How to Enliven Your Letters

☐ Add a P.S. at the end of your letter.

☐ Letters should look like letters.

☐ Use involvement devices.

☐ Enclose money.

☐ Use handwriting.

☐ Highlight with a second color.

☐ End each page with an incomplete sentence.

☐ Use a Johnson Box.

☐ Use short paragraphs. Vary the length.

☐ Use a rebus letter.

How to Get Your Envelopes Opened

☐ Use teaser copy.

☐ Use windows that generate interest.

☐ Make the envelope look important.

☐ Make it look like a personal letter.

☐ Use real stamps.

☐ Use special effects (stickers, cartoons, etc.).

☐ Use an unusual envelope.

How to Get Your Order Form Used

☐ Make it look like an order form.

☐ Keep it clear and simple.

☐ Print the reader's name and address.

☐ Limit the number of choices.

☐ Make sure your offer is clear.

☐ Make sure the form has all the details they need to place an order.

☐ State your guarantee.

☐ Use involvement devices such as stickers.

☐ Offer a toll-free phone order option.

☐ Include a reply envelope.

☐ Use two response devices rather than one.

☐ Print your name and address on every piece of the mailing.

Exhibit 4-1   Direct mail checklists.

Words That Work Checklist

advice to	here's why	risk-free	**Transitions**
amazing	how to	rush	All this and more!
announcing	hurry	safety	And here it is ...
at last	important	sale	And, if that's not enough, ...
bargain	improve	satisfaction guaranteed	And that's not all!
best	introducing	save	Best of all, ...
bonus	it's here	save money	But hurry!
breakthrough	just arrived	save time	But there's even more ...
cash	last chance	secret	Did you ever ask yourself ...?
challenge	limited edition	sensational	Don't forget ...
compare	love	a special invitation	Here's how ...
complete	low cost	sign up today	Here's why ...
comprehensive	magic	simple	How can ...?
deluxe	miracle	special	How many times have you said to yourself ...?
discovery	money	startling	In short, ...
don't delay	money back	step-by-step	Interested?
don't wait	money-making	success	It's that simple.
dream	new	suddenly	Most important, ...
easy	no-nonsense	tested	Now, for the first time, ...
easy to use	no obligation	time-saving	Simply stated, ...
enjoy	no risk	today	Sounds incredible?
exclusive	now	unforgetable	That's why ...
extra value	official	unique	The result?
fast	one of a kind	unmatched	The truth is ...
first class	order today	up-to-date	There's more: ...
fortune	powerful	urgent	These are just a few of the ...
found	proof	wanted	Think of it: ...
free	proven	wealth	Want proof?
free trial	P.S.	when	What's more ...
fully documented	quick	why	Why ...?
guarantee	ready-to-use	win	Yes, you too can ...
half price	remarkable	works wonders	
handy	results	yes	
happy	reveal	you	
health	revolutionary	your	
help	right now		

Exhibit 4-2   Words that work checklist.

```
                    Your Letterhead Here
```

Approval/Review Form

To: **Today's date:**

From: **Please return this form by:**

Re:

   Please read the attached draft of our new promotional literature. Then answer the following questions. Answer them as completely as you can. Please give us your honest opinion. You may also mark specific comments, corrections, and suggestions directly on the copy or attach a separate sheet, if necessary.

   When you have completed your review, return this form and the accompanying materials to me by the date noted above. Thank you for your help.

1. Do you understand the product being offered in this promotion? If so, please describe it in your own words. If you don't understand the product, what more information do you need?

2. Is the offer clear? Easy to follow? Effective? Please explain it in your own words.

3. If you were a member of the target audience, would you buy the product? If yes, why? If no, why not?

4. Is it clear how to respond to this offer? Is the order form easy to use? Is it clear and simple?

5. Is the rest of the promotional package easy to follow? Readable? Convincing? Please explain.

6. If you had the power to change any one thing in this promotion, what would it be? Why?

Exhibit 4-3 Approval/review form.

Coded Lists Track Record

Code:	Type of Request:
Company:	Date:
	Product:
	Source:

Date	Response: Offers	Response: Products

Date	Other Companies	Offer and Product

Exhibit 5-1   Coded lists track record.

LIST:

QUANTITY   DESCRIPTION   PRICE/M   DATE   UNIT OF SALE

PROFILE: SEX

SOURCE: ADDRESSING

SELECTIONS: MAINTAINED

SUGGESTED USES: SELECTIONS

REMARKS: KEYING

                                                        MINIMUM

Exhibit 5-2   List data card.

List Selection Checklist

Product:			Promotion:	

List Number	Description of the List	Qty.	List supplier (broker and/or company)
List #1			
List #2			
List #3			
List #4			

Question to Ask	List #1	List #2	List #3	List #4
Is this list related to the offer?				
Does the list consist of buyers?				
What is the source of the original sale?				
How recent are the names?				
Is the unit of sale similar?				
Can we select multi-buyers?				
Can we make other selections?				
Does list have similar demographics?				
Does list have similar psychographics?				
Does the list have a high dupe rate?				
Do others rent this list repeatedly?				
Do our competitors rent this list?				
Does this list have continuation usage?				
How did people on the list pay?				
Does this list have rollout potential?				
Is the list cost effective?				
Is this list clean?				
Is the list available in correct format?				
Are the delivery dates guaranteed?				
Any negative characteristics?				

Exhibit 5-3   List selection checklist.

List Rental Order Form

Vendor:

Purchase Order No.:

Date of Purchase Order:

Date List Wanted:

Mailing Date:

Ordered by:

Ship to:

Quantity	List / Selections	Price per M	Total Price

FORMAT (Material)
- ☐ Cheshire Labels
- ☐ Pressure Sensitive Labels
- ☐ 3 x 5 Cards
- ☐ Sheet Listing
- ☐ Magnetic Tape

GEOGRAPHIC SELECTIONS
- ☐ Complete List
- ☐ Cross-Section of U.S.
- ☐ Selected States
- ☐ Selected SCFs, Zips

List Subtotal	
Material	
Options	
Shipping	
Total Order	

SPECIAL INSTRUCTIONS
- ☐ Key Coding _____
- ☐ Title Address _____
- ☐ Sample mailing piece enclosed.

Exhibit 5-4   List rental order form.

Competitive Media Analyzer

	Direct Mail	Magazines	Newspapers	Network TV	Short-form TV Spot / Cable	Long-form TV Spot / Cable	Network Radio	Spot Radio	Outdoor Billboards	Telephone Marketing	Card Packs
Highly targetable audience											
Geographic selectivity											
Demographic selectivity											
Psychographic selectivity											
Low cost per thousand (CPM)											
Low cost per ad											
Inexpensive to produce											
Flexible costs											
Low clutter / no distractions											
Wide penetration of market											
Broad reach / mass market											
High frequency possible											
Flexible timing											
Short lead time / quick roll-out											
Quick response time											
Measurable response											
Numerous response options											
More testable / lots of options											
Lots of room to state message											
Lots of creative flexibility											
Excellent reproduction											
High graphic impact											
Involves all senses											
Highly participatory											
Intrusive											
Compatible editorial environment											
More flexibility in making changes											
A long life-span											
Great pass-along rate											
Repeated exposure											
Reach audience where you want to											
No wasted circulation											
Media help in preparing ads											

Exhibit 6-1   Competitive media analyzer.

Publication Data Record

Publication:	Key Code:	Space Deadline:
Address:	Frequency:	Art Deadline:
City/State/Zip:	Circulation:	Cover Date:
Contact Person:	Readership:	On Sale Date:
Phone:	Subjects:	
Fax Number:		

Size and/or Description of Ad Space	Cost of Ad	CPM (cost per thousand)

Date	Cost	Ad Size & Position	Ad Contents	Response	CPI/CPO

Exhibit 6-2   Publication data record.

Competition Ad Analysis Worksheet

Product:			Promotion:			Time Period:		
Magazines	**Competitor:**		**Competitor:**		**Competitor:**			
	Space	**Cost**	**Space**	**Cost**	**Space**	**Cost**		

Descriptive Codes:

FP — full page ad	1/3 — 1/3 page ad	IN — inserts	B/W — black & white	BL — bleed
2/3 — 2/3 page ad	1/4 — 1/4 page ad	2P — 2-page spread	2C — two colors	SE — special effects
1/2 — 1/2 page ad	1/6 — 1/6 page ad	PC — bind-in card	4C — full color	CP — coupon in ad
IS — island ad	1" — 1 inch by 1 col.	CA — classified ad	SP — special	PH — phone # in ad

Exhibit 6-3   Competition ad analysis worksheet.

Media Schedule

Product/Promotion: _____ **Period:** _____ **to** _____

Media Name	Items	January	February	March	April	May	June	July	August	Sept.	October	November	Dec.
Name:	Key:												
Circulation:	Size:												
Frequency:	Color:												
Rate (x):	Closing:												
Contract Period:	Cost:												
	Note:												
Name:	Key:												
Circulation:	Size:												
Frequency:	Color:												
Rate (x):	Closing:												
Contract Period:	Cost:												
	Note:												
Name:	Key:												
Circulation:	Size:												
Frequency:	Color:												
Rate (x):	Closing:												
Contract Period:	Cost:												
	Note:												
Name:	Key:												
Circulation:	Size:												
Frequency:	Color:												
Rate (x):	Closing:												
Contract Period:	Cost:												
	Note:												
Name:	Key:												
Circulation:	Size:												
Frequency:	Color:												
Rate (x):	Closing:												
Contract Period:	Cost:												
	Note:												
Name:	Key:												
Circulation:	Size:												
Frequency:	Color:												
Rate (x):	Closing:												
Contract Period:	Cost:												
	Note:												

Exhibit 6-4   Media schedule.

Your Letterhead Here

To the Publisher of:

Order No. _____

Date _____

Advertiser _____

Product _____

☐ This is a SPACE RESERVATION.

☐ This is an INSERTION ORDER.

☐ This ia a CANCELLATION or CHANGE of _____

Insertion Dates	Space	Position	Key	Caption / Description	Ad Rate

Additional Instructions:

Total Ad Cost	
Agency Discount	
Subtotal	
Cash Discount (%)	
Net Amount This Order	

Ad copy and materials ☐ Enclosed ☐ To Follow

Name _____

Phone _____

Signature

Exhibit 6-5 Ad insertion order.

Daily Record of Responses

Product:		Date:	
Key	**Number of Inquiries**	**Number of Orders**	**Cash Received**
No Key			
Total			
Refunds			
Net			

Exhibit 8-1   Daily record of responses.

Advertisement Response Record

Publication			Issue		Key	
Proposition			Page No.		On Sale Date	
Version			Size		Cost of Ad	
Circulation			Position		CPM	

	DATE	INQUIRIES		ORDERS		CASH SALES	
		Number Received	Total To Date	Number Received	Total To Date	Today's Sales	Total Sales
1							
2							
3							
4							
5							
6							
7							
8							
9							
10							
11							
12							
13							
14							
15							
16							
17							
18							
19							
20							
21							
22							
23							
24							
25							
26							
27							
28							
29							
30							

Exhibit 8-2   Advertisement response record.

Ad Comparisons Form

Product/Promotion: _____   Date: _____

Key	Publication / List	Cost of the Ad	# of Inquiries	CPI	# of Orders	CPO	I/O %	Order Income	Refunds	Gross Income	Net Income
TOTALS											

Exhibit 8-3 Ad comparisons form.

Catalog Sales Analysis

Catalog: _____   Date of Analysis: _____

Page Number	Item Number	Space Taken	Dollar Volume	Product Cost	Contribution Margin	Ad Cost	CM / AC Ratio	Item Profit / Loss
Totals for Page								
Totals for Page								
Totals for Page								
Totals for Page								
Totals for Page								
Totals for Page								
Total Sales for Pages								

Exhibit 9-1   Catalog sales analysis.

Merchandise Data Sheet

Manufacturer's Name	Sales Agent (if any)
Contact Person	Contact Person
Address	Address
City State Zip	City State Zip
Phone Number	Phone Number
Fax Number	Fax Number

Name of Product	Discount Schedule
Item Number	
Description of Product	

Size of Item	Weight of Item	# of Items Per Shipping Carton	Weight of Shipping Carton
Suggested Retail Price	Terms	F.O.B. Point	Shipping Point

Time required to ship merchandise after receipt of order

Items are packed as follows

The following are the major selling features of the product:

☐ The item is prepriced.

☐ We can remove the price from the item.

☐ The item is available for immediate delivery.

☐ The item will be available for at least one year.

☐ We guarantee no changes in price for one year.

☐ The item itself is guaranteed.

☐ We carry product liability insurance.

☐ The item can be dropshipped.

☐ The item can be modified per buyer's request.

☐ Line art or photos are enclosed.

☐ Descriptive literature is enclosed.

☐ Samples of the product are enclosed.

Signature   Date

Exhibit 9-3   Merchandise data sheet.

Inventory Record

Item				Reorder Point		
Product				Reorder Quantity		
Vendors for This Item —>						

Date	Carry-over	Received	In Stock	Usage	On Order	Total

Exhibit 11-1   Inventory record.

Receiving Inspection Report

RECEIVED FROM

Carrier Name _____

☐ UPS   ☐ Air Express
☐ Parcel Post   ☐ Express Mail USPO
☐ Truck   ☐ Rail
☐ Shipper's Truck   ☐ Other _____

☐ Prepaid   ☐ Collect $ _____

Our Order Number	Date Shipped	Date Received	Date Inspected	Inspected by

Quantity	Description of Item	Number of Cartons	Weight of Each	Total Weight	Condition of Carton	Condition of Items
		Total No. of Cartons		**Total Weight**		

Shipment	Number of Cartons	Number of Items
☐ Complete Shipment	☐ Received O.K. _____	☐ Received O.K. _____
☐ Partial Shipment	☐ Received Damaged _____	☐ Received Damaged _____

Exhibit 11-2   Receiving inspection report.

Appendix III

Sources and Resources

This appendix lists a few of the many resources available to direct marketers. Note that these listings are far from comprehensive. This appendix is only a beginning—a work in process that will get better with time. Although all addresses have been verified recently, there is a chance that some of the addresses or telephone numbers have changed.

AD AGENCIES

Business-to-Business Direct Mail
1341 Hamburg Turnpike
Wayne, NJ 07470
201-696-7843
    business-to-business direct
    marketing

Chapman Direct Advertising
Bill Sutherland
230 Park Avenue South
New York, NY 10003
212-614-3880

Donald D. Lewis Advertising
Gene Williams
Executive Vice-President
405 Riverside Drive
Burbank, CA 91506
818-841-4070; fax: 818-841-0694

Franklin & Joseph
237 Mamaroneck Avenue
White Plains, NY 10605
914-997-0212; fax: 914-597-0215
    direct marketing advertising
    agency

Gaylord Direct Marketing
Jeremy Gaylord
One Byram Brook Place
Armonk, NY 10504
914-273-2222

Hatchett & Fagan
P.O. Box 36099
Birmingham, AL 35236
205-991-9515

Haynes & Pittenger Direct
Tom Dittrich, Vice-President
5561 West 74th Street
Indianapolis, IN 46268
317-328-4650; fax: 317-328-4646

Interface Direct
250 Consumers Road, #802
Willowdale, Ontario M2J 4V6, Canada
416-490-8166; fax: 416-490-8172
    full-service direct marketing agency

Jackson & O'Malley
149 S. Main Street
Hightstown, NJ 08520
609-443-4112

Joel Alpert & Friends
404-636-5635

Lucien Cohen Advertising Design
1201 Broadway, #403A
New York, NY 10001
212-685-7455; fax: 212-779-8987
    circulation promotion, book direct
    marketing, insurance direct
    marketing

Marc Direct
4 Station Square
Pittsburgh, PA 15219
412-562-2000
    direct marketing advertising agency

Mecklerstone Inc.
Jeff Meckler
220A Moore Street
Philadelphia, PA 19148
215-271-9800; fax: 215-271-9803

Moreno Design
800 Hingham Street
Rockland, MA 02370
617-878-1101
    bank direct marketing

Powell Advertising
254 Park Avenue South
New York, NY 10010
212-473-0192
    specializes in direct mail

Princeton Direct
4105 U.S. Route 1 #8
Monmouth Junction, NJ 08852
908-329-3049; fax: 908-329-8424

Saugatuck Direct
18 Kings Highway N
Westport, CT 06880
203-226-8166; fax: 203-227-6667

SRH Direct Marketing
Steve Hoeft, President
1 Memorial Drive
Saint Louis, MO 63102
314-622-9400; fax: 314-622-9435

Trend Direct
300 Park Avenue South
New York, NY 10010
212-995-9100
    specializes in consumer retail
    catalogs

Trumbull Marketing Group
105 Beacon Street
Black Rock, CT 06605
203-367-0055

Westport Direct
1960 Bronson Road
Fairfield, CT 06430
    direct mail strategy and tactics

Wyse Direct
216-696-2427

ASSOCIATIONS

American Telemarketing
    Association
5000 Van Nuys Boulevard, #400
Sherman Oaks, CA 91403
818-995-7338

Australian Direct Marketing
    Association
52-58 Clarence Street, 10th Floor
Sydney 2000, Australia

Canadian Direct Marketing
    Association
One Concord Gate, #607
Don Mills, Ontario M3C 3N6,
    Canada
416-391-2362

Direct Marketing Association
11 West 42d Street
New York, NY 10036-9046
212-768-7277

Direct Marketing Creative Guild
516 Fifth Avenue
New York, NY 10036
212-947-7100

National Mail Order Association
3875 Wilshire Boulevard, #604
Los Angeles, CA 90010
213-380-3686

Third Class Mail Association
1333 F Street N.W., #710
Washington, DC 20004
202-347-0055

CARD PACK PRINTERS

Collated Products Corporation
7001 Pencader Drive
Newark, DE 19702
302-731-4800; fax: 302-731-2798

MGA Marketing
Metropolitan Graphic Arts
930 Turret Court
Mundelein, IL 60060
708-556-9502; fax: 708-566-9584;
    800-541-5936

Rose Printing Company
2503 Jackson Bluff
P.O. Box 5078
Tallahassee, FL 32314
904-576-4151; 800-227-3725

Schmidt Printing
1416 Valley High Drive N.
Rochester, MN 55901
507-288-6400

Scoville Press
14505 27th Avenue N.
Plymouth, MN 55441
612-553-1400; fax: 612-553-0042

Solar Press
1120 Frontenac Road
Naperville, IL 60566
312-983-1400; 800-323-2751

CLIPPING BUREAUS

Bacon's Clipping Bureau
332 S. Michigan Avenue
Chicago, IL 60604
312-922-2400; 800-621-0561

Broadcast Data Systems
1515 Broadway, 37th Floor
New York, NY 10036
212-536-5341; fax: 212-536-5310
    broadcast monitor for television
    and radio

Broadcast Information
501 Madison Avenue

New York, NY 10022-5602
212-385-1190
    clipping bureau for television
    broadcasts

Burrelles Press Clipping Service
75 E. Northfield Avenue
Livingston, NJ 07039
201-992-6600; 800-631-1160
    clipping bureau

Luce Press Clippings
420 Lexington Avenue
New York, NY 10170
212-889-6711; fax: 212-481-0105
    clipping bureau

Luce Press Clippings
42 South Center Street
Mesa, AZ 85210
602-834-6183
    clipping bureau

Mature Market Clipping Service
1326 Garnet Avenue
San Diego, CA 92109
619-272-2832
    200 mature market publications

Newsclip Clipping Bureau
213 West Institute Place
Chicago, IL 60610
312-751-7300; fax: 312-751-7306;
    800-544-8433

Pressclips Inc.
1 Hillside Boulevard
New Hyde Park, NY 11040
516-436-1047

COLLECTION AGENCIES

American Financial Management
3715 Ventura Drive
Arlington Heights, IL 60004
708-259-7000

Coleman & Coleman Consultants
28 Brookhaven Boulevard
Port Jefferson, NY 11776
516-331-3649

Gibson-Martin Associates
P.O. Box 637
Millbrook, AL 36054
205-285-3186

North Shore Agency
117 Cuttermill Road
Great Neck, NY 11021
516-466-9300; fax: 516-466-9391
     collection agency for direct
     marketers

Retrieval-Masters Credit Bureau
1261 Broadway
New York, NY 10001-3570
212-679-4025; 800-666-8097;
     fax: 800-843-8097
     collections, direct mail

Transworld Systems
633 N.E. 167th Street, #1205
North Miami Beach, FL 33162
309-654-1049

CONSULTANTS

Direct Marketing Management
     Consultants
151 S. Warner
Wayne, PA 19087
215-964-9200
     direct marketing consultants

Fenvessy Consulting
110 East 59th Street
New York, NY 10022
212-755-5050
     direct marketing management
     consultant

Rene Gnam
1 Response Road
Tarpon Springs, FL 34989-8500
813-938-1555; fax: 813-942-0416
     direct marketing consultant

Kobs, Gregory & Passavant
225 N. Michigan Avenue
Chicago, IL 60601
312-819-2300

Ed McLean
309 West 57th Street, #1608
New York, NY 10019
212-541-5772

Overton Direct Marketing Service
11511 Katy Freeway, #350
Houston, TX 77079
713-558-5333
     direct marketing and catalog
     consultants

Murray Raphel, Raphel Marketing
125 Virginia Avenue
Atlantic City, NJ 08401
609-348-6646
     marketing consultant

The Schmidt Group
119 Monroe Avenue
Spring Lake, NJ 07762
908-449-0076
     catalog consultants

Schober Direktmarketing
206 West 15th Street
New York, NY 10011
212-691-8869; fax: 212-206-1904
     direct marketing consultants for
     Europe

COPYWRITERS

John F. Bailey, The Copywriter
1 Mansfield Road
White Plains, NY 10605
914-997-1607
     direct mail copywriter, also
     sweepstakes

Bob Bly
174 Holland Avenue
New Milford, NJ 07646
201-599-2277; fax: 201-599-2276

Louis J. Boasi
56 Seventh Avenue
New York, NY 10011
212-741-7331

Hannah Brion
505 Court Street, #6C
Brooklyn, NY 11231
718-858-0362

Luther Brock
2911 Nottingham Drive
Denton, TX 76201
817-387-8058

Hugh Chewning
4 Candlebush
Irvine, CA 92715
714-854-2942

Communicomp
Herschell Gordon Lewis
P.O. Box 15725
Plantation, FL 33318
305-587-7500; fax: 305-797-9900

Copy That Pulls
Julie Riessman
7 East 14th Street
New York, NY 10003
212-691-1029

Creative Solutions
Barbara Wainhause
48 Karen Drive
Norwalk, CT 06851
203-853-1707

Stephanie Fogel
200 East 30th Street
New York, NY 10016
212-679-2978

Lila Freilicher
527 First Street
Brooklyn, NY 11215
718-768-1287
    also design and production

Rosalynd Friedman
171 East 83d Street, #3C
New York, NY 10028-1972
212-988-8189

Bob Gaines
33 Soulice Place
New Rochelle, NY 10804
914-633-1558

Karen Gedney
410 West 24th Street, #5C
New York, NY 10011
212-727-7885

Don Hauptman
61 West 62d Street
New York, NY 10023
212-246-8229; fax: 212-397-1964

Bob Kalian
23 Rosedale Road
Yonkers, NY 10710
914-337-4576

Andrew S. Linick
The Linick Group
Seven Linick Building
Middle Island, NY 11953
516-924-3888

Tom McCormick
1306 Vincent Place
McLean, VA 22101
703-356-7242

Larry Miller
408 Penwyn Road

Wynnewood, PA 19096
215-649-6170

Milt Pierce
162 West 54th Street
New York, NY 10019-5345
212-246-2325

Burton Pincus, Advertising Consultant
P.O. Box 194
Linwood, NJ 08221
609-927-1450

Suzanne Becker Ramos
237 East 20th Street, #5A
New York, NY 10003
212-674-2167

Steve Sahlein
30 Country Club Drive
Larchmont, NY 10538
914-834-4441; fax: 914-834-4695

Robert C. Schulte
Laughlin Studios, 4th Floor
156 West 44th Street
New York, NY 10036
212-921-2982

Robert Serling
3960 Laurel Canyon Boulevard, #380
Studio City, CA 91614-3791
818-761-2952

Ruth Koffler Sheldon
585 West End Avenue
New York, NY 10024-1721
212-873-0496

Pete Silver
P.O. Box 570217
Miami, FL 33257-0217
305-252-7757; fax: 305-252-7741

Richard Silverman
83-33 Austin Street
Kew Gardens, NY 11415
718-441-5358

Ernie Trecroci
1220 Valley Forge Road, #25
Valley Forge, PA 19481
215-933-0933

Marguerita Weiss
300 N. State Street
Chicago, IL 60610
312-467-0427

Bob Westenberg
6018 F Highway 179
Sedona, AZ 86336-8901
602-284-1111
    specializing in card pack sales

Amy Zipkin
31 Sniffen Road
Westport, CT 06880
203-226-7825
    also consulting

CREDIT CARDS

American Express Credit Cards
7300 N. Kendall Drive
Miami, FL 33156
800-528-5200
    American Express credit cards

Diner's Club
8430 W. Bryn Mawr Avenue
Chicago, IL 60631
312-380-5100; 800-525-7376

Discover Card
800-347-2000

Fraud & Theft Information Bureau
P.O. Box 400
Boynton Beach, FL 33425
407-737-7500; fax: 407-737-5800
    *The Complete Guide to Getting and
    Keeping Your Visa and MasterCard
    Merchant Status* report

DIRECTORIES

Adweek Agency Directory
49 East 21st Street
New York, NY 10010
212-995-7225; 800-3-ADWEEK
600 advertising and PR agencies

All-in-One Directory
Gebbie Press
P.O. Box 1000
New Paltz, NY 12561-0017
914-255-7560
    all media

Association Periodicals
Gale Research Company
835 Penobscot Building
Detroit, MI 48226-4094

313-961-2242; fax: 313-961-6083;
    800-877-4253

Bacon's Publicity Checker
R. H. Bacon Company
332 S. Michigan Avenue
Chicago, IL 60604
312-922-2400; fax: 312-922-3127;
    800-621-0561
    magazines and newspapers

Bacon's Radio/TV Directory
R. H. Bacon Company
332 S. Michigan Avenue
Chicago, IL 60604
312-922-2400; fax: 312-922-3127;
    800-621-0561
    9,000 radio and 1,300 TV

Book Marketing No-Frills Data
Ad-Lib Publications
51½ W. Adams Street
P.O. Box 1102
Fairfield, IA 52556-1102
515-472-6617; fax: 515-472-3186;
    800-669-0773
    book wholesalers, catalogs, book
    clubs, etc.

Book Publishers Resource Guide
Ad-Lib Publications
51½ West Adams Street
Fairfield, IA 52556
515-472-6617; fax: 515-472-3186;
    800-669-0773
    book wholesalers, catalogs, book
    clubs, media, etc.

Broadcasting and Cablecasting Yearbook
Broadcasting Publications
1735 DeSales Street N.W.
Washington, DC 20036-4480
202-638-1022
    radio and television stations (United
    States and Canada)

Business to Business Catalogs
Grey House Publishing
Pocket Knife Square
P.O. Box 1866
Lakeville, CT 06039
203-435-0868; fax: 203-435-0867;
    800-562-2139
    4,300 business catalogs

Cable Contacts
BPI Media Services
P.O. Box 2015
Lakewood, NJ 08701-9896

201-363-5633; 800-336-3533
575 cable TV networks and services

Catalog of Catalogs
Woodbine House
5615 Fishers Lane
Rockville, MD 20852
301-468-8800; 800-843-7323
12,000 catalog listings

The Catalogue's Catalogue
Information Publications
308 Hunters Run Lane
Mount Juliet, TN 37122
615-758-0088

Direct Marketing Market Place
Hilary House Publishers
980 N. Federal Highway, #206
Boca Raton, FL 33432
resources, catalogs, services, etc.

Directory of Book Printers
Ad-Lib Publications
51½ W. Adams Street
P.O. Box 1102
Fairfield, IA 52556-1102
515-472-6617; fax: 515-472-3186;
800-669-0773
1,000 book, catalog, and magazine
printers

Directory of Mail Order Catalogs
Grey House Publishing
Pocket Knife Square
P.O. Box 1866
Lakeville, CT 06039
203-435-0868; fax: 203-435-0867
800-562-2139
6,300 mail order catalogs

Directory of Major Mailers and What They Mail
Morgan Rand/Who's Mailing What
P.O. Box 8180
Stamford, CT 06905
203-329-1996; fax: 203-322-5009
4,000 mailers

Directory of Seed & Nursery Catalogs
National Gardening Association
180 Flynn Avenue
Burlington, VT 05401
802-863-1308
400 gardening mail order catalogs

Directory of Weekly Newspapers
National Newspaper Association
1627 K Street N.W., #400

Washington, DC 20006-1702
202-466-7200
weekly newspapers

Editor and Publisher Yearbook
Editor and Publisher
11 West 19th Street
New York, NY 10011-4236
212-752-7050
newspapers

Gale Directory of Publications and Broadcast Media
Gale Research Company
835 Penobscot Building
Detroit, MI 48226-4094
313-961-2242; fax: 313-961-6083;
800-877-4253
35,000 media

Gardening by Mail: A Source Book
Tusker Press
P.O. Box 1338
Sebastopol, CA 95473
1,200 gardening catalogs,
magazines, etc.

Great Book of Catalogs
Pinkerton Marketing
209 Change Street
New Bern, NC 28560-4906
consumer catalogs

How to Sell to Mail Order Catalogs
Ad-Lib Publications
51½ West Adams
P.O. Box 1102
Fairfield, IA 52556-1102
515-472-6617; fax: 515-472-3186;
800-669-0773
550 catalogs that carry books

Hudson's Newsletter Directory
Newsletter Clearinghouse
44 West Market Street
Rhinebeck, NY 12572-1403
914-876-2081
4,000 subscription newsletters

International Publicity Checker
R. H. Bacon Company
332 S. Michigan Avenue
Chicago, IL 60604
312-992-2400; fax: 312-922-3127;
800-621-0561
13,000 magazines and 1,000
newspapers

Kid's Catalog Collection
Globe Pequot Press
138 W. Main Street
P.O. Box Q
Chester, CT 06412
203-526-9571; fax: 203-526-2655
    400 kids' catalogs

Madison Avenue Handbook
Peter Glenn Publications
17 East 48th Street
New York, NY 10017-1046
800-223-1254
    sources for advertising
    professionals

Mail Order Business Directory
Todd Publications
18 N. Greenbush Road
West Nyack, NY 10994
914-358-6213; fax: 914-358-6213
    10,000 catalogs and mail order
    firms

The Mail Order Gardener
Harper Perennial
10 East 53d Street
New York, NY 10022
212-207-7000; 800-242-7737
    1500 gardening catalogs, maga-
    zines, etc.

Mature Market Finder Binder
P.O. Box 90279
San Diego, CA 92109-0279
619-272-1630
    450 media for mature adults

National Associations of the U.S.
Gale Research Company
835 Penobscot Building
Detroit, MI 48226-4094
313-961-2242; fax: 313-961-6083;
    800-877-4253
    19,500 associations

National Avocational Organizations
Columbia Books
1212 New York Avenue N.W., #330
Washington, DC 20005-3920
202-898-0662
    2,500 hobby, sporting, and cultural
    associations

National Directory of Catalogs
Oxbridge Communications
150 Fifth Avenue, #636
New York, NY 10011-4311

212-741-0231; fax: 212-633-2938
    7,000 catalogs

National Directory of Magazines
Oxbridge Communications
150 Fifth Avenue, #636
New York, NY 10011-4311
212-741-0231; fax: 212-633-2938
    12,000 magazines

National Directory of Mailing Lists
Oxbridge Communications
150 Fifth Avenue, #636
New York, NY 10011-4311
212-741-0231; fax: 212-633-2938
    30,000 mailing lists

National Directory of Newsletter and
    Reporting Services
Gale Research Company
835 Penobscot Building
Detroit, MI 48226-4094
313-961-2242; fax: 313-961-6083;
    800-877-4253
    newsletters and reporting services

National Trade & Professional Associations of
    the U.S.
Columbia Books
1212 New York Avenue N.W., #330
Washington, DC 20005-3920
202-898-0662
    associations

Oxbridge Newsletter Directory
Oxbridge Communications
150 Fifth Avenue, #636
New York, NY 10011-4311
212-741-0231; fax: 212-633-2938
    newsletters

PR FLASH No-Frills Database
Ad-Lib Publications
51½ W. Adams Street
P.O. Box 1102
Fairfield, IA 52556-1102
515-472-6617; fax: 515-472-3186;
    800-669-0773
    11,500 media

Senior Media Guide
CD Publications
8204 Fenton Street
Silver Spring, MD 20910
301-588-6380; fax: 301-588-6385;
    800-666-6380
    200 publications

Standard Periodical Directory
Oxbridge Communications

150 Fifth Avenue, #636
New York, NY 10011-4311
212-741-0231; fax: 212-633-2938
   78,000 magazines and newsletters

Standard Rate & Data Service
3004 Glenview Road
Wilmette, IL 60091-3065
708-256-8333; 800-323-4588
   Advertising Options Plus (out-of-home
   advertising opportunities)
   Business Publications Rates & Data
   Canadian Advertising Rates & Data
   Community Publications Rates & Data
   Consumer Magazines Rates & Data
   Hispanic Media and Markets
   Newspaper Rates & Data
   Spot Radio Rates & Data
   Spot Television Rates & Data

State & Regional Associations
Columbia Books
1212 New York Avenue N.W., #330
Washington, DC 20005-3920
202-898-0662
   regional associations

Who's Who in Direct Marketing Creative
   Services
Morgan Rand/Who's Mailing What
P.O. Box 8180
Stamford, CT 06905
   203-329-1996; fax: 203-322-5009

Working Press of the Nation
National Research Bureau
225 W. Wacker Drive, #2275
Chicago, IL 60604
800-456-4555
   all media, 5 volumes

DISKETTES, ADVERTISING COMPUTER

CompuDoc Inc.
1090 King George Post Road, #808
Edison, NJ 08837
201-417-1799

E.A.S.I.
J. G. Sandom
6 West 18th Street
New York, NY 10011
212-627-0970

The SoftAd Group
Paula George
207 Second Street

Sausalito, CA 94965
415-332-4704

FULFILLMENT SERVICES

ARM Fulfillment
180 S. Union Street
Battle Creek, MI 49017
616-968-2221; fax: 616-968-0340;
   800-562-9733
   promotional printing and fulfilment

Automated Resources Group
21 Philips Parkway
Montvale, NJ 07645
201-391-1500
   product and subscription fulfillment

Automatic Fulfillment Services
8 S. Morris Street
P.O. Box 305
Dover, NJ 07801
   circulation fulfillment

BSA Fulfillment Services
475 Oberlin Avenue S.
Lakewood, NJ 08701
908-905-7892
   catalog fulfillment

Burch Inc.
300 Riverview Drive
Benton Harbor, MI 49022
616-925-2121; 800-999-7212
   complete fulfillment services

Clover House
33 S. Maple Avenue
Park Ridge, NJ 07656
201-391-1305
   literature and product fulfillment

Directel
4151 Executive Parkway, #190
Westerville, OH 43081
614-383-5231
   direct mail fulfillment

Express Fulfillment Services
2515 East 43d Street
Chattanooga, TN 37406
615-867-9081
   full service fulfillment

Fosdick Corporation
500 S. Broad Street
Meriden, CT 06450
203-235-5558; fax: 203-238-9951;
   800-759-5558

Fulfillment Corporation of America
205 W. Center Street
Marion, OH 43302-3707
614-383-5231
    order processing and fulfillment

Georgetown Book Warehouse
34 Armstrong Avenue
Georgetown, Ontario L7G 4R9, Canada
416-792-8806
    Canadian fulfillment service,
    customs

JCI Data Processing
1911 Rowland Street
Riverton, NJ 08077
609-786-1160
    circulation fulfillment

Kistler
4000 Dahlia Street
Denver, CO 80216
    800-523-5485

Maxway Data Corporation
225 West 34th Street, #1105
New York, NY 10001
212-947-6100
    warehousing and fulfillment

Metro Services Inc.
6 Ram Ridge Road
Spring Valley, NY 10977
914-352-3900
    fulfillment services

Midpoint National
2215 Harrison
Kansas City, MO 64108
    fulfillment services for products,
    premiums, and inquiries

National Fulfillment Services
Holmes Corporate Center
100 Pine Avenue
Holmes, PA 19043-1484
215-532-4700; 800-345-8112
    fulfillment for books and magazines

Package Fulfillment Center
1744 Goldbach Avenue
Ronkonkoma, NY 11779
516-737-3000; fax: 516-737-3011
    all fulfillment services

Personal Reminders
777 Commerce Drive
Fairfield, CT 06430
203-371-6111; fax: 203-371-0626

Progressive Distribution Service
5505 36th
Grand Rapids, MI 49512
616-957-5900
    fulfillment services

RJV Computer Resources
135 Wood Road
Braintree, MA 02184
    circulation fulfillment (5,000
    to 100,000)

Sisk Fulfillment Service
P.O. Box 463
Federalsburg, MD 21632
301-754-8141

USA Fulfillment
P.O. Box 67
Church Hill, MD 21623
301-758-0803
    order processing and fulfillment

LAWYERS, DIRECT MARKETING

Winston & Morrone
18 East 41st Street
New York, NY 10017
212-532-2700

LETTERSHOPS

Lettershops can fold, insert, seal, affix
postage, sort, bag, and deliver the mail
to the post office.

David J. Thompson Mailing Corporation
85 Denton Avenue
New Hyde Park, NY 11040
212-869-4390; 516-352-7400

Direct Mail Services Inc.
P.O. Box 5000
Dover, NJ 07802-5000
201-328-2800

Focus Direct
301 N. Frio
P.O. Box 7789
San Antonio, TX 78207-0789
512-227-9185; 800-628-2528

The Inkwell
5190 N. W. 167th Street, #112

Miami, FL 33014
305-524-2747
     calligraphy, handwritten addresses

The Mail House
San Francisco, CA
800-350-3525

Mailing Services Inc.
1319 N. Broad Street
Hillside, NJ 07205
908-355-2300

Quality Letter Service
22 West 32d Street
New York, NY 10001
212-268-3400

Spring Hill Laser Services
79 Spring Hill Road
Sterling, PA 18463
717-689-0970

MAGAZINES, DIRECT MARKETING

Advertising Age
Valerie Mackie, Managing Editor
Crain Communications
740 N. Rush Street
Chicago, IL 60611-2590
312-649-5200

Adweek
Norren O'Leary, Managing Editor
49 East 21st Street
New York, NY 10010-6213
212-995-7323; fax: 212-529-7845

Adweek's Marketing Week
Rinker Buck, Editor
49 East 21st Street
New York, NY 10010-6213
212-995-7323; fax: 212-260-7919

Business Marketing
Steve Yahn, Editor
Crain Communications
740 N. Rush Street
Chicago, IL 60611-2590
312-649-5260; fax: 312-649-5462

Business Marketing Note Pad
Bernard Goldberg, Editor
1304 University Drive
Yardley, PA 19067
215-321-3068

Business to Business
Byron De Arakal, Editor
17222 Armstrong
Irvine, CA 92714
714-852-9300

Catalog Age
Laura Christiana, Editor
Six River Bend Center
911 Hope Street
P.O. Box 4949
Stamford, CT 06907-0949
203-358-9900; fax: 203-357-9014

Catalog Newsletter
11 West 42d Street
New York, NY 10036

Classified Communication
Agnes Franz, Editor
P.O. Box 4242
Prescott, AZ 86302-4242
602-778-6788; fax: 602-778-5447

Direct Magazine
Judy Evens, Managing Editor
Six River Bend Center
911 Hope Street
P.O. Box 4949
Stamford, CT 06907-0949
203-358-9900; fax: 203-357-9014

Direct Marketing
Gary Wojtas, Associate Editor
224 Seventh Street
Garden City, NY 11530-5771
516-746-6700; fax: 516-294-8141

Direct Marketing International
Boundary House
91-93 Charterhouse Street
London EC1M 6HR, England
071-250-0646; fax: 071-250-0637

Direct Response Newsletter
Kent Komae, Editor
Creative Direct Marketing Group
1815 W. 213th Street, #210
Torrance, CA 90501
213-212-5727

Direct Response Specialist
Galen Stilson, Editor
Stilson & Stilson
4036 Mermoor Court
Palm Harbor, FL 34685
813-786-1411

DM News
Ray Schultz, Editor
Mill Hollow Corporation
19 West 21st Street
New York, NY 10010-6805
212-741-2095; fax: 212-633-9367

4th Media Journal
Allen Weiner, Editor
Virgo Publishing
4141 N. Scottsdale Road, #316
Scottsdale, AZ 85251
602-990-1101; fax: 602-990-0819

The Gary Halbert Letter
Gary Halbert, Editor
423 Front Street, 2d Floor
Key West, FL 33040
305-294-8425; fax: 305-296-2296

Inbound/Outbound
Cameron Ives, Editor
Telecom Library
12 West 21st Street
New York, NY 10010
212-691-8215; fax: 212-691-1191

Journal of Business-to-Business Marketing
David Wilson, Editor
707-D Business Administration
   Building
Pennsylvania State University
University Park, PA 16802
607-722-2493; fax: 607-722-1424

Mail Order Briefings
Robert Teague, Editor
Teague Publishing Group
P.O. Box 14689
Dayton, OH 45413

Mail Order Digest
Paul Muchnick, Editor
National Mail Order Association
3875 Wilshire Boulevard, #604
Los Angeles, CA 90010
213-380-3686

Mail Profits Magazine
Gerald Carson, Editor
Carson Services Inc.
P.O. Box 4785
Lincoln, NE 68504
402-467-4230; fax: 402-467-4292

Mailing List Tidbits
Wayne Stoler, Editor
Letter Perfect Word Processing
4205 Menlo Drive
Baltimore, MD 21215
301-358-8973; fax: 301-764-0324

Newsletter on Newsletters
Paul Swift, Editor
Newsletter Clearinghouse
44 W. Market Street
P.O. Box 311
Rhinebeck, NY 12572-0311
914-876-2081; fax: 914-876-2561

Promo
Kerry J. Smith, Managing Editor
Smith Communications
47 Old Ridgefield Road
Wilton, CT 06897
203-761-1510; fax: 203-761-1522

Sales and Marketing Management
Louise Driben, Executive Editor
Bill Communications
633 Third Avenue
New York, NY 10017-6743
212-986-4800

Target Marketing
Mindy Drucker, Managing Editor
North American Publishing
401 N. Broad Street
Philadelphia, PA 19108-1074
215-238-5300; fax: 215-238-5457

Telemarketing
Linda Driscoll, Editor
Technology Marketing Corporation
One Technology Plaza
Norwalk, CT 06854-1924
203-852-6800; fax: 203-853-2845

TeleProfessional
Robert Van Voorhis, Jr., Editor
209 W. Fifth Street, #N
Waterloo, IA 50701-5420
319-235-4473; fax: 319-235-9850

Venture Views n News
Donna Cardillo, Editor
Venture Communications
114 East 32d Street, #1700
New York, NY 10016
212-684-4800; fax: 212-576-1129

Who's Mailing What
Denison Hatch, Editor
P.O. Box 8180
Stamford, CT 06905
203-329-1996; fax: 203-322-5009

MAIL MONITORS

Direct Mail Trackers
1001 Avenue of the Americas

New York, NY 10018
212-719-4626

Federal Monitoring Service
2 Horizon Drive
Fort Lee, NJ 07024
201-487-2845

Litle & Company
List Services Division
54 Stiles Road
Salem, NH 03079-2845
603-893-9333

U.S. Monitor Service
86 Maple Avenue
New City, NY 10956
914-634-1331

MAILING LISTS

Action Markets
1710 Highway 35
Ocean, NJ 07755
201-531-2212
    schools and teachers

ADCO List Management Services
Alan Drey Company
245 Fifth Avenue
New York, NY 10016
212-779-3650
    list managers

ADCO List Management Services
333 N. Michigan Avenue, #1725
Chicago, IL 60601-3901
312-236-8508
    list managers

AZ Marketing Services Inc.
31 River Road
Cos Cob, CT 06807
203-629-8088; 203-661-3004

Ad-Lib Lists
51½ West Adams
P.O. Box 1102
Fairfield, IA 52556
515-472-6617; fax: 515-472-3186;
    800-669-0773
    publicity outlets, wholesalers,
    printers, publishers, visitor bureaus

Aggressive List Management
3355 N. Arlington Heights Road

Arlington Heights, IL 60004-1437
708-577-4455
    list managers

AllMedia Inc.
4965 Preston Park Boulevard, #300
Plano, TX 75093
214-985-4060
    list managers

Alvin B. Zeller Inc.
224 Fifth Avenue
New York, NY 10001
212-689-4900; 800-223-0814
    catalog available

American Bar Association
Attn: List Manager
750 N. Lake Shore Drive
Chicago, IL 60611
312-988-5435
    official ABA lists

American Business Lists
P.O. Box 27347
5707 S. 86th Circle
Omaha, NE 68127-4146
402-331-7169; fax: 402-331-1505
    business lists compiled from yellow
    pages

American Direct Marketing Service
1120 Empire Central Place, #300
Dallas, TX 75247
800-527-5080
    763,000 businesses

American List Counsel
88 Orchard Road
Princeton, NJ 08540-8019
201-874-4300; 800-526-3973
    catalog available; list managers

American Student List Company
98 Cutter Mill Road, #347
Great Neck, NY 11021-3080
516-466-0602
    student lists (all grades)

Antigone Associates
51 Declaration Drive
Newtown, PA 18940
215-968-1619
    rural markets

Behavior Bank
Household Targeting Inc.
2200 Fletcher Avenue
Fort Lee, NJ 07024
201-586-8900

Bernice Bush Springdale Lists
15052 Springdale Street
Huntington Beach, CA 92649-1178
714-891-3344
　religious and general lists; list
　managers

Best Mailing Lists
38 West 32d Street
New York, NY 10001-3806
212-868-1080; 800-692-2378
　10 million business names, 82
　million consumers

Business Mailers Inc.
640 N. LaSalle Drive
Chicago, IL 60610-3794
312-943-6666; 800-888-8717;
　fax: 312-943-7509
　doctors and dentists

CMP Direct Marketing Services
600 Community Drive
Manhasset, NY 11030-3825
516-365-4600; 800-645-6278

CW Lists
Deb Goldstein, List Manager
5 Chrysler Road
Natick, MA 01760
617-879-0700
　computer lists

California Business Lists
19355 Business Center Drive, #7
Northridge, CA 91324
800-545-2254; CA: 800-899-8495
　business lists

Catholic Lists
100 Stevens Avenue, #410
Mount Vernon, NY 10550
914-668-7320
　Catholics lists

Channing L. Bete Company
200 State Road
South Deerfield, MA 01373
413-665-7611
　leaders in all fields

Charles Crane Associates
2050 Center Avenue
Fort Lee, NJ 07024
201-944-2240
　list managers

College Marketing Group
50 Cross Street
Winchester, MA 01890

617-729-7865; fax: 617-729-8413
　college faculty

Columbia House Lists
51 West 52d Street
New York, NY 10019-6101
212-445-4292
　Columbia House lists and package
　insert program

Compilers Plus
466 Main Street
New Rochelle, NY 10801
914-633-5240; 800-431-2914
　catalog available

Conrad Direct
80 West Street
Englewood, NJ 07631
201-567-3200
　list managers

Consolidated Mailing Service
Max Bradbard, Two Star Films
P.O. Box 495
Saint James, NY 11780
516-584-7283
　schools

Coolidge Company
25 West 43d Street
New York, NY 10036-7491
212-642-0300
　list brokers

CorpTech
12 Alfred Street, #200
Woburn, MA 01801
617-932-3939; 800-333-8036
　computer lists

Craver, Mathews, Smith & Company
300 N. Washington Street, #200
Falls Church, VA 22046
703-237-0600
　list managers

Curriculum Information Center
1020 15th Street, #42-C
Denver, CO 80202-2348
　school lists

Custom List Services
Three Metro Plaza, 107
8300 Professional Place
Landover, MD 20785
301-459-9885

D-J Associates
77 Danbury Road

Ridgefield, CT 06877
203-431-8777; fax: 203-431-3302
  list managers

Data Services
818 Brown Street
Salisbury, MD 21801
301-546-2206
  list managers

Demographic Systems
2 Executive Drive
Fort Lee, NJ 07024-3393
  catalog available

Dillon Agnew Marton
345 Park Avenue South, 8th Floor
New York, NY 10010
212-685-4600
  international lists

Direct Communications Corporation
24 Wales Street
Rutland, VT 05701
802-747-3322
  list managers

Direct Marketing Services
11 West 42d Street
New York, NY 10036
212-768-7277; fax: 212-599-1268

Direct Media List Management
200 Pemberwick Road
P.O. Box 4565
Greenwich, CT 06830
203-532-1000

Donnelley Marketing
70 Seaview Avenue
P.O. Box 10250
Stamford, CT 06904
203-353-7000; 800-433-LIST
  senior life-style lists, others

Dudley Jenkins Associates
77 St. John Street
London EC1M 4HH, England
01-250-1171
  international lists

Dun & Bradstreet Canada
4900 Yonge Street
Toronto, Ontario M5B 2E7, Canada
416-925-2861
  Canadian lists

Dun's Educational Directory
Dun's Marketing Services
3 Sylvan Way

Parsippany, NJ 07054
201-455-0900; 800-624-5669
  faculty, schools, and libraries

Dunhill International List
1100 Park Central Boulevard S.
Pompano Beach, FL 33064
305-974-7800

Ed Burnett Company
99 W. Sheffield Avenue
Englewood, NJ 07631-4804
201-871-1100; 800-223-7777
  list managers

Edith Roman Associates
875 Avenue of the Americas, #1603
New York, NY 10001-3592
212-695-3836; 800-223-2194
  catalog available

Education Mailings Clearinghouse
601 E. Marshall Street
P.O. Box 295
Sweet Springs, MO 65351
816-335-6373
  schools and teachers

Elsevier Business Lists
301 Gibralter Drive
Morris Plains, NJ 07950
201-361-9060
  business and computer lists

Executive Services Companies
Consumer List Division
901 N. International Parkway, #191
Richardson, TX 75081-2848
214-699-1271; 800-527-3933

Flynn Direct Response
62 Spring Hill Road
P.O. Box 759
Trumbull, CT 06611
203-452-1919
  list managers

Fred E. Allen Inc.
Allencrest Building
P.O. Box 1595
Mount Pleasant, TX 75455-1595
214-572-1701

Fred Woolf List Company
6 Corporate Park Drive
White Plains, NY 10604
914-694-4466; fax: 914-694-1710;
  800-431-1557
  catalog available

GMI/Uni-Mail Commercial
352 Park Avenue South
New York, NY 10010-1709
212-679-7000
 list manager for mail order and
 subscribers

Gary Slaughter Corporation
7101 Wisconsin Avenue, #1001
Bethesda, MD 20814
301-986-0840
 business and government executives

George-Mann Associates
20 Lake Drive
P.O. Box 930
Hightstown, NJ 08520-0930
609-443-1330
 list managers

Gnames Enterprises
1431 Green Way, #110
Irving, TX 75019
214-550-1140
 list managers

Greenfield Direct Response
3355 N. Arlington Heights Road
Arlington Heights, IL 60004
708-577-1540
 list broker

Hugo Dunhill Mailing Lists
630 Third Avenue
New York, NY 10017-6772
212-682-8030; 800-223-6454
 catalog available

IBIS Information Services
152 Madison Avenue, #803
New York, NY 10016-5424
212-779-1344; 800-433-6226
 international lists

IGL Direct Lists
4901 N. 57th Street
P.O. Box 5059
Lincoln, NE 68505-0266
402-466-8400
 business, medical, legal

Interface Group
300 First Avenue
Needham, MA 02194
617-449-6600
 business, computer lists

JAMI Marketing Services
2 Bluehill Plaza
Pearl River, NY 10965
914-620-0700

The Kaplan Agency
11 Forest Street
New Canaan, CT 06840
203-972-3600
 list managers

The Kleid Company
530 Fifth Avenue, 17th Floor
New York, NY 10036-5101
212-819-3400; fax: 212-719-9788
 catalog available; list managers

La Paz Computer & List Service
P.O. Box 4399
Santa Barbara, CA 93140-4399
805-966-1761
 government agencies

The Lake Group/Names in the News
Cowperwood-Osburn Building
411 Theodore Fremd Avenue
Rye, NY 10580-1497
914-925-2400; CompuName:
 914-925-2401
 list managers

Lakewood Publications Direct Mail Lists
50 S. Ninth Street
Minneapolis, MN 55402-3165
800-328-4329
 subscribers to trade magazines

Leland Company
1801 W. Leland Avenue
Chicago, IL 60640
312-561-4005; 800-621-5463
 business lists

Leon Henry Inc.
455 Central Avenue, #315
Scarsdale, NY 10583-1093
914-723-3176
 list managers

Lifestyle Change Marketing
5885 Glenridge Drive, #159
Atlanta, GA 30328
404-252-0554
 2.7 million retired people

List America Inc.
1202 Potomac Street N.W.
Washington, DC 20007
202-298-9206
 charitable and donor lists

List Brokerage and Management
145 Huguenot Street
New Rochelle, NY 10801
914-654-8900
 list managers

List Locators & Managers
5750 West 95th Street, #302
Overland Park, KS 66207
913-649-9362
    list managers

List Marketing Limited
247 Mill Street
Greenwich, CT 06830
203-531-0033

List Media International Ltd.
Media House, Weston Road
Slough, Berkshire, SL1 4HP, England
44-753-71011
    international lists

List Services Corporation
6 Trowbridge Drive
P.O. Box 516
Bethel, CT 06801
203-743-2600
    list managers

List Technology Systems Group
1001 Avenue of the Americas
New York, NY 10018
212-719-3850
    business and computer lists

Listco Mailing Lists
1 Haynes Avenue
Newark, NJ 07114
201-802-1893
    list managers

ListLine
50 Cross Street
Winchester, MA 01890
617-729-2757; fax: 617-729-8413
    list managers

Lists International
Accredited Mailing Lists
7316 Wisconsin Avenue, #220
Bethesda, MD 20814
202-652-8096
    business/international lists, list
    managers

Listworks Corporation
One Campus Drive
Pleasantville, NY 10570-1602
914-241-1900

MEDEC List Marketing
Medical Economics Company
5 Paragon Drive
Montbelle, NJ 07645
201-358-7200
    international medical mailing lists

Maclean-Hunter DM Services
481 University Avenue
Toronto M5W 1A7 ON, Canada
    business, science, medical,
    professionals

Mail Communications Inc.
721 Olive Street, #1200
Saint Louis, MO 63101-2235
314-241-5408; 800-325-7942
    religious lists

Mail Marketing Inc.
171 Terrace Street
Haworth, NJ 07641
201-387-1010
    list managers

Mailing List User Program
Superintendent of Documents
P.O. Box 1908
Washington, DC 20013-1908
202-275-3836
    35 government subscriber lists

Mailing Lists Asia
9/F Nin Lee Commercial Building
45 Lyndhurst Terrace
Central Hong Kong 5-430556
    international lists

Mal Dunn Associates
Hardscrabble Road
Croton Falls, NY 10519-9999
914-277-5558
    business/international lists, list
    managers

Management Associates
4676 Admiralty Way, #421
Marina Del Rey, CA 90292
213-822-4911

Mardev S. A. International Lists
9, rue Charles-Humbert
CH-1205 Geneva, Switzerland
022/28 75 36
    international lists

Market Data Retrieval
16 Progress Drive
P.O. Box 2117
Shelton, CT 06484-9990
800-243-5538
    schools and libraries

Market Street Lists
26 Millyard
Amesbury, MA 01913
508-388-6723
    list managers

Marketing Communications
10605 West 84th Terrace
Lenexa, KS 66214
913-492-1575; 800-821-5536
    sweepstakes list

Marketing Services International
625 N. Michigan Avenue
Chicago, IL 60611
312-642-1620
    list managers

Master Lists/Phelon, Sheldon & Marsar
15 Industrial Avenue
Fairview, NJ 07022
201-941-8804; 800-234-8804
    many business lists

Media Marketplace
6 Penns Trail
P.O. Box 500
Newtown, PA 18940-0500
215-968-5020
    list managers

Media Masters
51 Madison Avenue
New York, NY 10016
212-696-1244
    lists and package inserts

Medical Industry Direct Corporation
1 Lincoln Square Plaza
New York, NY 10023-7129
212-679-7000
    500,000 doctors, 680,000 others

Meredith List Marketing
1716 Locust Street
Des Moines, IA 50336-0001
515-284-2891

Metromail
901 West Bond Street
Lincoln, NE 68521-3694
402-475-4591
    consumers, students, newlyweds

Micro/Personal Computer Lists
40 Welles Avenue
Dorchester, MA 02124
617-825-8895; fax: 617-288-2999
    computers

Micromedia Ltd
158 Pearl Street
Toronto, Ontario M5H 1L3, Canada
416-593-5211
    Canadian libraries

Mike Wilson List Counsel
12120 Washington Boulevard
Los Angeles, CA 90066-5502
213-398-2754; 800-445-2089
    general, education, and family lists

Millard Group
10 Vose Farm Road
Peterborough, NH 03458
603-924-9262
    list managers

Name Finders
253 West 28th Street, #409
New York, NY 10001
212-239-0484; 800-228-8939
    list managers

Name Finders Lists
3180 18th Street
San Francisco, CA 94110
415-553-4177; 800-221-5009
    list managers

National Direct Marketing
1900 Quail Street
Newport Beach, CA 92660-2302
714-476-1154

National Fundraising Lists
2A Village Green
Crofton, MD 21114
301-721-5700

New Age Mailing Lists
P.O. Box 970
Santa Cruz, NM 87567
505-753-5086; fax: 505-753-9249
    list managers

North American List Marketing
20 Maple Avenue
Armonk, NY 10504-1824
914-273-8620
    political and charitable lists

The Other List Company
P.O. Box 286
Matawan, NJ 07747
201-591-1180

P&L Direct Marketing Group
4640 Lankershim Boulevard
North Hollywood, CA 91602
818-762-0036
    list managers

PCS Mailing List Company
85 Constitution Lane

Danvers, MA 01923
508-777-3332; 800-532-5478

Pacific Lists
131 Camino Alto, #D
Mill Valley, CA 94941-2295
415-381-0826
 list managers

Patterson's Mailing Lists
P.O. Box 199
Mount Prospect, IL 60056
 school directories

Postal Promotions
1100 Birchmont Road
Scarborough, Ontario M1K 5N9,
 Canada
416-752-8100; fax: 416-752-8239
 Canadian lists

Preferred Lists
5201 Leesburg Pike, #1007
Falls Church, VA 20041-3203
703-931-8000
 conservatives lists, list managers

Professional Mailing Lists
170 Fifth Avenue
New York, NY 10010-5911
 professionals and libraries

Qualified Lists Corporation
135 Bedford Road
Armonk, NY 10504-1831
914-273-6700

Quality Education Data
1600 Broadway
Denver, CO 80202
303-860-1852; 800-525-5811
 education buyers

R. L. Polk & Company
6400 Monroe Boulevard
Taylor, MI 48180
313-292-3200

RMI Direct Marketing
Johnson Publishing Company
4 Skyline Drive
Hawthorne, NY 10532
914-347-4949
 businesses and professionals

Religious Lists
86 Maple Avenue
New City, NY 10956-5019
914-634-8724-; 800-431-5303
 religious lists

Research Projects Corporation
4 S. Pomperaug Avenue
Woodbury, CT 06798
203-263-0100; 800-243-4360
 free catalog available; business and
 general

Roman Managed Lists
20 Squadron Boulevard, 6th Floor
New City, NY 10956
914-638-2530; 914-638-2631;
 800-322-5478
 list managers

Rubin Response Services
1111 Plaza Drive, 8th Floor
Schaumburg, IL 60173
 list manager

SmartNames Inc.
800 W. Cummings Park, #4400
Woburn, MA 01801
617-890-8900

Southam Direct Marketing Service
12 Nantucket Boulevard
Scarborough, Ontario M1P 4W7,
 Canada
416-759-4711
 Canadian lists; catalag available

The SpeciaLISTS
120 East 16th Street, Floor 12
New York, NY 10003-2150
212-677-6760
 catalog available; list managers

Taybi Direct
2560 Ninth Street, #317B
Berkeley, CA 94710
415-548-9181; fax: 415-548-1317
 business-to-business lists

Thor Lists
P.O. Box 158
Great Neck, NY 11022-0158
516-829-5151
 1,200 lists

Total Media Concepts
222 Cedar Lane
Teaneck, NJ 07666
201-692-0018

TransMark Inc.
555 West Adams
Chicago, IL 60661
312-431-5101
 new residents lists

Triangle Direct
P.O. Box 51637
Durham, NC 27717
919-683-1788
    medical lists

Twenty First Century Marketing
2 Dubon Court
Farmingdale, NY 11735
516-293-8550; fax: 516-293-8974
    list managers

Venture Communications
60 Madison Avenue, 3d Floor
New York, NY 10010
212-684-4800; fax: 212-545-1680
    list managers

W. S. Ponton Inc.
Ponton Building
5149 Butler Street
Pittsburgh, PA 15201-2606
412-782-2360; 800-628-7806
    business lists

Williams-Sonoma Mailing Lists
100 North Point Street
San Francisco, CA 94133
415-421-7900
    719,000 buyers from their catalogs

Woodruff-Stevens & Associates
345 Park Avenue South
New York, NY 10010-1707
212-685-4600
    list managers

World Innovators
72 Park Street
New Canaan, CT 06840
203-966-0374; fax: 203-966-0926
    international lists; list managers

Worldata
5200 Town Center Circle
Boca Raton, FL 33486
407-393-8200; fax: 407-368-8345
    general/international lists, list
    managers

Zeller & Letica
15 East 26th Street, #1708
New York, NY 10010-1567
212-685-7512; 800-221-4112
    catalog available, list managers

PLANNING CHARTS

Magna Visual
9400 Watson Road

Saint Louis, MO 63126
fax: 314-843-0000; 800-843-3399
    magnetic planning boards

PRINTING

For catalog printers, see the *Directory of Book Printers*

Action Graphics Network
14 East 4th Street, #604
New York, NY 10012
212-505-0400; fax: 212-505-6572
    inserts, brochures, catalogs, direct
    mail packages

American Webforms
Noble Street Extension
Kutztown, PA 19530
215-683-8848; 800-621-2121
    envelopes, padded forms

Amity Unlimited
531 N. Wayne Avenue
Cincinnati, OH 45215
513-554-4500; fax: 513-554-0450;
    800-544-2624
    direct mail packages

Amos Press/Direct Marketing
911 Vandemark Road
P.O. Box 150
Sidney, OH 45367
513-498-2111; 800-848-4406
    direct mail packages

Apollo Graphics
1085 Industrial Boulevard
Southampton, PA 18966
215-953-0500; fax: 215-953-1144;
    800-522-9006
    color catalog sheets, brochures

B&W Press
41 Pope's Lane
Danvers, MA 01923
508-774-2200
    bind-in envelopes

Business Envelope Manufacturers
900 Grand Boulevard
Deer Park, NY 11729
516-667-8500
    envelopes, letterhead

Caprice Printing Company
1655 Jarvis Avenue
Elk Grove, IL 60007

312-981-8650
direct mail packages

Catalog King
1 Entin Road
Clifton, NJ 07014
212-695-0711; 800-223-5751
color catalog sheets, brochures

Catalogs America
2911 Hunter Mill Road, #202
Oakton, VA 22124-9952
fax: 703-255-9857; 800-283-4666
color catalogs

CatalogueACE
Trade Litho Inc.
5301 N.W. 37th Avenue
Miami, FL 33142
305-633-9779; fax: 305-633-2848;
800-367-5871
color catalog sheets, brochures

Champion Printing and Mailing
3250 Spring Grove Avenue
Cincinnati, OH 45225
513-541-1100; 800-543-1957
self-mailers, catalogs

Color U.S. Inc.
4420A Commerce Circle
Atlanta, GA 30336
404-691-3201; 800-443-7377
color catalog sheets, brochures

ColorDirect Inc.
179 Spangler Avenue
Elmhurst, IL 60126-1523
312-279-7431; 800-828-3202
color two-way postcards

Colorlith Corporation
777 Hartford Avenue
Johnston, RI 02919
401-521-6000; 800-556-7171
color catalog sheets, brochures

Consolidated Printing & Envelope
502 Forest Avenue
Teaneck, NJ 07666
201-833-0268
direct mail packages

Direct Press Modern Litho
386 Oakwood Road
Huntington Station, NY 11746
516-271-7000; 800-645-5302
color catalog sheets, catalogs

Emergency Business Forms
6801 W. Howard Street

Niles, IL 60648
800-323-1479
direct mail packages

Envelope Marketing & Manufacturing
P.O. Box 74
Itasca, IL 60143
312-665-6606
printing of envelopes

Full-Color Graphics Inc.
P.O. Box 581
Plainview, NY 11803
516-937-0920; fax: 516-937-1547
800-323-5452
broker for color catalog sheets,
catalogs

Graphic Innovations
9 East 38th Street
New York, NY 10016
212-686-9123
snap-pak direct mail packages

Hi-Tech Color House
5901 N. Cicero Avenue
Chicago, IL 60646
312-478-3700; 800-621-4004
broker for color catalog sheets,
brochures

Insert Color Press
90 Air Park Drive
Ronkonkoma, NY 11779
516-981-3100; 800-356-3943
color inserts

Japs-Olson Company
30 N. 31st Avenue
Minneapolis, MN 55411
800-548-2897; fax: 612-522-3837
direct mail packages, catalogs

The Jemar Company
205 E. Ann Street
P.O. Box 460
Valdosta, GA 31603
912-244-1568; 800-841-4444
pads, brochures, and forms

Moore Response Marketing Service
1113 S. Milwaukee Avenue
Libertyville, IL 60048
708-680-0111; 800-722-9001
direct mail packages

MultiPrint Company
153 W. Ohio Street
Chicago, IL 60610
312-644-7910; 800-858-9999
color catalog sheets, catalogs

Nahan Printing Inc.
6380 Saukview Drive
P.O. Box 697
Saint Cloud, MN 56302
612-251-7611; fax: 612-259-1378
   direct mail printing

Ohio Valley Litho Color—Econocolor
   Catalog
7405 Industrial Road
Florence, KY 41042
606-525-7405; fax: 606-525-7654;
   800-877-7405
   color catalog sheets, catalogs

Parish Publications
760 Brooks Avenue
Rochester, NY 14619
716-328-7660
   direct mail packages

The Press Inc.
18780 West 78th Street
Chanhassen, MN 55317
612-937-9764; 800-336-2680
   color catalog sheets, brochures

Prestige Envelope
174 Marine Street
Farmingdale, NY 11735
516-249-5250; fax: 516-293-1068;
   800-835-1992

Rapidocolor Corporation
101 Brandywine Parkway
P.O. Box 2540
West Chester, PA 19380
215-344-0500; fax: 215-344-0506;
   800-872-7436
   color catalog sheets

Robert James Company
3600 7th Court South
P.O. Box 2726
Birmingham, AL 35202
800-633-8296
   envelopes and letterhead

Rotagraphics
1351 Conant
Dallas, TX 75207
214-634-2400
   bind-in envelopes and self-mailers

Service Web Offset
2568 S. Dearborn Street
Chicago, IL 60616
312-567-7000; 800-621-1567
   color catalog sheets, brochures

Tension Envelope Corporation
819 East 19th Street
Kansas City, MO 64108-1781
816-471-3800
   envelopes

U.S. Press
1628A James P. Rodgers Drive
P.O. Box 640
Valdosta, GA 31603-0640
912-244-5634; 800-227-7377
   color catalog sheets, brochures

Ultra Color Coporation
1814 Washington Avenue
Saint Louis, MO 63103
314-241-0300
   color catalog sheets, brochures

Unigraf Printers
511 North Main
East Longmeadow, MA 01028
413-732-3429
   envelopes

Valco Reproduction and Mailing
Hart Place
Brooklyn, NY 11224
718-372-0100
   direct mail packages

Web Specialties
401 S. Milwaukee Avenue
Wheeling, IL 60090
312-459-0800
   direct mail, envelopes, mini-catalogs

WebVelope Corporation
525 West 52d Street
New York, NY 10019
212-315-4713
   bind-in envelopes

RADIO COMMERCIALS

Dick Orkin's Radio Ranch
1140 N. LaBrea
Los Angeles, CA 90038
213-462-4966; fax: 213-856-4311

Hedquist Productions
1007 E. Madison
Fairfield, IA 52556
515-472-6708

RADIO REPS

Blair Radio
1190 Avenue of the Americas
New York, NY 10104-0101
212-603-5000

Caballero Spanish Radio
18 East 53d Street
New York, NY 10022-5202
212-223-6410

Hillier, Newmark, Wechsler & Howard
100 Park Avenue, 5th Floor
New York, NY 10017-5516
212-309-9000

Katz Radio
1 Dag Hammarskjold Plaza
New York, NY 10017-2289
212-572-5500

SERVICE BUREAUS

Service bureaus can provide
merge/purge output, NCOA
(National Change of Address) address
corrections, list enhancements, postal
presort optimization, database
modeling, and other services to make
mailings more effective.

Anchor Computer
1900 New Highway
Farmingdale, NY 11735
516-293-6100; 800-452-2357

Antares ITI
140 West 22d Street
New York, NY 10011
212-627-1400

Computer Strategy Coordinators
955 American Lane
Schaumburg, IL 60173-4971
708-330-1313

Creative Automation Company
220 Fenci Lane
Hillside, IL 60162-2098
708-449-2800

Fala Direct Marketing
70 Marcus Drive
Melville, NY 11747-4278
516-694-1919; fax: 516-694-7493

LCS Industries
120 Brighton Road
Clifton, NJ 07012
800-524-1388

Pagex Systems
77 W. Sheffield Avenue
Englewood, NJ 07631
201-871-0800

RMI Computer Services
4 Skyline Drive
Hawthorne, NY 10532
914-347-4949; fax: 914-347-2954

Sage Systems
4695 44th Street S.E.
Grand Rapids, MI 49512
616-940-8311; fax: 616-940-3383

SOFTWARE

Compass/Claritas
201 N. Union Street
Alexandria, VA 22314
703-683-8300
    product development software

The Controller+
Sigma/Micro Corporation
1238 N. Pennsylvania Street
Indianapolis, IN 46202
317-631-0907; 800-227-4462
    inventory control and catalog
    management

The Mail Order Accountant
Goldsmith & Associates
48 Shattuck Square, #86
Berkeley, CA 94704
415-540-8396
    mail order fulfillment software

The Mail Order Wizard
The Haven Corporation
802 Madison Street
Evanston, IL 60202
312-869-3434; 800-782-8278
    mail order fulfillment software

MailWorks Marketing Company
135 Vernon Road
Scituate, MA 02066
    list conditioning software

MarketPulse
Computer Corporation of America
4 Cambridge Center
Cambridge, MA 02142
617-492-8860

PostWare
Postalsoft Inc.
4439 Mormon Coulee Road
La Crosse, WI 54601-8220
608-788-8700
    mailing list software for postal
    discounts

Profile 90/Coral Companies
Prudential Plaza, 18th Floor
1050 17th Street
Denver, CO 80265
303-820-3000; 800-262-6275
    order processing software for mail
    order

Response/CoLinear Systems
1000 Johnson Ferry Road, #F-130
Marietta, GA 30067
404-578-0000
    order entry software for direct
    marketers

T.O.P.S. Software
P.O. Box 43161
Atlanta, GA 30336
404-949-4019
    mail order processing software

Tools for Sales
13335 Wildcrest Drive
Los Altos Hills, CA 94022
415-941-9191
    business and marketing plan
    software

SWEEPSTAKES

D. L. Blair
1051 Franklin Avenue
Garden City, NY 11530
516-746-3700

D-J Associates
77 Danbury Road
Ridgefield, CT 06877
203-431-8777; fax: 203-431-3302

Moore Response Marketing Services
Phil Brown
1113 S. Milwaukee Avenue

Libertyville, IL 60048
708-680-0111; 800-722-9001

Ventura Associates
1350 Avenue of the Americas
New York, NY 10019
212-586-9720; fax: 212-586-0844

TELEMARKETING

800-Connect
75 N. Main
P.O. Box 800
Driggs, ID 83422-0709
800-255-8989

Access 80 Answering Service
314 Fairmont Avenue
Fairmont, WV 26554
800-992-4045
    inbound telemarketing 800 number

Alert Communications
5515 York Boulevard
Los Angeles, CA 90042
800-333-7772
    outbound, 800 and 900 services

American Tele-Response Group
401 Pilgrim Lane
Drexel Hill, PA 19026
215-789-7000; 800-345-8501
    inbound and outbound services

Answer America
P.O. Box 435, Grand Central Station
New York, NY 10163
212-758-7664; 800-221-2145
    inbound and outbound
    telemarketing

Astro Marketing Services
5445 North 103d Street
Omaha, NE 68134
800-247-9999
    inbound telemarketing

AT&T American Transtech
Nick Covelli, Direct Marketing
    Services
8000 Baymeadows Way
Jacksonville, FL 32236
904-636-1128; 800-241-3354
    inbound and outbound
    telemarketing

Bayley Leighton & Ryan
355 East 50th Street

New York, NY 10012
212-888-0130; 800-288-4454
 outbound telemarketing, 800 lines

Britcom Telemarketing
2200 South Main
Lombard, IL 60148
708-932-7300
 outbound telemarketing

Budget Marketing
P.O. Box 1805
Des Moines, IA 50306
515-243-7000; 800-247-5000
 outbound telemarketing

Call Masters
6201 Frondosa Drive
Malibu, CA 90265
213-457-5601
 800 and 900 services

Centrac Telemarketing
48 Industrial Drive West
Clifton, NJ 07012
201-385-7171
 outbound telemarketing

Chicago Telemarketing Connection
380 Northwest Highway
Des Plaines, IL 60016
708-299-0400
 outbound and 800 services

Contact Telemarketing
120 Brighton Road
Clifton, NJ 07012
800-527-4669
 outbound, 800 and 900 services

Conversational Voice Technologies
4205 Grove Avenue
Gurnee, IL 60031
708-249-5560
 800 and 900 services

CRC Information Systems
435 Hudson Street
New York, NY 10014
212-620-5678
 outbound telemarketing

CSS Direct
313 North 30th Street
Omaha, NE 68131
402-341-3537
 outbound telemarketing

DialAmerica Marketing
960 Macarthur Boulevard

Mahwah, NJ 07495
201-837-7800; 800-531-3131
 outbound telemarketing, almost
 3,000 lines

The Direct Response Corporation
601 Skokie Boulevard
Northbrook, IL 60062
708-317-2320
 outbound telemarketing

Edward Blank Associates
71 West 23d Street, 8th Floor
New York, NY 10010
212-741-8133; 800-332-5265
 outbound telemarketing, 650
 outbound lines

Entertel
619 Massachusetts
Lawrence, KS 66044
913-841-1200
 outbound telemarketing

Executive Marketing Services
50 E. Shuman Boulevard, #300
Naperville, IL 60563-8473
708-355-3003; 800-367-7311
 telephone number lookup
 service

Grolier Telemarketing
Sherman Turnpike
Danbury, CT 06816
203-797-3106; 800-842-0014
 outbound telemarketing for
 magazines

Harte-Hanks Marketing Services
65 Route 4 East
River Edge, NJ 07661
201-342-6700
 outbound telemarketing

Heritage
2402 Wildwood Avenue
North Little Rock, AR 72116
800-633-1209
 outbound telemarketing

Hispanic Telemarketing
4550 N.W. Loop 410, #140
San Antonio, TX 78229
800-725-4672

ICR
605 W. State Street
Media, PA 19063-2620
215-565-9280
 outbound telemarketing

ICS—Integrated Customer Services
10509 Timberwood Circle, #101
Louisville, KY 40223
502-339-0339; fax: 502-339-0351;
    800-444-7487
    outbound telemarketing

ICT Group
800 Town Center Drive
Langhorne, PA 19047
215-757-0200; 800-535-3232
    outbound telemarketing, 750 lines

Idelman Telemarketing Inc.
7415 Dodge Street
Omaha, NE 68114
402-393-8000; 800-562-5000
    outbound telemarketing, 2,175 lines

Idelman Telemarketing Inc.
531 N. Wayne Avenue
Cincinnati, OH 45215
513-563-8666; 800-543-3005
    800 and 900 services

Impact Telemarketing
15 East Centre Street
Woodbury, NJ 08096
800-522-8446
    outbound and 800 services

Lester Telemarketing
19 Business Park Drive
Branford, CT 06405
203-488-5265
    outbound and 800 services

Mark Facey & Company
225 N. Main Street
Bristol, CT 06010
203-589-0221
    outbound, 800 and 900 services

Market Direct America
162 Wall Street
Princeton, NJ 08540
609-921-7200
    outbound and 800 services

Market Motivators
5201 W. Donges Bay Road
Mequon, WI 53092
414-242-9800
    outbound, 800 and 900 services

Market Track
2100 Powers Ferry Road
Atlanta, GA 30339
404-951-0681
    outbound telemarketing

Markline
P.O. Box 171
Belmont, MA 02178
617-891-8954; 800-343-8572
    inbound telemarketing, order
    fulfillment

Matrixx Marketing
One Matrixx Plaza
1300 West 4400 South
Ogden, UT 84405
801-629-6423; 800-543-6423
    inbound and outbound services,
    fulfillment

May Telemarketing
250 South 77th Street
Omaha, NE 68114
402-399-9700; 800-338-2600
    outbound marketing for
    magazines

MCI Direct
500 Second Avenue S.E.
Cedar Rapids, IA 52401
800-728-7000
    outbound, 800 and 900 services

Neodata/TMI
33 West 60th Street
New York, NY 10023
212-489-7038
    outbound (1,100 lines), 800 and 900
    services

Phone Marketing
P.O. Box 147
Lindenwold, NJ 08021
609-783-6070
    outbound and 800 services

Phone Power
16500 San Pedro Avenue, #400
San Antonio, TX 78232
512-822-4700; 800-683-5500
    outbound telemarketing

Pioneer Teletechnologies
102 Sergeant Square Drive
Sergeant Bluff, IA 51504
712-943-2308
    outbound (4600 lines) and 800
    services

Precision Response Corporation
4300 N.W. 135th Street
Miami, FL 33054
800-356-3279
    outbound, 800 and 900
    services

Premier Marketing Corporation
30700 Telegraph Road, #2550
Birmingham, MI 48010
313-645-1960; 800-755-0466
  outbound, 800 and 900 services

PSI Telemarketing
2945 W. Peterson
Chicago, IL 60659
312-878-0800
  outbound, 800 and 900 services

Results Telemarketing
499 Sheridan
Dania, FL 33004
305-921-2400; 800-284-5318
  outbound, 800 and 900 services

Ring Response
5309 W. Touhy
Skokie, IL 60077
708-673-6440; 800-338-3338
  inbound and outbound service

The Signature Group
200 N. Martingale Road
Schaumburg, IL 60173
708-605-4634; 800-521-6202
  outbound telemarketing, 1,200 lines

The Smith Company
1308 29th Street N.W.
Washington, DC 20007
202-298-7700
  outbound telemarketing

Sturner and Klein
11900 Parklawn Drive
Rockville, MD 20852
301-881-2720; fax: 301-881-3745
  outbound and 800 services

Tacticall
901 Bethlehem Pike
Spring House, PA 19477
800-544-3961
  outbound, 800 and 900 services

Tele America Inc.
1945 Techny Road, #3
Northbrook, IL 60062
708-480-1560
  outbound and 800 services

Telenational Marketing
7300 Woolworth Avenue
Omaha, NE 68124
800-333-6106; fax: 402-391-2044
  inbound and outbound service

Telequest
6301 Airport Freeway
Fort Worth, TX 76117
817-831-4381; fax: 817-834-7612;
  800-833-4443
  total telemarketing services

Teletech Communications
15355 Morrison Street
Sherman Oaks, CA 91403
818-501-5595; 800-835-3832
  outbound telemarketing

Touch Tone Access
9 Whippany Road
Whippany, NJ 07981
201-898-0999
  telemarketing, toll-free and 900
  services

U.S. Telemarketing
5300 Oakbrook Parkway
Norcross, GA 30093
404-381-0100
  outbound and 800 services

USA 800
9900 East 66 Terrace
Raytown, MO 64133
800-821-2539; 800-821-2280
  inbound telemarketing

WATS Marketing of America
2121 N. 117th Avenue
Omaha, NE 68164
402-498-4040; 800-351-1000
  inbound, outbound, and 900
  services

West Telemarketing Corporation
9910 Maple Street
Omaha, NE 68134
402-571-7700; 800-542-1000
  outbound, 800 and 900 services

TELEVISION ADS (LONG FORM)

Blue Marketing
20 Valley Stream Parkway
Malvern, PA 19355
215-648-9370

Hawthorne Communications
300 N. 16th Street
Fairfield, IA 52556
515-472-3800

Rocket Direct Marketing
209 East 25th Street
New York, NY 10010
212-532-5800

Worldwide 800
P.O. Box 613
Nanuet, NY 10954-0613
914-352-5560
        international toll-free telephone
        numbers

TOLL-FREE TELEPHONE NUMBERS

AT&T Communications
800-222-0400

MCI Telecommunications
800-444-4004

U.S. Sprint
P.O. Box 974
Burlingame, CA 94010
415-692-5600; 800-877-4000

VIDEO CATALOGS

Audio-Videographics
13801 East 35th Street
Independence, MO 64055
816-254-0400; 800-322-2832

Resolution
19 Gregory Drive
South Burlington, VT 05403
802-862-8881; 800-862-8900

Bibliography

In my various roles as marketing director of Open Horizons Publishing Company, as editor of the *Book Marketing Update* newsletter, as reviewer of books for *Small Press* magazine, and as consultant to many other publishers and direct marketers, I have read well over 500 books about direct marketing, advertising, copywriting, graphics, printing, publishing, and publicity. The books in this Bibliography are the ones I recommend most often.

Although I don't recommend that you buy every book in this list, read many of them, and have at least a few of them on your shelves for ready reference. Even after many years in this business, I still find inspiration, guidance, and good sense in many of these books.

All books listed in this Bibliography may be ordered from your favorite local bookseller, checked out at the library, or ordered direct from the publisher.

Adler, Elizabeth W., *Print That Works: The First Step-by-Step Guide That Integrates Writing, Design, and Marketing* (Palo Alto, CA: Bull Publishing, 1991), 400 pages, softcover, $29.95.
  A comprehensive guide to using computers and good design sense to create effective brochures, ads, fliers, newsletters, and other business communications. Step-by-step instructions cover all anyone needs to know to produce printed material quickly, easily, and cost-effectively.

Bayan, Richard, *Words That Sell* (Chicago: Contemporary, 1984), 127 pages, softcover, $10.95.
  If you have trouble finding the right words when you are writing catalog copy, advertisements, news releases, or book blurbs, this book is for you. It is a superb practical combination of a thesaurus and a course in advertising copywriting. Need help wording your guarantee? See page 87. Need a word to connote status or style? See pages 65 through 67. Want to

reword your order form? See page 88. Have trouble making snappy transitions? See page 11.

Beach, Mark, Steve Shepro, and Ken Russon, *Getting It Printed: How to Work with Printers and Graphic Arts Services to Assure Quality, Stay on Schedule, and Control Costs* (Portland, OR: Coast to Coast Books, 1985), 236 pages, hardcover, $42.50; softcover, $29.50.

Of all the books on printing and graphics that I have read, this book is a standout. It is detailed, well designed, and easy to use. It covers planning the printing job, writing specifications, requesting quotations, working with typesetters, preparing camera-ready copy, proofing, and working with your printer to get the best job, and it provides specific criteria for checking every step of the process. If every printer and print buyer had this book, 90% of all printing problems would disappear.

Beach, Mark, and Ken Russon, *Papers for Printing: How to Choose the Right Paper at the Right Price for Any Printing Job* (Portland: Coast to Coast Books, 1989), 40 sample sheets, 64 text pages, softcover, $34.50.

Shows how to buy and specify paper for various printing jobs. It includes 40 printed sample sheets, a chart that compares the costs of all 40 samples, a list of 678 paper brands, a list of 591 paper merchants, and a glossary of 214 paper terms.

Bencin, Richard L., and Donald J. Jonovic, Editors, *Encyclopedia of Telemarketing* (New York: Prentice-Hall, 1989), 726 pages, hardcover, $69.96.

Compilation of articles from 32 telemarketing pros that covers everything from how to design a telemarketing center to how to turn customer service into a potent marketing weapon. Other chapters focus on international telemarketing, business-to-business programs, catalog telemarketing, consumer programs, service bureaus, and hiring and training telephone salespeople.

Benson, Richard V., *Secrets of Successful Direct Mail* (Lincolnwood, IL: NTC Business Books, 1989), 208 pages, hardcover, $24.95.

A gem of inside secrets and tips from a man who has worked with such direct marketing programs as *American Heritage* and Time-Life Books. Includes lots of rules of thumb to show you how to increase response to your promotions.

Bird, Drayton, *Commonsense Direct Marketing, 2d Edition* (Lincolnwood, IL: NTC Business Books, 1990), 347 pages, hardcover, $29.95.

A basic guide to starting a direct marketing business that provides lots of commonsense advice for newcomers, but—and this is important—even seasoned veterans will find many ideas and reminders that could help them in their business as well. This book is a quick read and well worth the time.

Bly, Robert, *The Copywriter's Handbook* (New York: Henry Holt, 1990), 354 pages, softcover, $12.95.

Presents lots of advice on how to write copy that sells, including 8 headlines that work, 10 characteristics of successful print ads, 11 ways to make your copy more readable, and 15 ways to open a sales letter.

Bly, Robert, *Create the Perfect Sales Piece* (New York: John Wiley, 1985), 242 pages, softcover, $17.95.

If you want to design and write better brochures, promotional literature, and catalogs, here's help. How to find and evaluate talent, how to use the

11 basic types of sales literature, how to write benefit-oriented ad copy, how to get the best price on printing—these are just a few of the many topics covered in this book.

Bodian, Nat G., *Copywriter's Handbook: A Practical Guide for Advertising and Promotion of Specialized and Scholarly Books and Journals* (Phoenix: Oryx Press, 1984), 275 pages, softcover, $19.95.

Although this book is aimed at promoting professional and scholarly books, it still includes hundreds of copywriting tips and techniques of value to any publisher, regardless of subject or audience.

Bodian, Nat G., *NTC's Dictionary of Direct Mail and Mailing List Terminology and Techniques* (Lincolnwood, IL: NTC Business Books, 1990) 320 pages, hardcover, $49.95.

Defines 1,500 terms and concepts from the direct mail industry—everything from A/B split to zig-zag fold. If you are new to the industry and want to know what people are talking about, this book will tell you in clear and simple words.

Bodian, Nat G., *The Publisher's Direct Mail Handbook* (Phoenix: Oryx Press, 1987), 256 pages, hardcover, $39.95.

Another gem from Bodian, this book is a gold mine of ideas on how to sell books by mail. If you do any direct mail promotions for books, especially for professional or technical titles, this book will provide many inside tips based on years of experience.

Britt, Stuart H., *Marketing Manager's Handbook* (Chicago: Dartnell, 1983), 1135 pages, hardcover, $60.50.

A complete reference work for any marketing manager that covers everything from planning marketing strategy to dealing with the resulting sales. This is one of several superb Dartnell handbooks on marketing and promotion. This book is huge; you will need several weeks (even years) to digest all its details.

Brumbaugh, J. Frank, *Mail Order Made Easy* (North Hollywood, CA: Wilshire Books, 1979), 208 pages, softcover, $15.00.

Provides nuts-and-bolts know-how for mail order beginners. Contains chapters on choosing a product that sells, naming your price, using classified ads, choosing periodicals for advertising, designing and producing your sales package, and handling orders.

Burstiner, Irving, *Mail Order Selling* (New York: Prentice-Hall, 1982, 1989), 278 pages, softcover, $17.95.

Much of this book is simply regurgitation of various brochures from the Small Business Administration plus information from Burstiner's previous books on how to run a small business. As a result, most of the book really deals with starting up a business. In between those details, he does offer some basic information for mail order beginners.

Caples, John, *Tested Advertising Methods, 4th Edition* (New York: Prentice-Hall, 1981), 318 pages, softcover, $9.95.

Everything you want to know about writing ads that sell. The copywriter's bible, this book reveals proved selling techniques. Includes 20 formulas for writing winning headlines, 32 ways to increase inquiries, 20 ways to improve selling power, 17 ways to test ads, and much more. Useful for writing publicity releases and promotional brochures, as well as advertisements.

Chapman, Jr., Edward, *Exhibit Marketing: A Survival Guide for Managers* (New York: McGraw-Hill, 1987), 310 pages, hardcover, $21.95.

A detailed guide that describes how to plan, design, manage, and evaluate trade show exhibits to promote your products. It includes many examples and forms to make it easier for you to create a workable, attractive, and effective exhibit.

Chase, Cochrane, and Kenneth Barasch, *Marketing Problem Solver* (Radnor, PA: Chilton Books, 1977), 446 pages, hardcover, $37.50.

A comprehensive book packed with basic and advanced guidelines for any marketing situation—from market research and product development to advertising and sales promotions. Incredibly detailed.

Clip Away, *Direct Marketing Coupon Designs: 300 Creative, Copyright-Free Camera-Ready Professional Layouts* (Blue Ridge Summit, PA; TAB Books, 1990), 208 pages, softcover, $18.95.

This clip art book features 300 ready-to-use coupons, campaign ideas, and guidelines for designing your own direct marketing coupons.

Cohen, William A., *Building a Mail Order Business*, 3d Edition (New York: John Wiley, 1991), 565 pages, hardcover, $34.95.

A thorough guide for beginner and professional alike that details everything from financing and start-up to the most sophisticated new mail order techniques. Over 150 illustrations, case histories, graphs, and checklists show you exactly what to do. Highly recommended.

Cossman, E. Joseph, *How I Made $1,000,000 in Mail Order* (New York: Simon & Schuster, 1984), 267 pages, softcover, $11.95.

Cossman is famous for his one-shot mail order promotions (ant farms, fish lures, etc.). This book presents a commonsense, step-by-step procedure for promoting single items via mail order. Presents some creative direct marketing ideas.

Davidson, Jeffrey P., *Marketing on a Shoestring: Low-Cost Tips for Marketing Your Products or Services* (New York: John Wiley, 1988), 223 pages, softcover, $12.95.

While aimed primarily at local small businesses, this book contains many practical, low-cost, low-hassle strategies for marketing any product or service. Among the tips discussed are yellow pages advertising, business directories, brochures, bulletin boards, speaking, and marketing via the telephone.

Dunhill, Hugo, *How to Write an Effective Money-Making Direct Mail Letter* (New York: Hugo Dunhill Mailing Lists, 1989), three-ring binder plus two audiotapes and a wall chart, $79.95.

Written by a mailing list broker, this manual includes lots of tips and checklists to help you make your direct mail packages more effective.

Fidel, Stanley Leo, *Start-Up Telemarketing: How to Launch a Profitable Sales Operation* (New York: John Wiley, 1987), 287 pages, softcover, $12.95.

The best book on telemarketing I've ever read—simple, direct, and to the point. Comes complete with a sample telemarketing manual, including all the forms you'll need, plus a telephone presentation guide to answering questions and overcoming objections. Also has an extensive list of 700 resources, from automatic dialers to telemarketing consultants, from equipment suppliers to inbound and outbound services. If you are just getting started in telemarketing, this book is a must.

Gnam, Rene, *Direct Mail Workshop: 1,001 Ideas, Tips, Rule Breakers and Brainstorms for Improving Profits Fast* (New York: Prentice-Hall, 1990), hardcover, $49.95.
This new book contains many checklists and numbered tips to help anyone develop and carry out a direct marketing program, including 13 key steps for a successful direct mail launch, 49 ways to dramatize your offers, 41 tested ways to get your envelopes opened, 18 suggestions for more enticing sweepstakes, 40 tips for increasing renewals, 54 ways to get repeat sales, and much more. And the book comes with an unconditional lifetime guarantee—your lifetime!

Gosden, Jr., Freeman F., *Direct Marketing Success: What Works and Why* (New York: John Wiley, 1985), 225 pages, softcover, $12.95.
If you've ever wondered why there are certain direct marketing rules (and when and why you can sometimes break them), this book will answer many of your questions. It describes why long letters work, why teasers work, why picture captions are more important than pictures, why lift letters increase sales, why some lists do better than others, and much, much more.

Graham, Walter B., *Complete Guide to Pasteup, 3d Edition* (Omaha, NE: Dot Pasteup Supply, 1987), 236 pages, softcover, $19.95.
The classic book on how to prepare camera-ready copy for printing. If you are a newcomer to pasteup or have just hired a novice, this is the book to use. Detailed and complete. Indeed, if this book has any fault, it is that it could very well overwhelm you with its details.

Gross, Martin, *The Direct Marketer's Idea Book* (New York: AMACOM, 1989), 240 pages, hardcover, $19.95.
Not for beginners, this book includes lots of tips and examples for direct marketing professionals, including such topics as how to identify your best prospects, how to create a better offer, and how to head off buyers' objections.

Hill, Lawson T., *How to Build a Multi-Million Dollar Catalog Mail Order Business by Someone Who Did* (New York: Simon & Schuster, 1984), 304 pages, softcover, $19.95.
A practical handbook describing the basic steps and principles for establishing a successful catalog business—how to gain market leadership, design effective layouts, prepare selling catalog copy, get quality printing, forecast sales, market your catalog, and handle fulfillment.

Hodgson, Richard, *Direct Mail and Mail Order Handbook, 3d Edition* (Chicago: Dartnell, 1980), 1555 pages, hardcover, $60.50.
A classic so full of information that you won't be able to digest it in one reading. It's the kind of handbook you'll come back to again and again as you carry out direct marketing promotions.

Hodgson, Richard, *The Greatest Direct Mail Sales Letters of All Time* (Chicago: Dartnell), 450 pages, ring binder, $91.50.
A compilation featuring 100 of the most effective direct mail sales letters of all time—in their entirety. Also examines why each letter worked. A superb idea stimulator and a wonderful resource.

Holtz, Herman, *Starting and Building Your Catalog Sales Business* (New York: John Wiley, 1990), 272 pages, hardcover, $27.95
A basic introduction to selling via catalogs. For beginners only.

Judd, Karen, *Copyediting: A Practical Guide* (Los Altos, CA: Crisp Publications, 1988), 287 pages, hardcover, $19.95
 Answers questions regarding the appropriate places to use numerals versus spelling out numbers, how to use the standard punctuation marks, how to mark changes in a manuscript (with standard proofreading symbols), and how to typeset equations. A very complete and easy-to-use guide.

Kaatz, Ron, *Advertising and Marketing Checklists* (Lincolnwood, IL: NTC Business Books, 1989), 175 pages, softcover, $17.95.
 Contains 77 checklists—including 33 reasons to advertise, 9 tips for creating effective print ads, guidelines for creating selling television commercials, a 151-item checklist for conferences and special events, and many others.

Keding, Ann, and Thomas Bivins, *How to Produce Creative Advertising: Proven Techniques and Computer Applications* (Lincolnwood, IL: NTC Business Books, 1990), 181 pages, hardcover, $37.95.
 Illustrates how to use a computer to produce great print ads. While much of the discussion is based on Macintosh software, the basic principles apply to any advertising designs created with a computer.

Kiefer, Marie, *Directory of Book Printers*, 1992 Edition (Fairfield, IA: Ad-Lib Publications, 1992), 288 pages, softcover, $9.95.
 Lists 780 printers of books, catalogs, magazines, and other bound publications. With this edition, you can locate a quality printer who specializes in the quantities, sizes, and bindings you want to use—at a price you can afford. Not just for book publishers, this directory will save any direct marketer much time and money in selecting an appropriate catalog printer or a good local commercial printer that can handle almost any printing job.

Kobs, Jim, *Profitable Direct Marketing* (Lincolnwood, IL: NTC Business Books, 1979), 328 pages, hardcover, $27.95.
 One of the basic guides to direct marketing programs. Covers everything from selecting products to using and testing various media. It includes detailed examinations of 11 real-life examples, so you can relate the abstract principles to actual problems you might encounter in the day-to-day operation of a direct marketing program.

Kremer, John, *Book Marketing Made Easier: A Do-It-Yourself Marketing Kit for Book Publishers* (Fairfield, IA: Open Horizons, 1991), 384 pages, softcover, $19.95.
 A handy guide that features 120 worksheets and sample promotions to help anyone market books more effectively. This book covers everything from preparing a marketing strategy and planning budgets to setting up distribution and working with bookstores.

Kremer, John, *How to Sell to Mail Order Catalogs* (Fairfield, IA: Ad-Lib Publications, 1991), 50 pages, report, $30.00.
 Describes all the steps needed to sell a book or other product to mail order catalog houses and lists 550 catalogs that carry books, tapes, and other items. Current names, addresses, buyers, telephone numbers, subject interests, and products carried are listed for each catalog.

Kremer, John, *Mail Order Worksheet Kit* (Fairfield, IA: Open Horizons, 1991), 60 forms, master copies in a kit, $15.00.
 Contains full-size master copies of all the worksheets and sample letters

outlined in this book you are now reading. Use these master copies to organize your direct marketing programs.

Kremer, John, *Mail Order Spreadsheet Kit*, (Fairfield, IA: Open Horizons, 1991), 20 spreadsheets on disk, $29.95.

Have you ever wondered what would happen to your break-even point if you lowered postage costs by presorting? Or what effect a 10% change in response would have on the profitability of a mailing? Or how a small change in your selling price might affect your return on investment? The computer disk in this kit includes Lotus 123 or Quatro Pro spreadsheets for many of the worksheets included in this book. With these spreadsheets, you can explore all the possibilities of your promotions, playing **What if?** scenarios to your heart's delight—and to your pocket book's health.

Kremer, John, *1001 Ways to Market Your Books—For Authors and Publishers*, 3d Edition (Fairfield, IA: Open Horizons, 1990), 448 pages, hardcover, $19.95; softcover, $14.95.

Features more than 1,000 tips, techniques, and examples of how to market books more effectively. It covers traditional markets as well as special sales, subsidiary rights, direct mail, telemarketing, foreign sales, and much, much more. This book will help you to sell more books—and have fun doing it.

Kremer, John, and Marie Kiefer, *PR FLASH No-Frills Data Files* (Fairfield, IA: Ad-Lib Publications, 1992), 11,800 media records in various data formats for IBM-PC, Macintosh, or compatibles, $149.95.

Provides key contact names, addresses, telephone numbers, fax numbers, subject interests, and other important details for more than 11,800 media, including 3,845 newspaper editors, 3,690 magazine editors, 2,530 radio shows, 975 television shows, and 745 syndicated columns. The 11,800 records are available in a variety of file formats to use with many database programs on the IBM-PC, Macintosh, or compatibles. A great time-saver. No other directory or database offers so much for so little cost.

Lant, Jeffrey, *Cash Copy* (Cambridge, MA: Jeffrey Lant Associates, 1989), 480 pages, softcover, $24.95

This book has quickly become my favorite guide to writing promotional copy that sells. Chapter 11 on selling solutions is alone worth the price of the book. If you have ever been stuck when writing a direct mail letter, brochure, news release, cover letter, catalog copy, or advertisement, this book will open up new possibilities for you.

Lant, Jeffrey, *How to Make a Whole Lot More Than $1,000,000 Writing, Commissioning, Publishing and Selling How-To Information* (Cambridge, MA: Jeffrey Lant Associates, 1990), 552 pages, softcover, $35.00

A packed, detailed book about creating and selling books, tapes, reports, and other information products. Loaded with publicity and marketing ideas.

Lant, Jeffrey, *Money Making Marketing* (Cambridge, MA: Jeffrey Lant Associates, 1987), 268 pages, softcover, $30.00.

Another of Lant's exhaustive books, this one presents hundrds of creative, inexpensive, opinionated, and effective marketing techniques. His emphasis is on creating repeat customers for your products. This book is packed with detailed, money-making information.

Lem, Dean P., *Graphics Master 3* (Los Angeles: Dean Lem Associates, 1988), three-ring binder, $57.50.

A collection of production aids to make all the technicalities of graphics production much easier. This workbook includes a chart of paper sizes, drawings (and names) of common brochure folds, a scaling wheel, and other technical data charts. A useful collection for anyone who spends a lot of time doing layouts and graphic design.

Lewis, Herschell G., *Direct Mail Copy That Sells* (New York: Prentice-Hall, 1984), 196 pages, softcover, $14.95.

Gives specific techniques for writing irresistible copy, from attention-grabbing headlines to response-producing order forms. It also reveals dozens of common copy errors that can weaken the response to your promotional materials. These practical, high-impact ideas are presented with warmth and humor. Good reading.

Lewis, Herschell G., *How to Write Powerful Catalog Copy* (Chicago, Bonus Books, 1990), 331 pages, hardcover, $49.95.

Uses hundreds of examples from actual catalogs to show you how to create compelling copy that moves readers to buy your products. Lewis shows what works and what doesn't—and why. Learn how to match your copy to your catalog's image, how to put yourself in the buyer's shoes, how to write active copy, how to describe complicated items, and how to write headlines that attract attention.

Lewis, Herschell G., *More Than You Ever Wanted to Know about Mail Order Advertising* (New York: Prentice-Hall, out of print), 330 pages, softcover.

A wonderful collection of examples, techniques, and tidbits from a mail order professional. An easy-to-use guide to help you increase sales from all your promotions. Includes over 170 ideas.

Ljungren, Roy, *The Business-to-Business Direct Marketing Handbook* (New York: AMACOM, 1988), 400 pages, hardcover, $75.00.

This step-by-step guide is the only book I've seen that focuses solely on business-to-business direct marketing. Lots of details and good advice. It is a must if your primary market is other businesses.

Miller, Steve, *How to Get the Most Out of Trade Shows* (Lincolnwood, IL: NTC Business Books, 1987), 163 pages, hardcover, $19.95.

While not as complete as Chapman's *Exhibit Marketing*, this book is a good introduction to the subject that covers all the basics.

Muldoon, Katie, *Catalog Marketing: The Complete Guide to Profitability in the Catalog Business*, 2d Edition (New York: AMACOM, 1988), 410 pages, hardcover, $75.00

This book covers everything: how to get started, how to find your niche, how to select merchandise, how to create and produce a catalog, how to service your customers, and much more.

Nash, Edward, Editor, *The Direct Marketing Handbook* (New York: McGraw-Hill, 1984), 944 pages, hardcover, $54.95.

A classic in the field that covers everything—planning and budgeting, design and production, execution and fulfillment. Lots of inside secrets and top-of-the-line tips from people who have been in the business for years. Exhaustive.

Parker, Roger, *Looking Good in Print: A Guide to Basis Design for Desktop Publishing,*

2d Edition (Chapel Hill, NC: Ventana Press, 1990), 221 pages, softcover, $23.95.

Shows how to use computers to design and produce more effective brochures, newsletters, manuals, and catalogs. Also describes common design pitfalls and how to avoid them.

Playle, Ron, *Selling to Catalog Houses* (Des Moines, IA: R&D Services, 1982), 48 pages, saddle-stitched, $10.00

A succinct manual for selling books to major mail order catalog marketers. Includes sample letters, pricing guidelines, and addresses.

Pope, J., *Business-to-Business Telemarketing* (New York: AMACOM, 1983), 400 pages, hardcover, $75.00.

One of the first books on how to use telemarketing to sell products to other businesses. With all the new technology and new options (including 900 numbers), this book has become a bit dated.

Powers, Melvin, *How to Get Rich in Mail Order* (North Hollywood, CA: Wilshire Books, 1980), 336 pages, softcover, $20.00

Melvin has been publishing books, his own and others, for over 25 years (and sold millions of dollars worth of books). Although this book is about mail order, its primary focus is on selling information (books) by mail. The book is packed with examples of successful mail order ads and promotional literature.

Raphel, Murray, *Mind Your Own Business* (Atlantic City, NJ: Raphel Marketing), $19.95.

Raphel, Murray, and Ken Erdman, *The Do-It-Yourself Direct Mail Handbook* (Atlantic City, NJ: Raphel Marketing), $19.95.

Rice, Craig S., *Marketing without a Marketing Budget* (Holbrook, MA: Bob Adams, 1989), 317 pages, softcover, $9.95

A potpourri of brief ideas to help you get the most from your marketing dollars, this book offers good basic advice—not as good, however, as the similar do-less-and-accomplish-more books by Jay Levinson and Jeffrey Davidson.

Riso, Ovid, Editor, *Sales Promotion Handbook*, 7th Edition (Chicago: Dartnell, 1979), 1206 pages, hardcover, $56.50.

A standard in the field of sales promotion that is loaded with ideas, tips, examples, and much more—all showing you how to make better use of sales promotions. Like the other Dartnell handbooks, this book cannot be digested in one reading.

Robinson, William A., *Best Sales Promotions*, 6th Edition (Lincolnwood, IL: NTC Business Books, 1987), 372 pages, hardcover, $29.95.

If you've ever thought about using sales promotions (couponing, sampling, refunds, sweepstakes, continuity programs, premium packs, trade incentives, etc.) to promote your books, this book will stimulate your creative juices to overflowing. It describes and illustrates outstanding sales promotions. Provides a real boost to your idea quotient!

Sanderson, Steve, Editor, *Standard Legal Forms and Agreements for Small Business* (Bellingham, WA: Self-Counsel Press, 1990), 160 pages, softcover, $14.95.

Save time and money setting up your own legal forms and agreements. This set covers most small business needs, including a number of agreements for marketing and distribution.

Schultz, Don E., and William A. Robinson, *Sales Promotion Essentials* (Lincolnwood, IL: NTC Business Books, 1982), 240 pages, softcover, $14.95.
Another outstanding resource for those considering using sales promotions, this book describes the 12 basic sales promotion techniques and reveals how to use them most effectively: coupons, contests and sweepstakes, bonus packs, stamps and continuity plans, price-offs, trade coupons, refunds, free-in-the-mail premiums, self-liquidating premiums, sampling, and point-of-purchase displays.

Schwab, Victor, *How to Write a Good Advertisement* (North Hollywood, CA: Wilshire Books, 1962), 227 pages, softcover, $15.00.
Provides all you need to know to write good advertisements. It features 100 good headlines with explanations of why they worked, plus 22 ways to hold the reader's attention once you've attracted it.

Sewell, Susan, *Advertising Made Easy* (Los Angeles: Price Stern Sloan, 1990), 112 pages, softcover, $6.95.
Provides a basic overview to the current advertising world. It offers little in the way of practical advice but does tell a few good stories about the world of advertising today.

Shepard Associates, David, *The New Direct Marketing: How to Implement a Profit-Driven Database Marketing Strategy* (Homewood, IL: Business One Irwin, 1990), 535 pages, hardcover, $52.50.
Describes how to construct a customer database and how to use statistical analysis and modeling to build a profitable direct marketing business. Not for the beginner or anyone with a fear of numbers, this book goes deeply into measuring responses and using those measurements to forecast sales and profits.

Simon, Julian, *How to Start and Operate a Mail Order Business*, 4th Edition (New York: McGraw-Hill, 1987), 547 pages, hardcover, $44.95.
A comprehensive manual packed with sound advice and basic mail order techniques to help anyone make money in mail order. It covers everything you need to know to start and operate a successful mail order business. This is a book to be read more than once. It should be kept on your reference shelf at all times for easy reference. It's one of my first choices for an introduction to the business.

Smith, Richard D., and Ginger Dick, *Getting Sales* (Vancouver, BC: Self-Counsel Press, 1981), 110 pages, softcover, $14.95.
A basic guide to sales that covers telephone sales, publicity, direct mail, print advertising, and co-op advertising.

Sroge, Maxwell, *How to Create Successful Catalogs* (Lincolnwood, IL: NTC Business Books, 1985), 459 pages, hardcover, $79.95.
Shows how to improve the design, artwork, and copy of catalogs to create the most effective sales message. Special emphasis is given to the four major parts of any catalog: the front cover, the back cover, the order form, and the guarantee. Many examples and checklists make the information in this book easy to absorb and implement.

Sroge, Maxwell, Editor, *101 Tips for More Profitable Catalogs* (Lincolnwood, IL: NTC Business Books, 1990), 122 pages, softcover, $24.95.
Brings together 101 short tidbits of advice from dozens of catalog professionals covering choosing and testing lists, selecting products to sell, producing catalogs, telemarketing, and customer service.

Stilson, Galen, *59 Response/Profit Tips, Tricks, and Techniques to Help You Achieve Major Mail Order Success* (Fort Worth, TX: Premier Publishers, 1984), 26 pages, saddle stitched, $10.00.

A brief but excellent collection of tips and techniques for any direct marketer. It actually includes many more than 59 tips (one tip alone lists 23 rules for increasing response to your ads—this list itself is worth the small price of this manual).

Stone, Bob, *Successful Direct Marketing Methods*, 4th Edition (Lincolnwood, IL: NTC Business Books, 1988), 575 pages, hardcover, $34.95.

The professional's direct marketing bible, this book is not for beginners. For anyone with even an iota of experience in direct marketing, this book will quickly pay its own way. It is a superb overview of the entire business of direct marketing. In my opinion, it is the best book on direct marketing available anywhere: comprehensive, readable, and authoritative. A book to keep on your reference shelf for easy use at all times.

Stone, Bob, and John Wyman, *Successful Telemarketing* (Lincolnwood, IL: NTC Books, 1985), 206 pages, softcover, $15.95.

One of the best introductions to the new field of telemarketing. Read it carefully if you are considering using telephones to market books (whether for outbound WATS calls or inbound 800 calls).

Tharp, Louis, *The Complete Manager's Guide to Promotional Merchandise* (Homewood, IL: Dow Jones-Irwin, 1989), 176 pages, hardcover, $32.50.

Provides step-by-step guidance on how to evaluate, buy, and distribute promotional items—plus why you should use them. It includes many case histories that illustrate what works and what doesn't. It complements Robinson's *Best Sales Promotions*.

Ulanoff, Stanley, *Handbook of Sales Promotion* (New York: McGraw-Hill, 1984), 624 pages, hardcover, $49.95.

Like Ovid Riso's *Sales Promotion Handbook*, this one is an all-in-one-book compendium of sales promotion techniques and ideas. Very comprehensive. Useful if you are considering using sweepstakes, coupons, giveaways, rebates, or other promotional gimmicks.

Wallace, Carol Wilkie, *Great Ad! Low-Cost Do-It-Yourself Advertising for Your Small Business* (Blue Ridge Summit, PA: TAB Books, 1990), 340 pages, softcover, $19.95.

Focuses on low-cost advertising techniques for small retail businesses. Plenty of checklists for evaluating the pros and cons of various advertising media.

Weintraub, Diane K., *Trade Show Exhibiting: The Insider's Guide for Entrepreneurs* (New York: Liberty Hall Press, 1991), 203 pages, softcover, $14.95.

A good introduction to promoting products via trade shows, this book shows how to design effective exhibits, select the best shows and booth space, organize exhibits, and train staff to operate the exhibit. Also lists 77 practical tips for cutting trade show costs.

Weintz, Walter H., *The Solid Gold Mailbox* (New York: John Wiley, 1987), 268 pages, hardcover, $22.95.

An anecdotal yet detailed account of how to create mail order campaigns that work—all based on the experiences of a man who created such campaigns for *Reader's Digest*, Book-of-the-Month Club, Rodale Press, and many others. Interesting and informative.

Werz, Edward W., *Letters That Sell* (Chicago: Contemporary Books, 1987), 163 pages, softcover, $9.95; with the letters on IBM-compatible computer disc, $29.95.

If you've ever been at a loss for words when beginning a letter, this book of 90 easy-to-use letters will get you off to the right start. Includes letters for making direct sales, arranging appointments, following up on a meeting, and motivating salespeople, as well as goodwill letters, customer service letters, and six novelty letters. Also provides additional tips for salutations, headlines, transitions, openings, and closings. A handy guide that is well worth the price.

Williams, Lew, *Zip-Clip Library* (Dallas: Post Haste Publications, 1989), 7 pages per book, softcover, $14.95 each, $69.95 for the set.

A set of seven books featuring an average of 250 mail order clip art words and images per book: *Eye Catchers, Envelope Teasers, Response Devices, Toll-Free Telephones, Rubber Stamps, Script Teasers,* and *Information Sales.* A useful collection, especially when you need something in a hurry.

Wilson, Jerry R., *Word-of-Mouth Marketing* (New York: John Wiley, 1991), 256 pages, hardcover, $24.95.

Shows how to use satisfied customers to sell more of your product or service; in short, it shows you how to mount a word-of-mouth marketing campaign. Since customers are the most valuable assets of any direct marketing company, this book will quickly repay you for taking the time to read it and put its principles into action.

Index